How to Trace Your Jewish Roots

Discovering Your Unique History

How to Trace Your Jewish Roots

RABBI JO DAVID

CITADEL PRESS
KENSINGTON PUBLISHING CORP.
www.kensingtonbooks.com

CITADEL PRESS books are published by

Kensington Publishing Corp.
850 Third Avenue
New York, NY 10022

All Kensington titles, imprints, and distributed lines are available at special quantity discounts for bulk purchases for sales promotions, premiums, fund raising, educational, or institutional use. Special book excerpts or customized printings can also be created to fit specific needs. For details, write or phone the office of the Kensington special sales manager: Kensington Publishing Corp., 850 Third Avenue, New York, NY 10022, attn: Special Sales Department, phone 1-800-221-2647.

First printing 2000

10 9 8 7 6 5 4 3 2 1

Printed in the United States of America

Library of Congress Cataloging-in-Publication Data

David, Jo.
    How to trace your Jewish roots : discovering your unique history / Jo David.
        p.   cm.
    ISBN 0-8065-2042-6 (pb)
    1. Jews—Genealogy—Handbooks, manuals, etc.   I. Title.
CS21.D38   1999
929'.1'089924—dc21   98-52019
                                                                          CIP

This book is dedicated to Andrea Goodzeit, z'l, may her name always be remembered and blessed. She was talented, beautiful, loving, courageous, and beloved by many. Her heroic struggle with leukemia and her untimely death helped me to understand that each day of life is a precious gift to be cherished. None of us can accomplish in life all that we might wish, but each of us can focus on those things that are most important to us. By doing so, we can create a life of joy and fulfillment, a life lived without regret. Because of this insight, I made many changes in my life. Without those changes, this book would not have been written.

I will always be in Andrea's debt for the new life that her illness helped me to create. It is my hope that those who read this dedication may also be inspired to cherish each day and to live their lives fully and with joy.

Contents

Acknowledgments

An important rabbinic teaching is that each generation builds upon the work of previous generations. The same is true of this book. Without the groundbreaking work of Rabbi Malcolm Stern, of blessed memory, Arthur Kurzweil and other early Jewish genealogists, the book you are now reading could never have been written. They created the field of Jewish genealogy. I owe them all a great debt for what I have learned from their work and their writings.

I would also like to acknowledge the people and organizations that were especially helpful to me as I worked on building my family tree and doing special research for this project.

Audrey Sedita, a cousin I've spoken with many times but have yet to meet, provided excellent research advice, family documents and helped to fill in an important branch of our shared genealogy. Ms. Estelle Guzik of the Jewish Genealogy Society in New York City assisted me in a variety of ways, including helping to locate a copy of Malcolm Stern's Ten Commandments. My cyberspace genealogy pal, Harold Halpern, very kindly provided both a complete family genealogy and an in-depth report on his family's trip to Eastern Europe. Although this material was not used in the final version of the manuscript, it was very helpful as background material.

The staff at the National Archives and Records Administration, Regional Records Services in New York answered my many requests in a helpful and timely manner. The friendly and knowledgeable staff and volunteers at the Family History Library at Lincoln Center taught me to use their facility, enabling me to discover new information about my father's family.

A special thank you must be extended to my agent and friend, Richard Curtis, who suggested that this project might interest me, and to his associate, Laura Tucker, who was charged with my care. Thank you, Laura, for being encouraging, supportive and tactful at all times. I know that shepherding me through this project wasn't always easy.

This book underwent a metamorphosis during its creation. My original conception was to do a somewhat "cut and dried" "how to" manual. My editor at Carol Publishing, Hillel Black, challenged me to make it much more. For his insight into what this book could be, for his encouragement and patience, I am extremely grateful. Working with him has been a delight and has helped me to mature as a writer. I would also like to thank the support staff at Carol Publishing for their professionalism, their help, and their support, and to Carol Siegel for her copyediting.

This book could not have been written without the input and support of my family. My mother, Diana Marx, was extremely helpful in providing information about her parents' life and in finding important original family records and photographs. My uncle, Mortimer Marx, opened up new avenues of research into my father's family history, which would otherwise have been lost. My husband, Neil Yerman, patiently endured long months of hearing "I should be finished next week," with his typical good humor and love. My son and daughter-in-law, Justin David and Judith Wolf, were always encouraging and loving.

A special thank you must go to my father, Stan Marx z'l, who always encouraged my writing and who knew that I would be the family genealogist. Loving thoughts of him and the many lessons he taught me were a constant source of support and inspiration during the writing of this book.

Finally, I would like to ask for blessing for the souls of all my ancestors; those whom I know, those whom, perhaps someday, I will come to know, and those I will never know. Each of us is the genetic accumulation of the generations that preceded us. By understanding those who came before us, we better understand ourselves. What gifts I have, I owe

to them, and to the Creator who brings us into life and sustains us. I
give thanks to the One who guides and supports me for the privilege of
undertaking and completing this book.

New York City
December 29, 1998

Author to Reader

Where Did You Come From?

At a very young age children ask their parents, "Where did you come from, where were you born?" and most parents enjoy sharing the stories of their family life with their offspring. As a young child, I was fascinated with my grandmother's stories of her life in the Ukraine and of the long and difficult journey that she and my grandfather endured before they finally arrived in New York City. Her descriptions of life in "Kiev" fired my imagination and created a bond between us that was very precious. The fact that she didn't come frome Kiev, which I only found out as I was preparing to visit there, further whetted my appetite to trace my Jewish roots.

When I finally visited my grandmother's shtetl, I clearly understood why she claimed Kiev as her hometown. She was much too cosmopolitan to have ever lived, emotionally, in Skvira, a town about an hour outside of Kiev. I wish that we could have visited both Skvira and Kiev together, but I know that in all the ways that are important, she was with me on my pilgrimage.

Where did you come from? A recent survey showed that of the close to 6 million Jews living in America today, the majority are second-generation Americans. That means that their grandparents were born somewhere other than the United States. I'm one of those second-generation Americans, as is my husband.

I strong identify with the idea that I'm the granddaughter of immigrants. We lived with my mother's parents in Brooklyn for much of my childhood and I was especially close to my grandmother, Bessie Steinberg. I consider myself second generation, yet, on my father's side of the family, I'm actually a third-generation American Jew. My father's parents were both born here, to German Jews who emigrated in the 1880s.

For some reason, the German part of my heritage has no emotional pull on me. I identify completely through my maternal grandparents' immigrant experience and cherish that link to the past. I wonder why? Was it the fact that I didn't know my father's parents as well as I did my mother's parents? My father's parents both died before I was eight years old. Although I lost my maternal grandfather when I was eleven, I was lucky to have my maternal grandmother with me until I was in my early twenties. She even got to know her great-grandson.

Another possibility is that my father's parents were clearly Americans. They looked and sounded like my parents—like Americans. They were like everybody else's parents. They were so assimilated that our big family celebrations—mostly in the form of dinners and gifts—were Christmas and Easter. These celebrations, some of which were caught on "moving pictures," outdid, in their elaborate menus, wrappings, and gifts, the efforts of the few Christian neighbors who lived in our neighborhood. I was in my twenties before it really sank in that most Jewish families didn't have ceiling-high Christmas trees covered with angels, and parents who read Dickens by the fireplace on Christmas morning to the accompaniment of popovers and apple fritters.

Many Jews reading this last paragraph may find such experiences foreign, but for me they seemed normal, and I enjoyed them. I knew we were Jewish and that being Jewish was very important to who I was. But these family customs were part of the landscape of my life. They had no religious meaning. However, I think that to my father's parents and to my parents, and even to my mother's parents in some respects, our celebration of these "national" holidays meant that we were good Americans. And being an American, in the 1950s, was extremely important in our little corner of the world.

By contrast, my mother's parents were exotic, with their heavy Russian accents, their fluent Yiddish, spoken when they didn't want me to understand what they were saying, the different and wonderful foods they ate, and their stories—too few and too infrequent, I now understand—of the old country. They too leaned heavily into our American holiday celebrations. In addition, my grandfather loved cowboy movies and TV shows and was a staunch supporter of the Brooklyn Dodgers. He hated the New York Yankees, the Dodgers' mortal enemies. I've always thought that it was ironic that my grandfather should die, at the age of sixty, from Lou Gehrig's Disease.

There's a story my father told me that I believe is true. My father lived in Washington Heights, a German Jewish enclave in the first half of this century. He was a devoted Giants fan. The rivalry between the Giants and the Dodgers was even more bitter than that of the Dodgers and the Yankees, because they were both National League clubs and often played each other, for the bragging rights in New York.

My father told me that when he and my mother became engaged, my grandfather took him aside and explained the facts of life to him. If he was going to marry my mother, he had to convert! He had to give up the giants and become a Dodger fan! To a true New York baseball fan, such a conversion was as serious as changing one's religion. For some people, possibly more serious.

True love, however, can make all things possible, The depth of my father's conversion was demonstrated by the fact that by the time I was five years old, I could name the starting lineup for the Brooklyn Dodgers, but knew nothing at all about the Giants. Not only did my father convert, but he made sure that his oldest child would integrate the mysteries of the religion of baseball, as interpreted at Ebbett's Field, into her very being.

WHERE DID I COME FROM?

The question, "Where did you come from," has a corollary: "Where did I come from?" This is not a question about biology, per se, but about the forces in the lives of others that have come forward to shape the life of the questioner. Understanding the history of the ancestors in our own families helps us to understand who we are. The study of genealogy is directly concerned with these questions. Genealogy helps us to answer the question "Where did I come from" in a profound way. It links us with people we never knew and makes their experiences our own. It can explain why, in a family of dark-haired, brown-eyed people, a blue-eyed redhead is born. It can help us understand why there seem to be so many doctors or lawyers in one family and so many writers and teachers in another.

Working on a family tree can be a very effective tool for opening up a dialogue between generations in the same family. Usually we talk to each other in the time-honored, noncommunicative way:

"What are you doing in school?"

"The usual."

"What do you like to do when you're not in school?"

"Stuff."

Instead, in constructing a family tree, adults and children are forced to talk about and think about new ideas. Also, because often the people who are being traced are unknown both to the adults and the children, everyone is on an even playing field. Creating a four-generation family tree is most often the process of talking to relatives, writing down their stories, and unearthing existing family records. There are many different activities related to this project in which young people of all ages can be involved.

While many family-tree projects stop at the "What can we find out from our living relatives?" stage, more and more Jews today are beginning to ask, "Is it possible to trace my family through its 'old country' roots?" Fifty years ago, the answer to this question would probably have been, "Maybe, but not easily." There was no organized science of Jewish genealogy. Genealogists, both professional and amateur, did the best they could, but Jewish genealogy was not seen as a discreet discipline.

THE MODERN SCIENCE OF JEWISH GENEALOGY

The "dean" of modern Jewish genealogy was Rabbi Malcolm H. Stern, of blessed memory. He was born in 1916 and died in 1994 at the age of seventy-eight. Rabbi Stern served as genealogist to the American Jewish

Archives in Cincinnati from 1949 onward. He was a founding member of the Jewish Genealogical Society and its president from 1979 to 1984. He was the first Jewish Fellow of the American Genealogical Society, the founder of the Jewish Historical Society of New York, and a trustee of the Federation of Genealogical Societies. In his lifetime, he was honored numerous times for his contributions to the field of Jewish genealogy.

Rabbi Stern was a prolific writer, producing many articles for genealogical and historical publications. His best-known book is *Americans of Jewish Descent: 600 Genealogies (1654–1988)*. Its third edition, published in 1991, contains the names of approximately 50,000 people. It documents the genealogies of Jewish families that arrived during the American colonial and federal periods (1654 to 1838) and traces many families to the present. This book was a major research source for Stephen Birmingham's bestselling book, *The Grandees*.

Perhaps Rabbi Stern's greatest importance in the field of Jewish genealogy was his mentoring and support of individuals and organizations. He made himself available to both novice and professional genealogists alike. Many of the first Jewish genealogical societies in the United States were established as a result of his support and encouragement.

One of the genealogists influenced by Rabbi Stern was Arthur Kurzweil. It was Kurzweil's seminal work, *From Generation to Generation*, that helped to popularize Jewish genealogy. The book was revised and reissued in 1994. Since then there have been many exciting developments in the field including the birth of over sixty Jewish genealogy societies around the world, the establishment of countless Jewish archives, the development of genealogy software for computers, and, most recently, a dizzying proliferation of Jewish genealogy Web sites on the Internet.

There are also a number of new publications in the area of Jewish genealogy. Some are specific research guides like *Jewish Documentary Sources in Russia, Ukraine, and Belarus: A Preliminary List*, published by the Jewish Theological Seminary. Other, more general books, attempt to supply information and guide the novice genealogist through the research maze.

WHY IS THIS BOOK DIFFERENT FROM
ALL OTHER JEWISH GENEALOGY BOOKS?

Many of the books published for Jewish genealogists are written by professionals—either professional genealogists or Jewish historians or researchers with a specific specialization in documenting Jewish life. There are many wonderful books of this type. However, if you are a beginner, as I was some years ago, with a hobbyist's interest in tracing your family tree, many of these books can be overwhelming. There may be just too much information. Or the information given may assume a base of knowledge that you don't have. Personally, when I was starting out, many of these works made my eyes glaze over. I would have liked to have found a book that was written for someone like me—a real beginner.

How to Trace Your Jewish Roots is designed for the Jewish person who knows absolutely nothing about genealogy, but who would like to stick a cautious toe into the genealogical ocean. It was written, not by a professional genealogist, but by a professional writer and rabbi with an interest in Jewish genealogy. My goal was to create an easy-to-read, easy-to-follow manual that would lead a novice genealogist step by step through the process of creating a four- to six-generation family tree—a very satisfying and reachable goal for most individuals. In addition, I wanted to provide enough "meat" so that, once this initial goal was accomplished, the reader could continue to develop as a Jewish genealogist if he or she wished to do so.

TECHNOLOGY AND THE GENEALOGIST

When I began writing this book, I did what all writers do—I read a great number of books about genealogy in general and about Jewish genealogy in particular. With one exception, all these books referred me to information sources by providing book titles, phone numbers, mailing addresses, and an occasional fax number.

I had learned that a lot of computer software was available, but was unfamiliar with this type of programming. Several fact-finding missions to computer stores gave me a good overview of the computer software that deals with genealogical data and made me believe that the world of the Internet would probably yield some Jewish genealogical resources.

I'm a relative novice to the world of cyberspace and I assumed that my planned chapter on the use of computers in the practice of genealogy would revolve primarily around software and a few Internet addresses. I planned to write that the use of a computer wasn't really necessary for the Jewish genealogist, but that it could be helpful.

I didn't expect the genealogy on the Internet to be a significant portion of either my research or of the finished manuscript. However, as the famous saying goes, "The best laid plans of mice and rabbis . . ." Having now completed this book, I find that I must report a very different reality.

Access to the Internet is absolutely vital to the modern Jewish genealogist and to genealogists in general. Chapter 7, The Wild World of Genealogy in Cyberspace, and the many other chapters in which Internet sites are discussed and listed, will make the value of a computer completely clear to the reader.

If you have never used a computer before and find the idea of doing so rather daunting, don't despair. It is perfectly possible to become an accomplished Jewish genealogist without ever venturing into cyberspace. You should at least consider computer use, because once you get the hang of surfing the Internet, you'll save literally hundreds of hours of research time and also a great deal of money. And it's easy and endlessly fascinating! With a fifteen-minute introduction, anyone can now search the Internet with confidence.

I also must admit that there are many things that computers can't help you with. Nothing can replace a visit to your family village in the old country. Some records may only be found if such travel is possible. Also, even with the help of computers, many records will have to be requested by mail, E-mail, fax, or phone. For some records, a trip to a library will be absolutely necessary.

There are two different primary uses for a computer in genealogical research, each with its own joys and challenges. A computer is your door opener for the wide world of cyberspace genealogy and it can also be a helpful tool for data management.

Today there are many excellent computer software programs for compiling and managing the "results" of one's genealogical research. You can even create an online photo album with these programs.

Those readers who are comfortable with computer software will no doubt find these uses of the computer a real plus in managing their data. Personally, I'm still struggling in this area because I have a strong predisposition for writing things down on paper. However, I know that, given time and practice, I will come to love my software and feel comfortable with it.

The second use for a computer is in the area of genealogical research. For those readers uninitiated into the world of cyberspace, a word: Relax. Think of the Internet as a large library. Each "site" is like a book. It's really that simple, and once you get the hang of it, you'll enjoy it too.

Genealogy is addictive. The wonderful thing about this addiction, however, is that, while being incredibly satisfying and stimulating, it's not illegal, immoral, or fattening! Once you begin, you won't want to stop. Let's begin.

How to Trace Your Jewish Roots

1

Rabbi Jo David Searches for Her Roots: A Case History

I first became interested in genealogy when my husband began to create artistic renderings of family trees for people who had successfully compiled a family history. Most of the time he would be given handwritten, chaotic notes (this was before computer programs were invented to organize information). His job was to arrange the data artistically and then to develop suitable illustrations to enhance the artistic interest of the tree. He and I would spend hours trying to figure out, from the information we received, whether Aunt Sophie was Uncle Howard's wife, niece, sister, or no relation at all.

What especially fascinated me about these trees were the individuals who were born prior to 1900. I would find myself thinking about their lives. Before 1900, so many of the things that I take for granted—a car, air travel, television, the vote for women—did not exist. And yet, in many cases, much less than a century separated their lives and mine. I began to think about genealogy as a type of time travel. In connecting with one's ancestors, it was possible to link one's self to a very different time in history and, at least in some small way, to experience another type of existence and reality.

About fifteen years ago, I began to focus on capturing my own family history and preserving it. I would talk to older relatives about their memories. I wasn't particularly organized, but I was still able to begin to rough out a family tree for each of the four branches of my family. As I obtained information, I would throw it into a file marked "Jo's family." When I came across family photographs, especially old ones, I'd put these into the file also.

This method is directly opposite from the advice offered in this book. However, I mention it because I think it's important for beginning genealogists to know that you don't have to be either "perfect" or "professional" as you start out on your research. The most important thing to do is to begin. This was my way of beginning, and it suited the amount of time and energy I had available to devote to my research.

During the time that I started my genealogical research, I became ordained as a rabbi. As such, I found myself spending a lot of time in cemeteries and began to wonder where my relatives were buried. I made a list of who was interred where and kept it in my car. When I found myself in a cemetery in which I had a relative buried, I would search out the gravesite and copy down the information on the headstones that I found. I would also make notes about other stones nearby that might be related to me. I would add this information to my family file when I returned home. In this way, I was able to collect family names, including Hebrew names, as well as accurate yahrzeit dates (the anniversary of a person's death). I was also able to get information about the landsman-shaften organizations that my relatives belonged to and I would make notes on the location of the grave and the information on the stone. Some cooperative cemetery offices would give me a copy of the map of the group plot in which my relatives rested.

Visiting a gravesite is a very personal experience. Traditionally, one does not say the mourner's kaddish without a minyan (all male, of course). For this reason, since most people visit a gravesite alone or in small groups, most funeral homes supply booklets of inspirational readings—psalms and prayers—to be said by an individual who is visiting the grave of a loved one. Some people just like to come and talk to their loved ones. I once saw a young man set up a beach chair, get comfortable, and peruse the *New York Times!*

I personally believe that saying the mourner's kaddish by myself is respectful to the tradition and to the Holy One. Therefore, when I visit a relative's grave, I always say this prayer after filling my loved ones in on what's been happening in my life. Some people like to bring a stone from their home, or some flowers to leave behind as a personal touch.

I always leave a stone to show other relatives that the grave has been visited. This tradition dates back to a time when graves were covered with loose stones. When one visited the grave of a loved one, he or she would pile up the stones over the grave and replace those that had been shifted by the weather and by animals. This was the way of maintaining a gravesite and honoring the dead. Today, graves are covered differently, but we still leave a stone as a sign of love and respect.

Even at the time that I was first beginning my cemetery research, I recognized that my methods weren't particularly well organized or professional. However, my technique yielded the information that I wanted to collect and its very casual approach suited me then. Other relatives knew that I was interested in family history and on occasion someone would share a story with me or give me a photograph.

Along the way, I read *From Generation to Generation* by Arthur Kurzweil, which helped me to understand more about the methodology of genealogical research. My interest in genealogy led me to create genealogy projects for my religious school students. In preparing for these lessons, I reviewed several genealogy "workbooks" that also helped me in my own genealogical activities.

One of the wonderful things about genealogy is that even a child of nine or ten can create a pedigree chart for his or her family. In doing so, the child learns that older relatives have interesting stories to tell. It's important to teach young children this lesson. There are so many times when I've asked my own older relatives about their grandparents only to get the reply, "I wish I'd asked those questions when I was young, but I never thought to enquire and by the time I thought of those questions, those relatives were dead." In teaching young children about genealogy and the importance of asking older relatives questions about their lives, we are not only preserving important family memories, we are raising the consciousness of these children concerning the wealth of information an older person may have to relate. Hopefully, the generation of children learning about genealogy will not have to say, "If only I had asked when he [or she] was still alive."

I loved doing genealogy projects with my students because the results of these projects always proved fascinating. I would begin by teaching them about the family tree of our matriarchs and patriarchs—Abraham and Sarah, Isaac and Rebecca, Jacob and Leah, and Rachel and Jacob's twelve sons and one daughter. This four-generation model is perfect for beginners, because it is something that most people can understand in relation to their own family. After discussing how the tree is constructed, I would distribute a list of questions for the children to pose to relatives. This list was a simplified version of the family interview that appears in chapter 8. After talking about these questions, the students would be sent home to do their research and to create a pedigree chart.

A particular incident with a student taught me that genealogy "on the ground" was different from the way it was portrayed in helpful workbooks. One of my students handed in her pedigree sheet. It was filled in on the matrilineal side with a great deal of detail. However, the patrilineal side was blank. At first, I assumed that she hadn't done her homework completely, perhaps had run out of time. After class, I held her back and questioned her.

"Why didn't you fill in the patrilineal side of the tree? Was there a problem?"

"I don't have a father."

I explained to her that, even if her parents were divorced, or if her father had died, she still had a father for genealogical purposes. She insisted, however, that she didn't have a father. We went on in this fashion for a few minutes. I kept trying to explain that she had to have a father and she insisting that she didn't. Finally, in exasperation, I said to her, "The fact that you're here means that there was some man in your background."

"No," she said. "My mother went to a sperm bank."

That's when I learned that this is a new world, genealogically speaking, and that a broader view of family than is usually represented in traditional texts might be needed.

I Begin to Chart My Family Tree

Early in my genealogical "career," before I had read any books on the subject, I began to commit to paper the information I had collected. It never occurred to me to try to find preprinted forms to use. I just took typing paper, a ruler, and a pencil and began. I mention this to illustrate that to get started you need only the most rudimentary tools. And if you don't care about straight lines, you don't even need the ruler! One can purchase preprinted genealogy forms, and of course, today, computer programs make a pencil obsolete, but such programs are not absolutely necessary.

My first mistake: I tried to construct a family tree that encompassed my entire family. This project was much too complex for my skills. However, in making this mistake, I learned that it's much easier to build a family tree around the oldest relative you can find on one side of your family and then work toward the present. If you do this separately for the family lines of each of your four grandparents, you will have a complete overview of your family tree. Once you've done this, you can then put all the information onto one big tree, if you wish.

My purchase of an Arabian horse at about the time I began to document my family history formally, actually helped me in my genealogical research. Pure breed horses, like pedigreed dogs, come with their own genealogical papers. Paladin, my horse, had papers that traced his lineage back more than eight generations. I even found out that he was distantly related to the horse that Rudolph Valentino rode in *Son of the Sheik*.

The type of format used to trace animal genealogy is the pedigree form, which starts from the individual and works backward, allowing you to include all the mares and sires (mothers and fathers) in one tree. A lightbulb went on in my head. I could do this with my own genealogy!

I didn't know it then, but the pedigree form for human genealogy is well-known to all practitioners of the genealogical art. Discovering this form of documenting my own family helped me a great deal in organizing my information.

Once I had created a basic pedigree chart, I continued to add to it as I talked to various relatives, but didn't go much farther until a relative doing research on my grandfather's side of the family contacted me. He was looking for information that I could supply, and I did so. In return, he supplied information that I didn't have and I added that to my own work.

My grandmother's side of the family was more difficult to research. Her relatives who came to America had settled in the Midwest, while she and my grandfather remained in New York. I never knew anyone in my grandmother's family. However, in a conversation with my mother, she mentioned a cousin, Audrey Sedita. My mother had met Audrey many years ago, but they were no longer in touch with one another.

Some time after this conversation, as these things sometimes happen, Audrey called my mother because Audrey was also doing research on her family tree. My mother referred her to me and we were able to trade information. When I began this book, I called her and and she very graciously sent me photographs and copies of the naturalization papers she had collected in the interim.

In 1994, I was notified that the Rabbinical Council of UJA was sponsoring a trip for rabbis to Hungary, Kiev, and Israel to study the progress made in those Jewish communities since the fall of communism. As soon as I saw the word "Kiev" on the flyer, I knew that this was a trip that I had to take. Finally, a chance to visit my grandmother's home city! I had grown up with stories about Kiev and about the things that my grandmother loved there. I needed to see those things and experience them myself. I signed up for the trip.

In doing research for this trip, I was introduced to the Chicago Action for Soviet Jewry and its dynamic leader, Marilyn Tallman. I wanted to find out what I could bring for the Jews in Kiev and was told that this group, a chapter of the Union of Councils for Jews in the former Soviet Union, would know exactly what was needed. In speaking with them, I discovered that they had a liaison committee in Kiev and I agreed not only to take supplies and money that I collected from friends, family, and concerned citizens, but also to bring some materials that they needed to get to their workers in Kiev.

About two weeks before leaving on my trip, my mother said to me, "You know, your grandmother came from Skvira.

"Skvira?" I said. "All I ever heard about was Kiev!"

My mother explained that Skvira was a shtetl near Kiev, and that was where my grandmother grew up. I was dumbfounded. For more than forty years, my grandmother's persona was linked inextricably, for me, to a place called "Kiev" and now I had discovered that her home was somewhere quite different. Why hadn't I ever heard of this other place before? Why hadn't my mother mentioned it?

In the years that followed this experience, I had a great deal of contact with Jews from the former Soviet Union who had immigrated to the United States. I soon discovered that this type of regional generalization is quite common and learned to ask the question, "Are you really from X (the big city they had named,) or do you come from someplace else?" Almost without exception, they were really from a suburb or a small town near the metropolis they claimed as "home."

As for why my mother never mentioned this to me, I guess that while I was here in the United States, it didn't seem to make a difference to her. Not a genealogist herself, the importance of that specific name would not strike her as particularly significant. However, once I planned to visit the "homeland," the particularity of where my grandmother was born and lived became more important to her. Since I was going to be "in the neighborhood," I could visit the old homestead.

I was very grateful to discover this crucial piece of genealogical information and immediately made plans to break away from the group for a day to visit Skvira. I had no information about where the family lived, but I knew that there were some relatives who had never left the Ukraine. It was possible that I might be able to find a grave at the local cemetery, or perhaps someone who knew of my grandmother's family. To help me, I took along a copy of a family photograph, taken before my grandmother and her brothers emigrated. I had the vague idea of going to Skvira and showing this photograph to people. Who those people would be, I didn't know. I'd have to wait until I got there. I knew that if I tried, something would happen.

I Go to Skvira and Discover My Grandmother's Roots

Kiev is very cold and snowy in early February. It was exciting being in a city that I had heard about so often and never really believed I would visit. Our hotel, the Intourist, recently renovated to accommodate "Western" tourists, had not lost any of its pre-Glasnost charm. Every floor had a "matron" who carefully observed who went in and out of their rooms. I heard the rumor that the matrons could also provide tea and other comforts, but the matron on my floor never offered this service and I didn't ask for it. If she owned a smile, I certainly never saw it. Every time I came up to my room, she glared at me suspiciously.

The bedrooms did not have thermostats, so one was at the mercy of the central controller, who was stingy with the heat. There was at least a fifteen-degree difference in temperature between the rooms that were windward and those that were sheltered from the wind. I was initially stationed in one of the windward rooms like most of my rabbinic colleagues. However, because I was trained from infancy by my mother in how to deal with an unsatisfactory hotel room, I collared one of our Russian-speaking guides and returned to the front desk. Employing "stage one" tactics, I calmly and politely requested a different room on the other side of the hotel, explaining that my room was too cold. He repeated my request in Russian.

The clerk informed me, rather imperiously, half in Russian and half in English, that I had been assigned one of the "warm" rooms. She turned, as though to walk away. In her mind, the conversation was finished. However, she didn't realize that she was dealing not with just another westerner, but with a person in whose blood ran the iron of the "homeland." I smiled and explained to her back that the room was not satisfactory and repeated my request. She turned to me and repeated her mantra; I already had a warm room.

Time for "stage two," Ukrainian style. I stared at her, impassive. Our eyes locked. I told her that the room was unsatisfactory. My body language suggested that I was going to stand at the reception desk and be a pest until she changed my room. We glared at each other. She turned and took another key from the shelf. "Score one for the Jews," I thought. My new room, on the other side of the hotel, proved much warmer than the first one I had been assigned. It also had a shower that liberally dispensed hot water.

I had made arrangements, through the tour director who was traveling with us, to hire a car, driver, and interpreter to take me to Skvira on one of the days we were in Kiev. The day we were to leave was clear, bright, and, predictably, very cold. The driver, as it turned out, was a native of Skvira who was not Jewish. My interpreter, from Kiev, was a Jewish young man in his late twenties or early thirties named Sasha. It seemed to me that all Russian men were named Sasha and all women were named Natasha.

At the time I was in Kiev, in 1994, owning a car was a luxury out of the reach of most citizens. For this reason there was very little traffic on the highways, especially compared to other major cities around the world. As we drove out of Kiev, I plied Sasha with questions about the areas we passed. We saw many dachas, the summer homes maintained by Russian families. The dachas looked like they were literally rooted into the earth.

Occasionally we would pass a car pulled over to the side of the road. Underneath the car, there was often a small fire burning. Sasha explained that gasoline becomes frozen in the gas line. These people were defrosting the gas so that they could continue on their way. To Sasha, this was a routine sight, not even worthy of comment. To me, such a sight was astonishing. I wondered how many cars—and their owners—got blown up every year.

It took about an hour and forty-five minutes to drive the sixty-three miles to Skvira's city limits. There was a big sign and we pulled over, at my insistence, to take a photograph. I'm here, Grandma, I thought.

There were many groves of trees lining the roadway, and I thought of the stories about my grandparents escaping from Russia, traveling through the woods at night. Although I didn't know where they began their journey, it was easy to envision people moving quickly through those trees at night. There were no street lamps and it must have been very dark. I had a strong sense of my grandmother's presence.

We drove into town. Where did I want to go first? Sasha asked. My plan was to visit an area with a lot of people, show them the photograph of my grandmother's family, and ask them if they knew of any people with that name. It seemed to me that a central shopping area might be a good place to start. Sasha and the driver discussed this idea and decided that we should begin at the central department store.

The central department store was dark, depressing, and virtually empty of what a westerner would consider "merchandise." A light film of dust covered the shelves and some of the goods that were lined up in straight rows. I found some toys on a shelf—plastic soldiers—lying down and standing up. In the clothing department, there were a few dresses, utilitarian rather than fashionable, in various sizes, no two alike. There were a couple of boxes of bubble gum, whose labels, printed in Arabic, suggested that the gum was not made in the United States or Israel.

Several "salesladies" stood behind the counters, talking to one another. There were no shoppers in the store, other than us. It was so different from any store I had ever been in. I was literally speechless. I didn't want to stare, but I couldn't help myself. There was such an air of poverty and hopelessness in that place. I felt like a visitor from another planet.

Sasha nudged me out of my stupor and asked me what I wanted to do. I took the Xerox of my family photograph out of my tote bag and suggested that we should show it to one of the salesladies and inquire if she recognized any of the people. We approached the "candy counter," home of the Arabic bubble gum, and the saleswoman approached us.

Sasha explained that I was an American whose family originally lived in Skvira. I was trying to trace my relatives. He showed her the photograph and asked her if she recognized any of the people in the photograph.

As soon as he took out the photograph, the other saleswomen, who had been hovering on the edge of our little group, came over. A conversation ensued. Another woman was called over. Another discussion.

It was decided that the director should be consulted. Why? The director was Jewish. He would be in shortly. Would we wait? Of course.

In the meantime, one of the women told Sasha that her husband was an historian and a writer and had written a history of Skvira for the town's six-hundredth anniversary. Would I care to come to their home for potatoes?

Sasha explained to me that this was an invitation to lunch. I gladly accepted and the woman went off to alert her family that a visitor would soon arrive. As she did so, the director arrived. The situation was explained to him and he looked at the photograph. He didn't recognize either my family name or anyone in the photo, but he suggested that we call the oldest Jewish man in Skvira. This was done, but the man was not home. It was suggested that we might phone later in the day.

We went home with our hostess, Luda Ivanovich, and met her husband Vasil and her extended family—her mother, her daughter, and grandson, who also lived with them. Her daughter's husband was at work, as was her older son. The family, about eight people in all, lived in a four-room house. I wasn't given the tour, but I did see the dining room, which I think doubled as a bedroom at night, and the "living room/study" where Vasil worked, which I think also served as a bedroom for him and his wife.

The house was situated on a very large piece of land planted with fruit and nut trees. In the summer, they also planted vegetables, which were then preserved for the winter. We ate some of these at lunch.

As we waited for the food to be served, Vasil presented me with an inscribed copy of his book and we spoke about the history of Skvira. He told me that before World War II, 30,000 people, including 16,000 Jews, resided in Skvira. The general population in 1994 was 20,000, with only about 100 Jews left. He said that many of the Jews had immigrated to Israel or the United States. He refrained from telling me that many had died during the war in a massacre similar to the killings at Baba Yar. I found this out later when I visited the local cemetery, which has a monument to the Jews of Skvira who had been murdered there.

Recently, a friend, Cantor Natasha Jitomirskaia, who is from the Ukraine, looked through the book that Vasil had given me and translated the inscription. It reads, "For good memory of our meeting in Skvira—with utmost respect to Jo David with the best wishes of happiness and goodnes in life. Author Tzymbaliuk." The book is written in Ukranian and was published in 1990. Natasha told me that the language is a curious combination of politically correct Communist language with overtones of Ukrainian nationalism. She suggested that my host was probably a "closet" Ukrainian nationalist. Interestingly, there is no mention of the Jewish community of Skvira.

I discovered, from our driver, that Skvira had been the home of an Hassidic sect—the Skvira Hasidim. This group had relocated to the United States. I later found out that they were settled almost in my backyard—in a northern suburb of New York in a town called, appropriately, "New Square."

We ate a wonderful lunch washed down with a great deal of champagne. Luda's daughter, a doctor, told me about the problems in the local hospital. There were no anesthetics or analgesics available, so the staff was being taught reflexology to help manage pain. The idea behind reflexology is that specific parts of the foot are connected in some way to other parts of the body. If one has pain in the lower back, for example, it is believed that massaging the part of the foot that correlates to the lower back can relieve this pain.

We took our leave of our friendly hosts in the early afternoon to see some other sites. Hoping that I would have occasion to distribute them, I had taken a number of different gifts with me. I left some of these with the family, including the Russian language baseball cards that I had purchased in the United States, scented hand creams, panty hose, lipsticks, and a nice tie for Vasil.

We took a tour of the town, with our driver pointing out the sights. I saw the building that had been the town's major synagogue, now turned into a factory. It was behind a locked gate guarded by a drunk and belligerent watchman. When I wanted to take a picture of the building through the rails of the gate, he became quite threatening. Sasha gave him a couple of dollars and he grumbled, but spared me a few moments to take my picture. It was still possible to see the outline of a Jewish star on the red brick wall.

We also passed a building that had been a seltzer factory. Skvira was a center for seltzer production and, in fact, my great-grandfather and several of his brothers had been in this business together. Apparently, at the turn of the century, making seltzer was a Jewish trade, one of the few businesses in which Jews could engage. When my great-grandfather's brothers immigrated to the United States, they went into the business that they knew and prospered.

The Jewish immigrant seltzer connection had never had any particular meaning to me before going to Skvira. Getting our regular seltzer delivery in Brooklyn, where I grew up, was a normal part of our lives. In the winter, we would be aware of when our seltzer delivery was coming. We didn't want the bright green and blue bottles to freeze and burst in the metal delivery box that stood next to our front door. That the seltzer delivery man and the companies that made the seltzer were Jewish were a fact of life, not something to be questioned. Now I understand why they were Jewish.

After my trip, the words, "Your great grandfather was in the seltzer business," had a different ring. I had seen one of the factories. I had seen the small houses and the fruit trees. I had met some of the people, including the non-Jews who lived there. I could envision a close-knit community supporting itself in a hostile environment with limited resources. I could understand the feelings of the immigrants taking the trade they knew and transferring those skills to the New World. And I could understand that, as their children and grandchildren became Americanized, those skills would no longer be valued as a source of income. Thus, today, seltzer comes in plastic bottles with twist-off caps. There are no more deliveries and rarely, if ever, does one see a "real" seltzer bottle with its silver metal "spritzer."

When we finished our tour of Skvira, we headed back to Kiev. I hadn't met anyone who knew my relatives, but I had been given a glimpse of life that, I suspect, was not all that different from that which my grandmother knew. It may not have been the most "efficient" use of my limited time, but it was emotionally very rewarding. That was not the end of my Skvira experience, however.

The itinerary for the group with whom I was traveling included a trip to Israel with Jews who were making aliyah. At the Kiev airport, one of my rabbinic colleagues who spoke Yiddish fell into a conversation with the family sitting next to him. Suddenly he turned to me and said, "Jo, this family is from Skvira."

It was true. Seventeen members of a Jewish family sat next to us. The grandfather, Isaac Damsky, a man who I judged to be in his mid-sixties, was introduced to me. I was immediately offered vodka, which I accepted, and we began to talk, through our interpreter. I took out the picture of my family and showed it to the man. No, he didn't know anyone in the photo and didn't recognize the family name. To console me, he opened a yellow cast-iron pot and offered it to me.

Inside were cold beef patties. As soon as I smelled the garlic, I knew exactly what they were and I started to cry. These were no mere cold hamburgers. These were *cutlyeten*, patties made with ground beef, eggs, bread crumbs, and garlic and fried in chicken fat. My grandmother used to make them when we lived in Brooklyn. I hadn't smelled or eaten one for more than thirty years. I practically inhaled the first one, and then several more. The taste was the same, only in my childhood I had never washed them down with vodka.

I told this family about my trip to Skvira and my search for my relatives. The vodka continued to flow. In a somewhat alcoholic and garlic-filled haze, we finally got on the plane. I wished them well and thanked them for the food and drink. I felt like I had had a special "visitation" from my grandmother and her Skvira family. I hadn't found specific individuals, but I had discovered a sense of "home."

My trip to Skvira was emotionally satisfying. I was lucky that our driver was a local resident and could give me a guided tour. However, from the point of view of practical genealogy, there were many opportunities that I missed. Also, given the cost of visiting the old country, I wouldn't suggest my rather casual approach if you're interested in trying to get some "hard" results.

There are three things that you can do to maximize your search for records or existing family members in the old country and to prepare for a trip.

1. Hire a local genealogist, Jewish, if possible, to do some research for you, either in lieu of actually making a trip yourself or to help you prepare for your trip before you go. This person can also be your guide when you are in the country, and may be able to assist you with transportation and accommodations by referring you to a local resource for these services. Remember, the genealogist is a genealogist, not a travel agent. A list of genealogists appears in chapter 18.

2. Work with a company that specializes in organizing genealogical trips to your family's hometown. These companies can provide a variety of services including setting up interviews with local officials and making appointments for you to visit local records archives. In Eastern Europe, vital records offices may not have regular visitor's hours, so it's a good idea to find out what the local situation is before you arrive.

3. Do your own research on the history of the Jewish community in your family's hometown. Current travel books often have excellent histories of the cities you might want to visit. The embassy or consulate of the country in which your city/town is located may also be able to give you helpful information. Libraries are also a good resource.

WORKING WITH A LOCAL GENEALOGIST

There are many ways in which a local genealogist can help you.

Phone Book Research

- The local genealogist can check the current local phone book and the phone book in the largest nearby city for individuals with your family surname. If people with that surname are listed, he or she can supply you with a list of their names, addresses, and phone numbers.

- He or she can also check the current phone books of any other cities where you think your family might have relocated. If anyone with that surname is listed, follow the steps above.

If you locate anyone with your family name, you can write a letter that your genealogist can translate into that country's language. In the letter, introduce yourself and explain why you think you may be related. Give as many family details as possible. Ask the genealogist to accept responses and translate them and forward them to you or have the letters come directly to you and arrange for them to be translated by someone locally. With your letter, enclose a self-addressed envelope and include a check or international money order to cover return postage.

- Have the geneaologist check the local phone books for your family surname during the years when you know your family lived in that town. Write down the addresses and phone numbers of all the people with that surname. You may find names you would recognize.

Local Life-Cycle Records—Birth, Death, Marriage

The local offices that house life-cycle records for birth, death, and marriage certificates for your relatives should also be checked. A local geneaologist can be very helpful with this task. The accuracy of the information you provide will determine the success of this type of search.

Local Synagogue Records

In some communities where an active Jewish community no longer exists, the records of local synagogues have been preserved as part of the town's history. These records, especially membership lists and yahrzeit lists, may provide family clues.

Local Jewish Cemetery Research

- The local Jewish cemetery may have an office that contains records of graves that no longer exist. Such records may give you clues about family relatives.

- Individual or family headstones may still be in existence. These headstones could be photographed for your family records.

NEXT STEPS

For some time after I returned from Skvira, I put a hold on my genealogical research. There were a great number of things going on in my life and I didn't have the time to focus on that project. However, in late 1997, I was approached about doing this book, and that assignment rekindled my interest in my own family history project.

It was at this time that I invested in some computer software and began to chart my family tree more clearly. I spoke to other family members, attempting to get more information. I also began collecting family documents and photographs. I wrote to the regional NARA office (National Archives and Records Administration) for my maternal grandparents' petitions for naturalization and to the appropriate local registry and archives offices in New York City for documents related to my father's genealogy.

I'm focusing on my maternal line, but will eventually begin to work in earnest on my paternal genealogy. I plan to work with a local genealogist in the Ukraine not only to trace back my grandparents' roots, but to see if we can find living relatives.

I'm also beginning to think about how I want to preserve all our documents and replicate them for our family. I became a grandmother last year and I want my grandson to know about his heritage. A copy of my in-progress family tree appears at the end of this chapter. Chapter 5 has detailed information about how to create your own family tree.

WHY I'M HOOKED ON GENEALOGY

I was explaining to someone just the other day how to use one life-cycle document—like a birth certificate—to get information about previous generations. "It's just like a jigsaw puzzle," she said.

It's true. There are no straight lines in genealogy. It's very much a matter of laying out the "corner pieces" and then working your way into the puzzle in whatever way you can. You can do everything just right—by the book—and come up with nothing, or do something completely "wrong" and hit the jackpot. I like that. The advice can help, but there's a great deal of serendipity involved in putting together a family tree.

Recently, at my grandson's first birthday party, an unexpected piece of the puzzle fell into my lap. I was talking to my mother about this book and asking her questions about my grandmother's family. I had brought pictures that her cousin Audrey, the genealogist I mentioned earlier, had sent me to show to my mother. As we looked at the photographs, I asked her why my grandmother had never had much of a relationship with her uncles who came to the United States. The rest of her siblings had stayed behind in the Ukraine.

Then I remembered that my grandmother used to get letters from these relatives and talk to them on the phone. I remember her sending them packages. I had never asked specifically who these relatives were or where they were calling from. She wasn't sure who it was that my grandmother had been talking to except that she thought that they were the children of my grandmother's brother Toddle.

"Were they calling from Skvira?" I asked.

"No," my mother said. "I think they were calling from Moscow." After the party, she went home and found some postcards at home that had been sent to my grandmother from Moscow.

Moscow! A new trail. Will the descendents of Toddle Pokrashevsky, born in Skvira, Ukraine, please phone home!

RABBI JO DAVID—FAMILY TREE AS OF JUNE 1998
(Combined matrilineal and patrilineal)

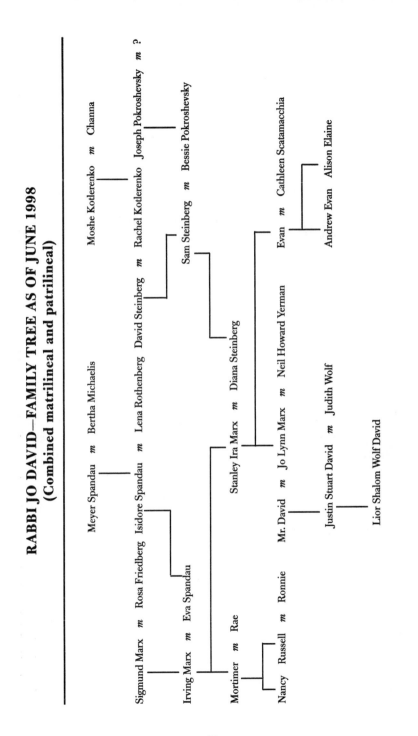

2

Genealogy: It's Very Jewish

GENEALOGY IN THE BIBLE

"Now the man knew his wife, Eve, and she conceived and bore Cain.... She then bore his brother, Abel.... Cain knew his wife and she conceived and bore Enoch. And he then founded a city, and named the city after his son Enoch. To Enoch was born Irad, and Irad begot Mehujael, and Mehujael begot Methusael, and Methusael begot Lamach. Lamach took to himself two wives: Adah and Zillah. Adah bore Jabal; he was the ancestor of those who dwell in tents and amidst the herds. The name of his brother was Jubal; he was the ancestor of all who play the lyre and pipe. As for Zillah, she bore Tubal-cain, who forged all implements of copper and iron. And the sister of Tubal-cain was Naamah. Adam knew his wife again and she bore a son and named him Seth.... And to Seth a son was born and he named him Enosh. It was then that men began to invoke YHVH by name." (Genesis 4:1–26)

This first genealogy in the biblical book of Genesis is a blueprint for modern genealogists. Although presented in narrative form, which is not the modern genealogist's "format of choice," it clearly shows how to present a linear description of a family's history. It also demonstrates the way in which personal names, place names, occupations, and important historical events are intertwined with a family's history. As we will see, such information can provide important clues for a genealogist.

If this were the only genealogical account in the Bible, we might assume that its purpose was merely to answer the question, "Where did people come from?" However, there are dozens of genealogies in the Bible. Each genealogy has a specific purpose. Some genealogies serve to link the development of the Jewish people to its earliest roots. The first genealogy in the Torah is important because it establishes *yichis*—the legitimate and prestigious family lineage—for the various characters that will later be introduced onto the stage of biblical history. Other genealogies seem to be constructed to "fill in the blanks" for a major figure whose antecedents are unclear.

The background of Moses is an excellent example. At the beginning of the book of Exodus, we are told that the Pharaoh's daughter pulls Moses from the river and gives him the name "Moses." (Exodus 2:5–10) However, the names of his father, his mother, his sister, and even the Pharaoh's daughter are missing. We only know that "a certain man of the house of Levi married a Levite woman." (Exodus 2:1) It's not until Exodus 6:14 that a genealogy is introduced that establishes Moses as the son of Amram and Yocheved and as the younger brother of Aaron.

From a genealogist's point of view, the mention of Moses' parents as being Levites is important because the Levites will become recognized as the "priestly class," the God-ordained spiritual leaders of the Jewish people. Moses is a Levite on both sides of his family tree, as are his brother Aaron and his sister, Miriam. This lineage is meaningful because it justifies the right of leadership for Moses, Aaron, and Miriam.

Interestingly, Miriam is not mentioned in the genealogy that links Moses and Aaron. The first mention of her relationship to this family line occurs in Exodus 15:20, when she is introduced as "Miriam the prophetess, Aaron's sister." The fact that she is not mentioned as Moses' sister raised a red flag for biblical commentators and biblical historians.

Some scholars have suggested that Moses was not really the brother of Aaron and Miriam, but rather an Egyptian who identified with the Jewish people and their god. As proof for this argument, they point to the etymology of Moses' name. The Hebrew text says that he was named Moses because he was drawn out of the water. This relates to the Hebrew word *masha,* which means "to draw out." However, this is an incorrect etymology. More likely, scholars say, the name was Egyptian. Moshe is related to the Egyptian word that means "born of" as in the name of the Pharaoh Thutmosis, which means "born of Thut."

Other scholars point to the story of Moses being found in the river in a reed basket. They suggest that this story was a literary convention used in the ancient Near East to fill in the background of a leader whose origin is unknown. As proof, they point to the story of Sargon, the Semitic conqueror of Babylonia who ruled at about 2300 B.C.E. A similar story is told about his birth.

On the other hand, Rashi, the great Jewish biblical commentator, upholds the tradition that Moses was the brother of Aaron and Miriam. Rashi suggests that Miriam is called Aaron's sister, rather than Moses' sister, in the text because Miriam was a prophetess even before Moses' birth.

To a modern reader, this may seem like a nonsequitur. The traditional rabbinic mind, however, accepts the concept that the Torah was given to us by God and is therefore perfect. The tradition teaches that Moses, Miriam, and Aaron were siblings. Therefore, rather than look for proof that this is not the case, the rabbinic commentator seeks to resolve problems in the text.

For Rashi, since the relationship between Moses, Aaron, and Miriam is a given, the only problem in the text is to explain why Miriam is not linked to Moses as well as to Aaron in Exodus 15:20. Rashi's conclusion suggests that Miriam was much older than Moses and closer in age to Aaron. Aaron and Miriam had a close relationship because of their relative ages, whereas Miriam and Moses were so far apart in age that Moses was like an "only child." For this reason, Miriam is mentioned only as Aaron's sister.

Biblical genealogies were constructed along the patrilineal line. This gave authority to the assumption that the stories of men were more important than the stories of women. Of the thirty-nine books in the Hebrew Bible, only two have "leading ladies"—the Book of Esther, and the Book of Ruth. However, these two women were very important. Esther, through her influence as the Queen of Shushan, saves the Jewish people from annihilation. Ruth, a convert to Judaism, becomes the grandmother of King David, from whose genealogical line the Jewish messiah will come.

These two Biblical books demonstrate that women's lives are as important as those of men. Without Esther, there would be no Jewish people. Without Ruth, there would be no messiah.

Establishing Your Jewish Lineage

The history of genealogy can be traced back to the earliest Jewish stories in the Bible. Throughout Jewish history, establishing one's Jewish parentage and lineage has been extremely important in the continuity of the Jewish people. The biblical injunctions against intermarriage (Exodus 34:15–16; Deuteronomy 7:3–4) make it imperative for two Jewish people about to be married to be able to assure the religious authorities that they are both Jewish. For the last 2,500 years or so, the document most important for this purpose has been the ketubah.

The ketubah is a Jewish wedding contract that acted as both a life insurance policy for the bride—it established the amount of money her future husband would settle on her, to be hers in case he predeceased her—and it also established the participants' Jewish lineage. Every ketubah contains the Hebrew name of both the bride and the groom and their fathers. The names of their mothers were rarely, if ever, included. The status of "Cohen" and "Levi," if applicable, were also reflected in a father's Hebrew name.

Every ketubah notes the geographical location at which the wedding takes place. In ancient times, the nearest major body of water was also listed so that common place names would not be confused—i.e., Haran in Iraq and Haran in Syria. In wealthy and established Jewish communities like those of Italy in the eighteenth-century, ketubot were beautifully illuminated and illustrated. Family trees and family portraits were often incorporated into the illustrative border. Today, Jewish marriages still require a ketubah. Many modern ketubot incorporate family trees and other types of family history. We will discuss ketubot at greater length in another chapter.

SPECIAL CHALLENGES FOR THE JEWISH GENEALOGIST

A trip through your local bookstore's genealogy section will make the special problems of a Jewish genealogist crystal clear. Most books about genealogy written for English speakers assume that one's family came over on the *Mayflower* or have an English-speaking background. For most Jews living in English-speaking countries today, that is not the case.

If your American family roots go back less than four generations, it's a good bet that your family came from Russia, Poland, or Eastern Europe. If your American roots begin somewhere around 1850, your family most likely came to America from Germany. If you've been here longer than that, your family is probably of Sephardic origin, coming to the United States from Latin America, Holland, Spain, or Portugal. The bottom line is that probably sooner rather than later you will need to deal with archives and research materials in languages other than English. This need not create an insurmountable barrier for your research. Easy ways of negotiating this situation are discussed in several chapters in this book.

Another challenge for Jewish genealogists is the idea that many Jewish records were destroyed during the Holocaust. While it is true that many records were destroyed, more and more records previously thought missing have come to light in the past few decades. One should not assume that records are not available just because one's family is from Russia or Eastern Europe.

Fifty years ago, the science of Jewish genealogy was literally unknown. Groundbreaking work was done in the 1970s and 1980s by Rabbi Malcolm Stern, Arthur Kurzweil, Dan Rottenberg, Gary Mokotoff, and Avotaynu (the "think tank" of Jewish genealogy). Today, the resources available to Jewish genealogists are multiplying at a dizzying rate. JewishGen, the premiere online Jewish genealogy Web site, is a link to hundreds of other resources. Countless Jewish archives, libraries, Jewish historical societies, and Jewish genealogy associations now exist to support the growing ranks of amateur and professional Jewish genealogists.

Jews are called "the People of the Book," because the Torah guides and inspires our lives. The Torah and other sections of the Hebrew Bible, through their many genealogies, teach us the importance of family and of knowing who we are and where we came from. They also teach us the importance of conserving and adding to this knowledge. When we embark on the search for our own family history, we not only add to the richness of our own lives, but we also leave a priceless inheritance for our descendents, adding details and texture to the ongoing story of the Jewish people.

Every Pesach (Passover) we read in the Haggadah a passage from the Torah: "My father was a wandering Aramean who went down to Egypt and dwelt there." (Deuteronomy 26:5) The "father" referred to is generally understood to be Abraham, whose name in Hebrew can be understood as meaning "father of many." Abraham's wanderings are seen as the genesis of the Jewish people as a distinct group on the world stage. Through the yearly repetition of this story, we are reminded of where our Jewish roots are planted. As Jewish genealogists, our challenge is to work backward, reaching toward those roots. An awesome task, but then, as Ben Hei Hei tells us in the *Pirke Avot:* "According to the labor is the reward." (5:26) A good motto for a Jewish genealogist.

3

An Historical Look at Jewish Emigration and Immigration

One day, a few years ago, I had the thought that, since I'm here and I'm Jewish, one of my ancestors must have crossed the Reed Sea with Moses and Miriam. It was a powerful idea that gave me a strong sense of being connected to Judaism and to the history of the Jewish people. It made the story of the Biblical exodus come alive for me. The broad sweep of Jewish history was no longer just a confusing bunch of dates and place-names but a very personal aspect of my own family history.

This idea, that I personally had family roots that connected me to ancient times, was one of the factors that stimulated my desire to do genealogical research. Of course, I later thought of several reasons why some ancestors of mine might not have crossed the Reed Sea with Moses and Miriam. However, by the time I had figured this out, I was hooked on genealogy.

Another way that some families can trace themselves back to biblical times is through inherited priestly status. In the Torah, the tribe of Levi is designated as the tribe that will serve God in the Temple. Because of this, the Levites did not receive any land when the Israelites conquered Canaan under Joshua's leadership. Instead, the Israelites supported them by bringing special offerings to the Temple at the three harvest festivals—Sukkot, Pesach, and Shavuot.

All members of the tribe of Levi are Levites. However, only the descendents of Aaron the priest have the special designation of "Kohen." Only a member of the family of a Kohen could become the Kohen Gadol, the High Priest. The Kohen Gadol was responsible for the proper functioning of the Temple in Jerusalem.

The maintaining of accurate genealogical records was very important to Levitical families even in biblical times. When the Jews returned to the land of Israel after the Babylonian exile in about 500 B.C.E., priestly families that could not provide documentation to prove their right to claim levitical status were disqualified as Levites and Kohanim. (Ezra 2:62)

Today, the "proof" of a genealogical link to the tribe of Levi is contained in the Hebrew name of a Jewish man. If his Hebrew name has the suffix "haKohen," he is recognized as being a descendent of the family of Aaron. If his name has the suffix "haLevi," he is recognized as being a descendent of the tribe of Levi, but not of the family of Aaron.

For practical purposes, the functioning of Levitical families as servants of God goes back about three-thousand years to the time of the building of the First Temple in Jerusalem and to about 500 B.C.E. in terms of establishing a firm genealogical link. For most Jewish families, the passing down of the status of Kohen and Levi has been an oral rather than written tradition. Very few Jewish families, if any, have written genealogies that date back to 500 B.C.E. For this reason, in the modern Jewish community, the oral tradition is respected and considered to be accurate. However, there is little hard genealogical proof in most families to substantiate the link to the biblical Levites.

This situation points up one of the central challenges a genealogist faces. We can go so far and then the trail disappears. Working on our family tree is a process of working backward from the known to the unknown. Once we hit the disappearing trail, what do we do next? Is there some way that we can perhaps generalize about our family's background? We find evidence of our family in Poland or Spain or Italy. But how did we get there?

This chapter answers that question in a general way. There are many reasons why Jewish populations emigrated throughout ancient and modern history. Sometimes these movements were voluntary, undertaken for financial reasons. All too often, however, Jewish populations were relocated by those hostile to our community. Many of us may not be able to trace our roots to a time before the mid-eighteenth century. However, perhaps by looking at an overview of Jewish migrations throughout the ages, we can get a feeling for what the lives of our early ancestors were like. Perhaps we can even begin to feel that they are truly part of our family tree.

The various peoples of the ancient Near East inhabited the areas that today we call Israel, Lebanon, Syria, Saudi Arabia, Iraq, Jordan, Iran, and Egypt. Our story as a people with a unique god and a unique mission in the world begins in the ancient Near East with the story of a man named Abraham and a god whose name is YHVH.

The letters *YHVH* represent the four letters that spell the unpronounceable name of the God of the Israelites, sometimes referred to as the "tetragrammaton." In Hebrew, the letters for this name are *yod hey vav hey*. Incorporated into this name are all the letters needed to create the past, present, and future of the Hebrew verb "to be." Thus, the name of this god can be understood to be "I was, I am, I will be." For this reason, some English translations of this name in prayer books translate the tetragrammaton as the word "Eternal."

The Tetragrammaton was considered to be so sacred that it was only pronounced once a year by the High Priest on Yom Kippur. After the fall of the Second Temple, the tradition developed that the name was not to be said aloud at all.

When Jews pray to this god and invoke this name in prayer, the word substituted for the unpronounceable name is *Adonai,* which means, "my Lord." In printed English translations of the Torah, when YHVH is on the scene, the word used to substitute for the unpronounceable name is *Lord*. The word *God* refers to one of the other seven sacred names for the same deity. The seven sacred names of God in the Torah are: YHVH, Adonai, El, Eloah, Elohlm, Shaddai, and Tzevaot. When speaking of the god of the tetragrammaton, or even of God in general, some Jews use the term *Hashem*—the name—as a way of further distancing themselves from inadvertently saying the holy name or taking the name of the Holy One in vain.

The god of the Israelites has seven different sacred names in the Torah and well over a hundred different names that are used in Jewish liturgy. Most of the hundred or so names refer to specific aspects of God—i.e., the Shechina—God's female presence in the world, Tzur Yisrael—Rock of Israel, Melech—King. The tetragrammaton might be considered to be God's special "parental" name.

What is a special parental name? The word *mother* designates a formal relationship between a parent and child. However, few children call their female parent "mother" (except perhaps when they're angry). Most substitute another particular name—mom, mommy, ma, mama— that signifies a warm, loving relationship. For the Jewish people, the tetragrammaton is this special, particular kind of name for their God.

The other six sacred names might be compared to the other types of family-related titles used to designate a particular person. For example, the same woman, me, might be called Mrs. Yerman (by someone who doesn't know that I'm a rabbi and that I use a different name from my husband), Justin's mother, Neil's wife, Mrs. Marx's daughter, Lior's grandmother, and Judy's mother-in-law.

Despite the Jewish tradition of not pronouncing the tetragrammaton, scholars working on the biblical texts have speculated about how the name should be pronounced. The two most common name forms that have emerged to refer to this god are Yahweh and Jehovah. Jews never use these names in worship, although some Jewish academicians use these names when doing scholarly work on the Bible or on Jewish liturgy.

THE JOURNEY BEGINS

Our story begins with Abraham and Sarah, who are considered to be the "George and Martha Washington" of the Jewish people. Historical estimates put Abraham's birth sometime between 1800 B.C.E. and 1500

B.C.E. with the later date (1500 B.C.E.) being somewhat more in favor these days. Sarah's birth date has never been considered important by either secular or religious researchers. However, the Torah tells us that Sarah was about ten years younger than Abraham.

The Torah tells us that Abraham's father Terach and his family—Abram (later Abraham), Abram's wife Sarai (later Sarah), and his grandson Lot—moved from the city of Ur sometime after Lot's father's death to the city of Haran. (Genesis 11:31) Ur, which was located near the southern part of the Euphrates River, is in modern Iraq. Haran was near the northern Syrian-Turkish border.

At some point after settling in Haran, Abram was told by the god YHVH to leave his father's home and to begin a journey toward the land of Canaan. (Genesis 12:1–8) Canaan at this time encompassed roughly the area of modern-day Israel and Lebanon. At the time of this journey, Abram was seventy-five and Sarah about sixty-five.

Abraham and Sarah went to Canaan, but, being somewhat nomadic, moved from place to place within the country, venturing, for a brief period, into the land of Egypt during a time of famine in Canaan. (Genesis 12:10–20) In time, Abraham had a son with Sarah's maidservant, Hagar. The name of the son of Hagar and Abraham was Ishmael, which means "God will hear." According to Moslem tradition, Ishmael is the founder of one of the major Arabic groups.

When Ishmael was about fourteen, Sarah gave birth to a son who was named Isaac. Isaac and his descendents remained in Canaan. During a period of famine in Isaac's lifetime, Isaac was specifically warned by God not to go back to Egypt. (Genesis 26:2) The descendents of Abraham and Sarah followed this commandment until a terrible famine struck the biblical world in the time of Joseph, Abraham's great-grandson.

Jacob, one of Isaac's two sons, was the father of twelve sons and a daughter. Unbeknownst to Jacob, his son Joseph, whom he thought had been killed, was the regent of Egypt at the time of the famine. Joseph was in charge of dispensing food supplies. Because of the famine, Jacob sent his sons, who were responsible for selling Joseph into slavery, into Egypt to buy food. At first, the brothers didn't recognize Joseph. Finally,

Joseph revealed himself to them and reconciliation was effected. As a result, the entire family received an invitation by the Pharaoh to relocate to the northern section of Egypt—Goshen, the Nile delta. They settled there and became very wealthy.

Several hundred years later, sometime around 1225 B.C.E., a "mixed multitude" led by a man named Moses left Egypt. Their destination was Canaan, the land that had been promised as a homeland to the three patriarchs Abraham, Isaac, and Jacob. The exodus group included descendents of Jacob's twelve sons as well as other people living in Egypt at that time.

According to the Torah, a set of laws that would guide this group in their relationship to their special god, YHVH, was given to them somewhere in the Sinai desert. They spent a period of forty years in the desert, traveling to forty-two different places until finally entering Canaan sometime in the early twelfth century B.C.E.

THE POST-TORAH PERIOD

In about the year 1000 B.C.E., King David established Jerusalem as the capital of a united Israelite kingdom. The First Temple was built by King Solomon, King David's son, in the mid-tenth century. Its purpose was to serve as a symbol of national unity based on the tradition of the twelve tribes. However, many of the tribes, especially those in the north, did not accept Davidic rule.

At the end of the tenth century, ten northern tribes broke away from the unified kingdom and established their own temple at Shechem, presided over by leaders of their own choosing. There were now two "Jewish" states. The northern kingdom was called "Israel" and occupied the area north of Bethel and Jaffa to an inland area somewhat above Tyre (modern-day Lebanon). Judea, the southern kingdom was an inland state that included Jerusalem in the north and Kadesh-barnea in the south.

Between 732 and 712 B.C.E., the Israelite kingdom was conquered by the Assyrian rulers Tiglath-pileser III and Sargon. During this time, many of the Israelites living in the northern kingdom were "relocated" to other parts of the Assyrian empire. This was the first of many forced emigrations for the Jewish people. Israelites were sent to cities in Syria, Iraq, and Iran, forming the first Jewish communities in these areas. It is also likely that refugees from the northern kingdom made their way into Judea, bringing their traditions and stories with them.

The kingdom of Judea, with its Jerusalem temple, was spared at this time. During the reign of King Josiah (628–609 B.C.E.), at a time when the power of Assyria was waning, Judea underwent a religious and political renewal. During this time, parts of the Israelite kingdom that had been ruled by the Assyrians were retaken and combined into the kingdom of Judea. However, just a few years after the death of King Josiah, Nebuchadnezzar, the king of Babylon, took control of the kingdom of Judea.

Local rulers were selected by Nebuchadnezzar. However, these rulers became embroiled in a number of rebellions against the rule of Babylon. Finally, in retribution, Nebuchadnezzar destroyed all of the fortified cities of Judea, including Jerusalem as well as the Temple, in the fall of 587 B.C.E. This time it was the inhabitants of Judea who were relocated, many to Babylonia.

In 586 other Israelite families fled Judea for Egypt after the murder of the ruler selected by Nebuchadnezzar. These families founded Jewish military colonies. Of these, the most famous is the colony at Elephantine in southern Egypt. This was the beginning of the Jewish presence in Egypt in "modern" times.

THE EXILES RETURN HOME

With the fall of the kingdom of Babylon to Cyrus the Persian in 539, the fortunes of the former citizens of Judea were reversed. Cyrus built his vast kingdom on the principle of religious tolerance. In 537, the first of the exiles from Judea returned from Babylonia with permission to rebuild the Temple in Jerusalem. This project was completed in 515. While many of the exiles returned to Judea, others chose to stay in the areas of Iraq, Iran, and Syria, where they had been relocated.

The Syrian Greeks appeared on the scene in the person of Alexan-

der, son of King Phillip II of Macedonia, in 332. This eventually led to
the rise of Antiochus IV, against whom the Maccabees rebelled in 167.

In the period between the third to the first centuries B.C.E., it became
very hard for the land of Judea to sustain the material needs of its population. Families began to relocate, looking for better opportunities for
themselves and their children. Some families moved to Egyptian military
colonies like Elephantine and Cyrene. Others emigrated to Egyptian
cities like Alexandria, Thebes, and Leontopolis, where they worked at
farming, crafts, and government service. There were Israelite temples of
note at Alexandria and Leontopolis. The temple at Leontopolis stood
until sometime after the destruction of the Second Temple in 70 C.E.
During this time, some Israelites also migrated into Turkey, Cyprus, and
parts of Greece.

During the first century B.C.E., the hold of the Selucid empire weak-
ened. The Selucid empire, which was composed primarily of the area of
modern-day Israel, Lebanon, Syria, Iraq, and Turkey, was eventually
taken over by the conquering Roman invaders. In 63, Pompey conquered Jerusalem after a siege. Pompey took many Jewish slaves who
had been acquired during his campaign through Palestine, back to Italy.
These slaves were the founders of Italy's Jewish community, especially
the community in Rome.

In 70 C.E., after a prolonged revolt against Roman rule, on the ninth
of Av, the Romans burned the Temple to the ground. By the decree of
Titus, all the people of Jerusalem were taken prisoner and the upper
city was leveled. Many of those captives were exiled to Babylonia or
sent to Rome. However, some Jews managed to remain in Jerusalem
during this time. In Rome, the Arch of Titus depicts the sacking of the
Temple and the carrying away of the golden menorah that was one of
the most important religious artifacts in the sanctuary.

THE LAST ATTEMPT AT JEWISH NATIONALISM

In 131 C.E., Jews living in Jerusalem heard that Hadrian had plans to
found a Roman colony, complete with pagan temples, in Jerusalem. Ever
since the destruction of the Second Temple, the Jewish community had

been seeking an opportunity to overthrow Roman rule and rebuild the Temple. The rumor about Hadrian's plans provided a trigger for the smoldering Jewish rebellion.

Rabbi Akiva proclaimed that Simeon Bar Kosiba (later known as Bar Kochba—son of the star) was the Messiah. Under Rabbi Akiva's spiritual leadership, the Bar Kochba rebellion was born. In order to mobilize support for the revolt, Rabbi Akiva traveled to Jewish colonies in the Diaspora. These included Gaul (France) and Africa as well as the more well established Jewish communities of Babylonia and Media. Unfortunately, we don't know how Jews reached Africa and Gaul, but because of Rabbi Akiva's journey, we know that these communities already existed by the middle of the second century of the Common Era.

The Bar Kochba revolt was put down in 135 C.E. During the war, over 500,000 Jews were killed. This was the last major uprising of the Jewish people in the land of Israel until 1948, when the Jews living in Palestine went to war to secure their homeland.

THE WORLDWIDE DISPERSAL BEGINS

At the end of the Bar Kochba rebellion, Jewish literary and religious creativity became focused in the Diaspora communities, especially those in Babylonia. Jewish communities there flourished during the third through the fifth centuries of the Common Era. It was here that the Babylonian Talmud was developed in the academies. The Babylonian Talmud was the first Jewish "encyclopedia," covering all phases of Jewish life, law, and lore. It became the source text for the development of Jewish law through the ages and up to the present time.

However, as Islam began sweeping through the eastern regions of the Roman empire in the late sixth and early seventh centuries, many Jews fled west to the relative safety of Spain, Germany, Italy, France, and England. Some Jews made their way from Egypt into northern Africa. Still others moved further east into Russia, India, and China. Jews in Spain during this period made their mark in the arts and in a variety of professions and gained favor with many monarchs.

Jews who found their way to China and India generally received a friendly welcome. There were well-established Jewish communities in these areas in the Middle Ages. The Chinese community in the city of Kaifeng existed into the nineteenth century, after which it disappeared as a distinct community, as had the other Jewish communities in China, through intermarriage and assimilation. Several of the Jewish communities in India exist to this day.

Scholars do not agree on how Jewish communities formed in Africa. However, the Ethiopian Jewish community, which was recently relocated to Israel, was long known to be a community with legitimate Jewish status.

During the Middle Ages, Jews found themselves persecuted by the Catholic church in many different countries. Jews were expelled from England in 1290, from France in 1394, from some parts of Germany during the fifteenth century, and from Spain and Portugal at the end of the fifteenth century. Some Jews went north to Amsterdam. Others made their way to Hungary, Poland, and Italy. Still others went to South America and the Caribbean. The ancestors of these Sephardic travelers were the first Jews to settle in colonial America.

Because the political situation in Italy was fragmented, Jews tended to do better in Italy during this period than in other parts of Europe. In fact, the Jewish community in Rome is the only European Jewish community that can trace its roots back to antiquity.

Despite the persecution and expulsions of the Jews in Germany, life in Eastern Europe flourished in the Middle Ages. Because Germany was called by the biblical name "Ashkenaz" in medieval Hebrew, the Jews who populated Germany and who later spread out into Poland, Lithuania, and the Ukraine were called "Ashkenazim."

JEWS IN MODERN TIMES

In modern times, each country in Europe has had a very complicated relationship with its own Jewish community. Jewish immigration from the seventeenth century to the present is covered in some detail in chapter 8.

Prior to the Holocaust, Eastern European Jewish communities, especially those of Poland, Germany, Lithuania, and Austria-Hungary, were the major centers of Jewish learning and Jewish life. Israel didn't exist as a Jewish state. American Jews were battling anti-Semitism and generally figuring out how to make it in the American melting pot. Russian Jews were dealing with communism.

The Second World War decimated European Jewry. Many communities where Jews had lived for hundreds of years no longer existed. In those countries where some Jews managed to live through the war, their numbers were radically diminished.

Today, there are four major Jewish population centers. Israel is the largest. In the Diaspora, the other major Jewish communities in order of size are the United States, the former Soviet Union, and France. However, it's hard to visit any country that does not have some Jewish population. There are Jewish communities in Australia, Hong Kong, Japan, Khazakstan, New Zealand, Slovakia, St. Croix, Panama, Brazil, Ireland, South Africa, Chile, and Zimbabwe. There is even a Jewish community in Uganda.

In the light of the Holocaust, the importance of protecting and preserving the cultures and traditions of Jewish communities has become a priority for a number of different organizations. One of the most prominent of these is Beth Hatefutsoth, the Museum of the Diaspora in Tel Aviv. Beth Hatefutsoth was established to study and preserve the history and life of Jewish Diaspora communities. Its excellent Web site offers a wide range of information and services. Their Web site address is: http://www.bh.org.il/.

Another excellent source for in-depth information about specific Diaspora communities is the *Encyclopedia Judaica*. The "EJ" can be found in most synagogue and Jewish research libraries. For some time, most of the research done on Diaspora communities has focused on Ashkenazic customs and lifestyles. However, in the past few years, there has been a renewed interest in studying Sephardic customs and traditions. There are now a number of excellent organizations and Web sites dealing with the Sephardic community. On the Internet, BSZNet, http://www.bsz.org/ provides a wide range of Sephardic links as well as information on Sephardic genealogy, communities around the world, synagogues, recipes, and music. There are Sephardic Jewish communities all around the world, including Morocco, the Balkans, Guatemala, Bulgaria, Turkey, Cuba, Lebanon, Yemen, and the United States.

Another important center for Sephardic education is the Sephardic Educational Center: http://www.primenet.com/~sec/. The center is dedicated to creating programs around the world which are focused on Judaism, Sephardic heritage, and the centrality of Israel. Its headquarters are located at 6505 Wilshire Blvd., Ste. 403, Los Angeles, CA 90048; Tel. (213) 653-7365; Fax (213) 653-9985; E-mail: sec@sephardic.org.

ELLIS ISLAND—THE GATEWAY TO THE GOLDEN LAND

Ellis Island. The name of this American gateway located in New York Harbor is famous all around the world. It symbolizes the door to freedom and a fresh start for people whose homelands no longer felt like home. For the 20 million immigrants who passed through Ellis Island between 1892 and 1924, the period of peak immigration in America, Ellis Island was the gateway to the fabled *Goldene Medina,* the "Golden Land."

Since colonial times, New York has been the primary entry point for European immigrants with eighty percent of all immigrants to America coming through this small island. In 1882, Congress assumed its Constitutional power to regulate immigration, but it was not until about 1890 that the federal government actually assumed the role of examining immigrants arriving in New York. Until 1848, this duty was performed by local New York City officials, after which New York State supervised the process.

Coming into the New World was a risky business for the immigrants. Strangers in a strange land, often without friends or family, unscrupulous city officials and others preyed on them. In an effort to protect the new immigrants, the state commissioners decided that it would be helpful to have a somewhat secluded area in which to control the immigration process. After much discussion, Castle Garden was leased for this purpose and formally opened on August 1, 1855, as the "Emigrant Landing

Depot." Castle Garden was an abandoned military station located on what is now Battery Park at the tip of the island of Manhattan.

When the federal government took over the job of regulating immigration in 1890, the New York authorities refused to permit them to continue to use Castle Garden. It was decided that an island would be more secluded and would make it more difficult for the immigrants to be robbed and cheated by the local population. Ellis Island, which the federal government owned, was finally chosen.

The Immigration Service officially opened on January 1, 1892. In 1898 and 1905, two additional islands were created by dumping earth and rock taken from subway tunnels and from the Grand Central Station excavation. The Immigrant Station consisted of administration buildings, dormitories, hospitals, kitchens, a baggage station, an electrical plant, and a bath house. The cost of the buildings and the hiring of all the personnel, including Immigration and Naturalization Service officers, interpreters, clerks, guards, cooks, maintenance staff, and doctors, and nurses came to approximately $500,000.

THE EXPERIENCE OF ELLIS ISLAND

First Steps

When an immigrant boarded the ship that was to take him or her to the New World, a form, called a "manifest," was filled out. This form contained a wide variety of information including the person's name, age, nationality, marital status, occupation, amount of money in the person's possession, whether the person was going to meet a relative, and other pertinent information. Despite the many stories of name changes on Ellis Island, most often the change occurred on the manifest that was made out on board the ship before the voyage began. For a genealogist, finding a ship's manifest for a relative who came through Ellis Island can provide a wealth of information.

Once docked in New York Harbor, a variety of different things could happen. As in many other situations, money gave some people privileges denied to others. First- and second-class passengers were inspected onboard. Once approved, they would disembark at the pier at which the ship docked. These passengers were only taken to Ellis Island if they were detained or held for special inquiry.

For third-class and steerage passengers, the routine was different. These passengers were often offloaded from their ship onto a barge or ferry and taken to Ellis Island. Other steerage passengers disembarked from the ship in Manhattan, Hoboken, or wherever the ship's dock was located. They then boarded a ferry that took them to Ellis Island.

After 1924, when immigration declined because of changes in the immigration laws, all immigrants were inspected while onboard ship. From this time until 1954, the only arriving immigrants taken to Ellis Island were those who faced detention or Board of Special Inquiry hearings. Today, the many details involved in admitting new immigrants are taken care of in the person's home country and steamships have given way to jumbo 747s. Interestingly, many people now refer to flying "economy class" as flying "steerage."

The Inspections

Once a new immigrant set foot on Ellis Island, there was still the possibility that that individual might not be admitted to the United States. The first stop was the main building's reception area. The first floor was a luggage check and a railroad ticket office. Very often, luggage was lost or misplaced. Missionaries, religious aid societies, and welfare workers assisted the immigrants in finding their lost luggage.

After this was taken care of, the immigrants climbed the stairs to the registry room on the second floor. The climb to the second floor was monitored by medical officers who stood at the top of the stairs watching for signs of lameness, shortness of breath, heart conditions, and mental problems. This inspection served as a preliminary screening process, although the immigrants were unaware of the doctors' scrutiny. As the immigrants moved through a series of examinations, about one in every five would receive chalk marks on their clothing, indicating the need for further medical inspection.

Immigrants who passed the medical exams were then questioned by an examiner and an interpreter to verify the twenty-nine items of information contained on the manifest. Ninety-eight percent of the immigrants passed this test. The literacy tests were also given. All adults and children over sixteen had to be able to read and write in their native language.

Finally, the immigrants who had passed the screening process could exchange whatever foreign money, gold, or silver they had for American dollars. They then bought railroad tickets, if necessary, for their final destinations in America.

It took between two and five hours for an immigrant to be processed. However, when there was more than one person in a family, the actual stay on Ellis Island could be considerably longer. For this reason, a variety of facilities, including sleeping facilities, were provided.

Until the late 1920s, when new facilities were built to accommodate families, immigrant families were separated by sex. The men and older boys were sent to the men's dormitory, while the women and younger children were kept in their own facility. I remember my grandmother telling me of this experience and how frightening it was—and it took a lot to frighten my grandmother! She told me that it was the first time that she and my grandfather had been separated since their marriage.

The Daughters of the American Revolution and various welfare agencies provided other facilities for the immigrants. These included a nursery where mothers were instructed in child care, a kindergarten which introduced children to English, a library with books and magazines in a wide variety of languages, recreational facilities, religious services, and even an occasional concert. In addition, clothing was given to people in need.

When an immigrant was approved for immigration, there were a number of different scenarios for that person's actual entry to the United States. Many immigrants were capable of taking care of themselves and were left by themselves to continue their journey. However, some immigrants expected to be met by friends and family. If these people did not show up on time, or not at all, and if the immigration officer felt that the individual should not be released alone, the immigrant would be discharged into the care of a social service agency worker or a member of one of the missionary groups that "worked" Ellis Island.

HIAS (Hebrew Immigrant Aid Society) was a very important link for many Jews coming through Ellis Island. HIAS was established to aid Jews in the process of their emigration worldwide. When the steamship company that was to take my grandparents from Turkey to the United States went bankrupt and stranded them in Constantinople for two years, it was HIAS that helped them through that period and that finally arranged for their passage to New York.

HIAS helped Jews in a number of different ways, as did other immigrant aid societies. Some immigrants arrived in the United States without sufficient money to enable them to reach their destinations. In such a situation, these people might be released to a social service agency or a missionary group that would care for them until enough money was raised to finance the rest of their journey.

Women and girls who had no friends or relatives in the country were also not released by themselves. Under the law, "unaccompanied" women and children were not admitted as immigrants unless met by a husband or a relative. If a relative could not be present, very often a social service agency would assist in locating relatives or friends willing to accept the responsibility for the new immigrants. If this was not done, these women could be returned to their home country.

The Medical Examination and Its Consequences

The most frightening experience for many people was the medical inspection. From the late nineteenth century on, immigrants with dangerous contagious diseases and those who suffered any physical or mental disability that would make it difficult for that individual to make a living were denied entry. Public Health Service physicians stationed at Ellis Island screened the new immigrants. If the doctors thought that an arriving immigrant was medically unfit, they would "certify" that illness with a "medical certificate."

Immigration officers could accept the medical certificate and use it as grounds for rejecting an immigrant or they could overrule the certificate and admit the immigrant. An appeals process allowed immigrants to challenge the medical certificates and many immigrants who were initially rejected were ultimately permitted to enter the United States. If the illness was curable, the immigrant would be admitted to a hospital until the condition was cured. Once the person was well, grounds for exclusion no longer existed and he or she could be admitted. Most of the time, those immigrants with incurable diseases were returned to their country of origin unless their situation was noncontagious and someone was willing to accept responsibility for their care.

I remember hearing a story when I was very young about a woman someone knew who came to America with her husband and a number of children. One of the children was diagnosed with an eye infection at Ellis Island. For whatever reason, rather than admit the child to the hospital for treatment, the mother and the young child were forced to return to Russia while the husband and the older children were admitted to the United States. Several years passed before the family was reunited in America.

I remember thinking how awful it must have been for the woman to have to take that journey back. Who knew what kind of situation she had left? It might have been dangerous for her to return, but she had no other option. Was there anyone to help her and care for her and her child when they returned to the "old country"? Her anxiety over her child's health and their uncertain future must have been unbearable. And to have to travel steerage again! Did they have enough money and food to make the journey? Were there medical facilities on the boat to treat her child? Many young children died on those crossings. And then, if her child recovered, she would have to go through the journey yet again! If the money could be found! And how would her husband and children manage without her in the new land? The pain, worry, and suffering of this family boggles the mind.

One of the little-known facts about people who were rejected for entrance into the United States was that there were some other options. If an immigrant was sent back to his or her original destination, the cost of the trip came out of the pocket of the ship's captain. Therefore, he had a vested interest in returning as few people as possible. Some captains would therefore take "rejected" immigrants to another port, where they could come into the United States or Canada without going through Ellis Island.

So often, when the media depicts our immigrant ancestors, the picture drawn is of impoverished "country folk," trodden down by life, desperate for the freedom of America. Emma Lazarus, a Jewish woman, wrote the "The New Colossus," the poem that is at the base of the Statue of Liberty. The picture that it draws of an immigrant formed our national consciousness and our social policies for immigration.

> Give me your tired, your poor, your huddled masses yearning
> to breathe free,
> The wretched refuse of your teeming shore,
> Send these, the homeless, tempest-tossed, to me:
> I lift my lamp beside the golden door.

What could be more demeaning than to term our immigrant ancestors "wretched refuse"? In fact, they were brave, incredibly courageous pioneers. How many of us today would be willing to give up everything for an uncertain chance at a new life?

Many of our ancestors were not poor, but the journey to freedom often cost them a great deal, both emotionally and financially. Some of our ancestors were not people who were worldly travelers or otherwise well prepared for the hazards of making such a difficult journey. But their desire to secure a better life for their children drove them to leave loved ones behind and venture forth into an unknown future. This is a family legacy to cherish, no matter what the final outcome.

I remember my grandmother telling me that my great-grandfather lost all the jewels they had over the side of the ship in a storm. As a young child, it didn't occur to me to ask how that could happen, and now my grandmother is not here for me to pose the question. But such stories were not uncommon. If people didn't lose at least some of their money to robbers, to con men, or through other misadventures, they were very, very lucky. And yet, even without the jewels, my family, like so many immigrant families, put down strong roots and prospered.

Welcome to the New World

For immigrants arriving on Ellis Island who passed all of their inspections, their entry to America could still be very confusing and difficult.

Very often, these difficulties were ameliorated by social service agencies. In the Jewish world, there are several agencies that have been long associated with Jewish immigration, not only in America, but throughout the world.

HIAS　　Hebrew Immigrant Aid Society aided many Jews around the world traveling to America. While HIAS originally worked primarily in the Jewish community, today it helps both Jews and non-Jews with a wide variety of immigration issues. HIAS is one of the resources for genealogists looking for information about their ancestors.

Jewish Agency　　The Jewish Agency has many different roles. However, for most of its existence, its primary role has been to help get Jews out of places that have become too dangerous and to help support Jewish life for those Jews who remain behind. A couple of years ago, for example, I was in Budapest and witnessed the successful rescue mission of Jews (and non-Jewish family members and close friends) from Sarajevo. It was an overwhelming experience. What struck me most at the time was that the Jewish Agency had also rescued the pet dog of a young orphaned non-Jewish boy, both of whom had been adopted by a Jewish playmate from Sarajevo. After the refugees had rested from their bus ride, they would be going to Israel to start a new life.

Landsmanshaften　　These were organizations made up of settled immigrants from a particular town or city. The landsmanshaften offered a variety of services and help, including loans, matchmaking, and help in getting settled in general.

For years, our family belonged to a credit union formed by one such organization. It had an unpronounceable name. This was where we went when we needed help. I remember my own first trip there. My mother said to me, "Let me talk to them. You have to know what to say to them." I let her talk and I got the loan, the first of many that I took and paid back. I recently received a letter from them telling me that they were having a contest to find a new, "modern" name. It saddened me, because it made me realize that talking to their loan officer would now be the same as talking to a loan officer in any other financial institution. In a way, I guess this is progress, but I also felt a sense of loss.

Representatives of these and other Jewish social service agencies aided the immigrants in a variety of ways. Some of these services included:

- letter writing to help the immigrants get in touch with friends or relatives in this country
- help in locating lost baggage
- assistance with transportation difficulties
- contacting relatives with the time of a train's arrival
- distribution of newspapers, periodicals, and other literature
- providing representation before boards of inquiry on behalf of detained immigrants; advice on how to appeal their cases
- help with securing bonds and accepting responsibility for their discharge
- making marriage arrangements in the case of girls coming to meet their fiancés.

ELLIS ISLAND TODAY

Ellis Island continued to do some immigrant processing until the mid-1950s. During World War II, Ellis Island was used as a detention center for enemy aliens. In March 1955, it was declared surplus property by the federal government and was turned over to the General Services Administration. In May 1965, Ellis Island was declared part of the Statue of Liberty National Monument. After a successful campaign to raise the funds to restore both the Statue of Liberty and Ellis Island, Ellis Island was reopened and dedicated on September 10, 1990.

The "new" Ellis Island boasts three major new projects.

The Ellis Island Immigration Museum has 200,000 square feet of exhibit space, restored areas, and educational facilities including an interactive learning center for children. There are also two theaters that show a documentary film entitled, *Island of Hope, Island of Tears*. The museum is self-guided and also offers an audio tape guide.

Some of the exhibits and restored areas of the museum include: the Great Hall where immigrants waited to begin their processing; a collection of "Treasures From Home," artifacts donated to the museum by descendents of the immigrants who brought them to America, including religious articles, family photographs, clothing, and jewelry;

more than thirty separate galleries filled with artifacts, historic photos, posters, and maps; and the Immigrant's Living Theatre. Tickets must be purchased on arrival.

The American Immigrant Wall of Honor is a memorial to those who came through Ellis Island. Names of relatives or family names continue to be added to the wall. This can be done by making a donation to the fund that supports this project.

The American Family Immigration History Center is a genealogy center that is currently under development. The first phase of the project is to create a centralized data base with all of the data for the 20 million immigrants who arrived through New York Harbor and Ellis Island from 1892 to 1924. This information will include the names of ships, their dates of arrival, cities and countries of origin, marital status of the immigrants, the names of their relatives in America, their planned destinations in America, and much more. Given the difficulty of finding this information, the creation of a central data base will be a tremendous boon to genealogists around the world.

Ellis Island is a major tourist attraction today. It is located in New York Harbor and is open every day except Christmas from approximately 9:30 A.M. to 5:00 P.M. The Ellis Island Immigration Museum and the exhibit in the base of the statue are both fully accessible to persons with disabilities. Access to both Ellis Island and the Statue of Liberty is by the Circle Line Statue of Liberty Ferry, which leaves from the Battery in Lower Manhattan and from Liberty State Park in New Jersey. For boat schedules and prices and for information on visiting the statue or Ellis Island, you can call the following numbers:

National Park Service: (212) 363-3200

Statue of Liberty and Ellis Island, National Park Service, Liberty Island, New York, NY 10004; (212) 363-7620

Circle Line: (212) 269-5755

Immigration Wall of Honor: (212) 883-1896

Internet: http://www.ellisisland.org/

Ellis Island Wall of Honor: http://www.wallofhonor.com/

WHO ARE WE? WHERE DID WE COME FROM?

Many of the immigrants who came through Ellis Island wanted to draw a curtain over their past life. Some were quite successful in doing so, remaking themselves into their image of "real Americans." Because of this change of persona, sometimes genealogists like ourselves have difficulty obtaining real "facts" about our background. On occasion, our relatives may have even lied when they related their history, or glossed over facts they preferred to keep hidden.

What should we believe? What do we want to believe? Sometimes we accept the stories that jibe with our self image and do not ask the probing questions. Our focus may get so narrow that we lose track of the bigger picture.

Recently I've been thinking about a story that my father, of blessed memory, told me many years ago. I've been wondering what it means in the light of what I think I know about his family and what I've more recently learned about the movement of Jews over Europe.

My father's family was very proud of their German-American heritage. Relatives came to the United States in the mid-nineteenth century. They had settled in German-Jewish Washington Heights for several generations. No greenhorns they! I grew up thinking that my father's side of the family belonged to a kind of middle class "Our Crowd." My mother, on the other hand, was born here, but her parents had emigrated from the Ukraine in the early 1920s. My maternal grandparents spoke with distinctive Russian accents.

When my father was introduced to my mother's paternal grandmother, who was herself from the Ukraine, she looked at my father and made a remark in Yiddish. On the maternal side of my family, we're all very fair skinned with blue eyes and light hair. The remark my great-grandmother made was that she thought my father was Sephardic! My father had dark curly hair, brown eyes, a "Roman" nose, and a cast of olive in his complexion. My great-grandmother didn't accept my father as an Ashkenazic Jew!

While there are certainly dark-haired, dark-eyed German Jews, lately I've been wondering if my great-grandmother didn't have a piece of genealogical truth about my father's family. Perhaps someday I'll find out.

4

Thirteen Steps to Becoming a Jewish Genealogist

If you, the reader, are a novice genealogist, much of what will be presented in this chapter will be new to you. However, don't worry. Each of these steps is detailed in its own chapter later on in the book. The purpose of this chapter is to serve as a road map for "next steps" as you do your own genealogical research.

Rabbi Malcolm Stern, one of the most important figures in the development of modern Jewish genealogical research, developed a guideline for genealogists. These "Ten Commandments" set the ground rules for all genealogists and serve as a guide to creating an accurate family history.

TEN COMMANDMENTS FOR GENEALOGISTS BY RABBI MALCOLM H. STERN

1. I am a genealogist dedicated to true knowledge about the families I am researching.

2. Thou shalt use family traditions with caution and only as clues.

3. Thou shalt not accept as gospel every written record or printed word.

4. Thou shalt not hang nobility or royalty on your family tree without verifying with experts.

5. Thou shalt clearly label the questionable and the fairy tale.

6. Thou shalt handle all records in such a way that the next users will find them in the same condition you did.

7. Thou shalt credit those who help you and ask permission of those whose work you use.

8. Thou shalt not query any source of information without supplying postage.

9. Thou shalt respect the sensitivities of the living in whatever you record but tell the truth about the dead.

10. Thou shalt not become a genealogical teacher or authority without appropriate training and certification.

While most of the above are self-explanatory, a few words about commandment 4 might be helpful.

Most Jews don't think of "royalty" as being a concept that is consonant with being Jewish. However, a type of Jewish "royalty" does exist. Some Jews are descended from famous rabbinic or Chassidic families. Most of the time, people who are descendents of these families are well aware of their lineage. Written documentation usually exists to support it. In some families, however, the tradition that "we are descended from a famous rabbi" exists without documentation of any kind. Other people believe that if they came from a town that was home to a particular rabbinic or Chassidic dynasty, they must be related to that family. Commandment 4 is a warning not to make any assumptions.

The genealogies of famous rabbinic and Chassidic families are very accessible for research. For example, the Index volume of the *Encyclopedia Judaica* contains the patrilineal genealogies of many of the major Chassidic sects. Another important resource is *The Unbroken Chain: Biographical Sketches and the Genealogy of Illustrious Jewish Families*

from the 15th–20th Century, by Neil Rosenstein (Elizabeth, New Jersey:
Computer Center for Jewish Genealogy, 1990). This book is available
through Amazon.com and may also be found in Jewish bookstores.

There are a number of other books that list and describe the biogra-
phies and genealogies of famous rabbinic families. These books, however, are mostly in Hebrew. They can be found in most major Judaic
libraries. The most important of these is the *Otzar Harabanim: Rabbi's
Encyclopedia* by Rabbi Nathan Zvi Friedman. This is a directory of
twenty thousand rabbis from 970 to 1970. The rabbis are cross indexed
by name, town, publications, and male relatives, if these relatives were
rabbis.

Of particular interest to me, since my grandmother was born and
raised in Skvira, was the development of the Skvira Chassidim. I was
surprised to discover that the Skvira Chassidim are a branch of the
learned and prolific Twersky family, which emigrated to the United
States and Israel. The Skvira Chassidim were founded by Rabbi Isaac
Twersky in the 1840s. Rabbi Isaac was the grandson of Menachem
Nahum Twersky of Chernobyl. The Skvira Chassidim immigrated to
Rockland County, in New York, and established a town called "New
Square." I know that I'm not related to this family, but it's always nice to
keep up with what the "neighbors" are doing.

It doesn't matter whether you're the descendent of a "royal" Jewish
family, a family of Cohens or Levis, or just an "Israelite" like most of
us. The work needed to document your family line is the same for all of
us. Here is a thirteen-step guide to help you get started.

STEP ONE: GET STARTED BY TAKING THE PLUNGE

Genealogy is like putting together a puzzle that has no corners. Starting
out, you know that some of the pieces will fit together very easily. However, the design of the puzzle is such that you may not know when it's
finished, except by trial and error.

In "real life," my favorite puzzle is one that has one thousand pieces—
all white. Although it's a puzzle with edges, the designers managed to
create interior pieces with straight edges, too, so a straight edge is no

guarantee of an easy placement. Working on that puzzle is a lot like working on a family tree; you pick up a piece, look at it, and then try to find a relationship to another piece. It takes time, patience, and a willingness to permit yourself to stop when you get tired, cranky, or a little crazed. I've been working on that puzzle for years. I've never felt that I have to finish it; I just like the feeling of working on it from time to time. Making a match—even a small one—is a big accomplishment.

I feel the same way about my family tree. When I first began working on it, I was very intimidated by the undertaking. My father showed me a "professional" tree that had been done for his mother's family in the early 1950s tracing the line of the German-based Spandau family. I couldn't imagine how I would ever be able to create a similar tree for the Russian side of my family. However, my closeness to my maternal grandparents made me want to document as much as I could about their lives for future generations.

Little by little, I worked away. I discovered that tracing one's roots is something anyone can do today. Genealogy at its most basic level—working with a three- to four-generation family tree—is relatively simple research, once you know how to do it, and great fun. The important thing to remember is that every journey starts with a single step. The way to get started is to get started.

The first thing to do is to write down everything you know about your family. Use four separate pieces of paper—one for each of your grandparents—and use these pages to organize your information. Chat informally with close relatives to fill in some of the gaps.

STEP TWO: SET RESEARCH GOALS

In order to set your research goals, you need to get a clear picture of what you know and what you need to know. Follow these simple steps.

1. Write down everything you know on four pieces of paper. This will create a visual image of the information you've collected. When you feel that you've gotten as much information as you can through informal conversations and you've written it all down, spread the four sheets of paper out in front of you. The amount of research

that needs to be done will be very clear for each of the four branches. The sheet with the least amount of information will probably be the most difficult to research. The sheet with the most amount of information may give you a fairly complete multi-generational tree.

2. Using the information that you have on each page, create a pedigree chart. A pedigree chart contains information about your directly related ancestors—parents, grandparents, great-grandparents, but doesn't show other relatives like siblings or cousins or your own children. A pedigree chart will help you keep track of your research as you progress by reminding you which relationship line you're working on and who's related to whom.

3. Create a family tree for each of the four branches of your family based on the oldest relative for whom you have information.

4. Decide which branch to begin with based on how easy you feel it will be to get information about that side of your family. This will depend on many different factors including the number of older living relatives, where they live and your access to them, the availability of documents, and the level of your own motivation to pursue a particular family line. In general, it's best to begin with the situation that is easiest to research so that you don't run into major research problems before you've had a chance to build your research skills and experience.

STEP THREE: INVOLVE FAMILY MEMBERS AND INTERVIEW THEM

Don't assume that because you tell your family members that you're doing research on your family tree that they'll immediately help you. For one thing, although this is important to you, it may not be important to them. Also, this is your project; it's top of mind for you, but they have other things to be concerned about. It's not that they intend to be unhelpful; it just isn't their project. Individual family members may also have private reasons for wanting to conceal parts of their own family history. It's important to remember that your research may stimulate conflicts or disturbing feelings of which you may be unaware.

For these reasons, a genealogist should be respectful of family members' hesitation in offering information, if such a situation should present itself. Going slowly and being welcoming when inviting family members to become involved in your genealogical research will increase your family's willingness to cooperate with you.

Once you have decided which line of your family tree you're going to research, you'll want to conduct in-depth interviews with family members. Careful planning of these interviews will help guarantee your success. It's also very important to follow up these interviews, as details may be remembered days, or even weeks after your initial meeting.

STEP FOUR: DOCUMENT WHAT YOU KNOW

Writing down what you discover about your family is vital for several reasons. If you don't commit your ideas and notes to paper, you may forget the information. Also, at some time, another family member may want to continue the research. It will be helpful for you to be able to pass along what you've discovered. Finally, remember that the reason that you're doing this research is that no one else in your family—that you know of—has done this before. Keeping written records will ensure that future generations will have the benefit of your hard work.

STEP FIVE: BECOME FAMILIAR WITH RESEARCH SOURCES AND JEWISH GENEALOGICAL ORGANIZATIONS

Your family will form your first source of information about your family tree, but sooner or later you will need to explore archives and other research depositories. For this reason, it will be helpful for you to search out the genealogy research sources in your area and those that exist on a national level. These include municipal archives for life-cycle records, the nearest Family History Center; the National Archives Research Administration; JewGen—the largest Jewish genealogy research hub on the Internet; Avotaynu, the premier publisher of

Jewish genealogy research materials, and your local Jewish genealogy society.

In addition, there are many specialized groups that can aid the Jewish genealogist in his or her research. Landsmanshaften groups are organizations founded to help people from a particular town or region. Although many of these are now no longer active, many of these organizations provided burial sites for their members. Finding a landsmanshaften organization for a family member can lead to finding other family members.

Many areas, both in the United States and abroad, now have Jewish heritage societies. These societies often house local archives and books that can be of help. There are also a number of Jewish archives that store Jewish family trees. Becoming familiar with these resources will help you expand your research.

STEP SIX: RESEARCH FAMILY SURNAMES AND PERSONAL NAMES

Family surnames and personal names offer many clues about your family's development and history. It can be especially important to create a directory of family Hebrew and Yiddish names. Since these names are often passed down in a family, knowledge of the names used in the last few generations can help you uncover relatives even farther back. In addition, by creating such a directory, you will be preserving an important part of your family's history.

Sometimes, family names can prod one's memory about important genealogical information. For example, when I was doing some research on my father's matrilineal line, no one could remember his maternal grandmother's name. Then I remembered that one of my Hebrew names—Leah—came from my paternal grandmother, and I recalled that I had been told that her name was Lina. I remembered that my father told me that his mother's mother lived with them when he was growing up. Although I didn't know when Lina died, this information, added to the fact that I was named after her, helped me narrow the time band for the purpose of researching her date of death.

STEP SEVEN: COLLECT AND PRESERVE FAMILY DOCUMENTS

Collecting and preserving family documents is an excellent way to extend your research and also preserve information for future generations. Many families retain important documents like naturalization papers, birth certificates, and marriage certificates. Because these documents usually include information about more than one generation of a family, getting access to these papers and preserving them is extremely important if you want to extend your research past the immediate living generations of your family.

Even if these records are not in your possession, there are many different ways to find them and get copies. Learning how to do this will be an important aspect of your development as a Jewish genealogist.

STEP EIGHT: EXAMINE FAMILY PHOTOS AND HEIRLOOMS

Family photographs and heirlooms can provide important clues about your family's history. For example, the dress of family members can help to date a photograph. Sometimes postcards sent by family members can give clues about a family's migration. In researching my mother's photographs, we found a postcard with Russian writing on the back. When we had it translated, it turned out that the photograph was from one of my grandmother's sisters who had moved from Kiev to Moscow and lived there during the 1930s. Until I found this photograph, I was unaware that any of my grandmother's family had left the Ukraine. It was an important clue.

Family heirlooms can also provide information about family members. A wimple, which is a Torah binder made from a baby's swaddling blanket, may contain the birth date and name of a child. A kiddush cup given as a wedding gift may have the name of the bride and groom, as well as their wedding date, engraved on it. Even Aunt Fanny's candlesticks, received as a wedding present and brought from the old country, may contain a date of manufacture or origin that can help in expanding your knowledge of your family's history. For this reason, it's very important to ask family members about photographs and heirlooms retained in the family, and to look at them yourself.

STEP NINE: PRESERVE YOUR RESEARCH, PHOTOS, AND HEIRLOOMS

It's not enough to collect documents, photographs, and heirlooms. In order to make sure that future generations will be able to appreciate their worth, it's vital to catalogue, label, and preserve them. It's also important to make sure that they will be passed on, after your death, to someone in the family who will take the responsibility of caring for them and making them accessible to future family genealogists.

STEP TEN: COMPILE HISTORICAL INFORMATION ABOUT YOUR FAMILY'S PLACE OF ORIGIN

Learning about the history of your family's place of origin can help you find clues about your heritage. I was recently on a plane with a man who told me that it had been suggested to him that he had Jewish ancestry. Since his father was a Baptist minister, he didn't see how this could be. We began to talk and I asked him where his family originally came from. It turned out that one set of grandparents had immigrated to the United States from Germany right before World War II. In addition, these relatives had personal names and surnames that suggested some Jewish ancestry. Since many of the Germans who immigrated to the United States in the 1930s were Jewish, I suggested that he begin to research his family background.

He was surprised to think that he might actually have Jewish ancestry. He asked, "Did Jews who came from Germany hide their Jewish background?" I explained that, while this was not usual, there were many who did. The most famous instance of a Jewish family that changed its religion in America is the family of Secretary of State Madeleine Albright. Although she grew up as an Episcopalian, her Jewish grandparents died in concentration camps during the Holocaust. This was a situation of which she had been unaware until very recently.

Another possibility is that one of this man's grandparents or great grandparents had been Jewish. In Nazi Germany, even partial Jewish identity was a ticket to the gas chambers. This man was unaware of the

Jewish history attached to the time during which his family immigrated to the United States. Learning just a few facts encouraged him to begin his own genealogical research.

STEP ELEVEN: TALK TO PEOPLE

The Jewish world is very small. Talking to other Jews you meet about your family research is not the most "scientific" method. However, it is easy to do and can sometimes lead to good results. Recently I was on a plane and fell into conversation with a young Jewish man from Omaha. Since I have relatives in Omaha, I asked if he knew them. It turned out that not only did he know them, but that he and I were distantly related, through a family connection of which I had been previously unaware.

STEP TWELVE: DISTRIBUTE YOUR INFORMATION TO JEWISH FAMILY TREE ARCHIVES AND FAMILY MEMBERS

In order to make sure that your work will be available to future genealogists, it's very important to make the tree available to other family members. In addition, your completed tree should be stored with all appropriate Jewish archives.

STEP THIRTEEN: CREATE GENEALOGICAL HEIRLOOMS FOR FUTURE GENERATIONS

You are a link in the chain of your family. As you become more involved in the study of your ancestors, you may find the feeling of being a link between the past and the future will grow stronger. As a link, you can do many things to facilitate the work of future family genealogists. You may want to create many different genealogical heirlooms for life-cycle events. You can make sure that your own family documents are preserved and stored in a place that will make them easily available to your descendents. By doing these things, you will not only be linking the past to the future, but you will be sending a message to descendents you may never meet about your own life and times.

A Stress-Free Guide to Constructing a Four-Generation Family Tree

 When thinking of genealogy, many beginners initially feel overwhelmed. The task of going back in time to find lost relatives can seem daunting. However, many of us forget that, if we can't go back too far, we can certainly lay the groundwork for those who come after us. This too, is an important part of genealogy—saving what we know for future generations.

The purpose of this chapter is to help you get started with your family tree by focusing on what you already know. In this chapter, we're going to look at how to construct a four-generation family tree. The techniques used for this exercise will help you establish a solid basis for further research, if you wish to continue.

START WITH WHAT YOU KNOW

Almost all of us know who we are and where we live, so this is a logical place to start. In genealogy, we use a variety of forms and charts to track and collect different types of information. The chart we're going to use for this first exercise uses yourself as the focus of your family tree. Follow the simple directions and fill in the Four-Generation Family Tree Worksheet on the following page. See my husband's filled-in family tree draft as a sample. If you have more than four generations of information, feel free to add it. Once you have filled in this form, you will have a partially completed four-generation (or more) family tree.

BEGINNING TO FILL IN THE BLANKS

Very often there is information that we don't know, but which is available by asking close relatives. If you have parents and/or grandparents still living, this is a good time for a phone call. Tell them that you're constructing a family tree and that you need some specific information. Suggest that at sometime soon in the future, you would like to interview them in depth, but that right now you need some basic information. Don't let them sidetrack you with long family stories about Aunt Harriet and the butcher's son in the old country. Right now, you just want basic facts.

If your parents or grandparents aren't around, you might try speaking to an older aunt or uncle. In many families, you most likely will find a "family historian" who knows everything. While you're not ready for "everything" right now, identifying this person at this stage of your research can prove very helpful. Older family friends may also be able to give you information about your family. They are resources who should not be overlooked.

Before you make a call to an older relative or family friend for information, make sure that you are prepared with a couple of pens, your family chart, and a pad for note taking. During your conversation, write down everything your relative says. Don't let them tell you that they'll send you the information. Explain that you need it *now*. People mean well, but they don't always follow through. Your job as a genealogist is to be persistent and to insist, nicely, on getting the information that you need. Persistence and perseverance are among the most important skills a genealogist can cultivate. As you get more information, add it to your

FOUR-GENERATION FAMILY TREE WORKSHEET

Instructions: Fill your name and as much other information as possible. Continue to add information to this worksheet as it becomes available.

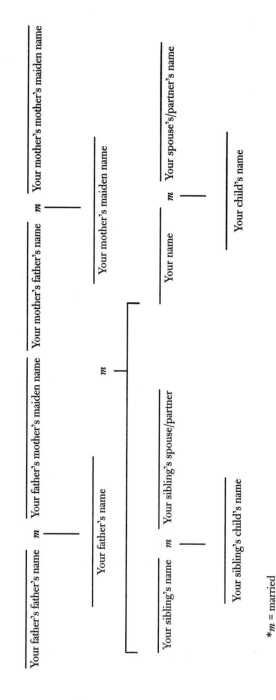

Your father's father's name

m — Your father's mother's maiden name

Your mother's father's name

m — Your mother's mother's maiden name

Your father's name

m

Your mother's maiden name

Your sibling's name — *m* — Your sibling's spouse/partner

Your name — *m* — Your spouse's/partner's name

Your sibling's child's name

Your child's name

m = married

SAMPLE FOUR-GENERATION FAMILY TREE—NEIL HOWARD YERMAN

Michael Yerman *m* Ida Tuck

Charles Markowitz *m* Sophie Denowitz

Melvin Jerome Yerman

Sylvia Markowitz

m

Barry David Yerman Neil Howard Yerman *m* Jo Lynn Marx David Philip Yerman *m* Gloria Manning Lawrence Jay Yerman
(dec.)

Melanie Yerman

Stephanie Yerman

family tree worksheet, your pedigree chart, your descendent chart, your personal record charts, and your family group worksheets, all of which are discussed in this chapter.

If you've followed the steps in this chapter, your family tree chart should begin to grow. Now let's discuss how to go from your family tree worksheet to a family history with a great deal more detail.

USING THE TOOLS THE PROS USE

Over the years, professional genealogists and hobbyists have developed a number of standardized forms for recording genealogical information. Copies of these forms are printed at the end of this chapter. Working copies can be purchased through a number of different sources including genealogy societies and companies that specialize in products for the genealogy market. The names and addresses of these resources are listed at the back of this book. While it's not necessary to use any of these forms—you're free to create one or more for yourself—it may help you to begin with those tools which others have found helpful. At the very least, it's important to know how to read certain standard forms, since you may come across some of these in your own research.

There are four basic forms that genealogists use to collect family information. These are the ascendant chart, the descendent chart, the family group sheet, and the personal record sheet. Computer programs that are available on the market have these and other forms built into them. It should be noted that these forms were not created with Jewish genealogy in mind. Therefore, if one wishes to keep track of Hebrew names in the family, for example, it will be necessary to add that information to the forms. One may also include Jewish birth dates and yahrzeit dates (the date of a person's death.) Let's now look at the three standard forms.

Ascendant/Pedigree Chart

An Ascendant or Pedigree Chart begins with a specific individual (you, for example) and shows all the parents who are direct ancestors on both the matrilineal and patrilineal lines. It does not show the siblings of any of the people listed. Pedigreed animal owners will recognize this chart because it is the one used to trace the pedigree of animals such as horses, dogs, and cats that have special breeding.

There is room for a great deal of information on an ascendant chart. Each entry is numbered so that you can tell at a glance how the individuals are related. Except for number one, which is you, under the convention for inserting information, even numbers represent males and odd numbers represent females. Most charts include the following information for each person listed: name of individual, date of birth, place of birth, date of marriage, date of death, place of death, name of spouse, and relationship to previous generation—i.e., mother of, father of number _____.

On my pedigree chart, which is offered as a sample, I added both the father of my son, my present husband, and my son. My brother and his family, however, are not listed. Although most commercially available pedigree charts do not ask for information about the spouse and child of the primary person, it seemed to me that the story of my life would be incomplete without these additions, so I added them. A sample worksheet of a "Jewish" pedigree chart appears on pages 66–67.

Descendent Chart

A descendent chart begins with the oldest known person, called the "progenitor" in your family. The descendent chart shows the way in which the family has descended from this individual. In the sample provided, the Spandau Descendent Tree, you can see how my family descended from my father's mother's family.

A descendent chart is usually constructed once some research is done and several generations have been delineated. Descendent charts generally indicate only dates of birth, death, and marriage and serve as an "at a glance" picture of one's family structure rather than as a source of in-depth information.

PEDIGREE CHART

Your Name

1 _____

Hebrew name _____
Date born _____
Place born _____
Date married _____
Place married _____

Name of Your Spouse/Partner

_____

Hebrew name _____
Date born _____
Place born _____

Name of Your Child/Children

_____

Hebrew name _____
Date born _____
Place born _____

Your Father's Name

2 _____

Hebrew name _____
Date born _____
Place born _____
Date married _____
Place married _____
Date died _____
Place died _____
Buried _____

Your Mother's Name

3 _____

Hebrew name _____
Date born _____
Place born _____
Date married _____
Place married _____
Date died _____
Place died _____
Buried _____

Your Father's Father's Name

4 _____

Hebrew name _____
Date born _____
Place born _____
Date married _____
Place married_____
Date died_____
Place died _____
Buried _____

Your Father's Mother's Name

5 _____

Hebrew name _____
Date born _____
Place born _____
Date married _____
Place married_____
Date died_____
Place died _____
Buried _____

Your Mother's Father's Name

6 _____

Hebrew name _____
Date born _____
Place born _____
Date married _____
Place married_____
Date died_____
Place died _____
Buried _____

Your Mother's Mother's Name

7 _____

Hebrew name _____
Date born _____
Place born _____
Date married _____
Place married_____
Date died_____
Place died _____
Buried _____

Your Great-Grandfather's Name

8 _____
Date born_____
Place born _____
Date married _____
Date died _____

Your Great-Grandmother's Name

9 _____
Date born_____
Place born _____
Date married _____
Date died _____

Your Great-Grandfather's Name

10 _____
Date born_____
Place born _____
Date married _____
Date died _____

Your Great-Grandmother's Name

11 _____
Date born_____
Place born _____
Date married _____
Date died _____

Your Great-Grandfather's Name

12 _____
Date born_____
Place born _____
Date married _____
Date died _____

Your Great-Grandmother's Name

13 _____
Date born_____
Place born _____
Date married _____
Date died _____

Your Great-Grandfather's Name

14 _____
Date born_____
Place born _____
Date married _____
Date died _____

Your Great-Grandmother's Name

15 _____
Date born_____
Place born _____
Date married _____
Date died _____

SPANDAU DESCENDENT TREE

Author's note: Specific details of branches of my family other than my direct branch have been left out to protect the privacy of the individuals concerned. On my completed tree, which is not shown here, all the information for all the branches is given in as much detail as possible.

Meyer Spandau *m* Bertha Michaelis

Isidore Spandau *m* Lena Rothenberg
b. Nov., 1855
Bonn, Rheinland

Hattie *m* Nat Miller   Sam *m* Ethel   Dora *m* David Queen   Max
m. 1952

Leo *m* Helen *m* Irving Marx   Sidney G. *m* Lucille   Hy L. *m* Isabelle   Marilyn *m* David M.   Irwin

Irving Marx *m* Eva Spandau
b. 1888   b. 1889
d. 7/31/56   d. 10/21/51

Stanley Ira Marx *m* Diana Steinberg   Mortimer *m* Rae
b. 8/12/19—NYC   b. 1/5/28—Brooklyn, NY
m. 11/11/45—NYC
d. 7/13/94—NYC

Evan *m* Cathleen Scatamacchia
b. 2/19/52
m. 5/30/77—Haverhill, MA.

Jo Lynn Marx *m* Neil Yerman
b. 3/18/49—NYC   6/21/81
Carmel, NY

Irma *m* Rudolf   Seymour *m* Birdie   Jesse *m* Henrietta   Bea *m* Alvin *m* Renee

Alison Elaine
b. 6/1/86
LI, NY

Andrew Evan
b. 6/28/82
LI, NY

Mr. David *m* Judith Wolf

Justin David *m* Judith Wolf
b. 11/22/68
m. 6/13/93

Lior Shalom Wolf David
b. 8/10/97—NYC

68

Family Group Sheet

The purpose of a family group sheet is to segregate information about each distinct family and its members. The sheet includes room for all the information on an ascending chart and also for occupation of both parents. A separate section of the sheet makes room for all the children of the couple, their dates and places of birth, marriage, and death and the same information for the spouses of the children.

If desired, additional information can be included on attached pages or on the back of the master sheet. One might also want to note if pictures of the individuals are available and if so, where these pictures can be found.

Personal Record Sheet

This form is designed to help you keep track of each individual's personal information. It usually has room for notes and other material not usually transferred to one of the other charts.

COMPUTER PROGRAMS FOR MANAGING FAMILY INFORMATION

Let me suggest why you should use a computer to manage your family information. As you work on your family tree, you will need to make all kinds of additions, changes, deletions, notes, and comments. At some point in your research, you will want to e-mail information to someone else who has also been working on your family tree. You will also want to generate a copy of your tree for relatives who have helped you. And you will certainly want to contribute your family tree to the various Jewish family tree archives that now exist. If your material is on computer, whenever you want to do any of these things, you'll be able to create a beautiful, clean, readable copy with a couple of clicks of a button.

There are many computer software programs available to help you organize your family records and print charts and family trees. Some programs even let you insert photos of each person into the tree. That

FAMILY GROUP SHEET _____ (Family Name)

Husband's Name _____
Hebrew Name _____
Father's English Name _____
Father's Hebrew Name _____
Mother's English Name _____
Mother's Hebrew Name _____
Date of Birth _____
Place of Birth _____
Date of Death _____
Hebrew Calendar Date of Death _____
Place of Death _____
Place of Burial _____
Occupation _____
Notes:

Wife's Name _____
Hebrew Name _____
Father's English Name _____
Father's Hebrew Name _____
Mother's English Name _____
Mother's Hebrew Name _____
Date of Birth _____
Place of Birth _____
Date of Death _____
Hebrew Calendar Date of Death _____
Place of Death _____
Place of Burial _____
Occupation _____
Notes:

Children

Name	Date/ Place of Birth	Marriage	Death	Married to	Date/ Place of Birth	Date/ Place of Death
1.						
2.						
3						
4.						

70

PERSONAL RECORD SHEET

Fill in a copy of this form for each individual whom you are researching.

English Name _____

Hebrew Name _____

Date of Birth _____

Place of Birth _____

Time of Birth _____

Date of Bris/Naming _____

Place of Bris/Naming _____

Name of Officiant _____

Date of Pidyon Haben (Usually only for boys) _____

Place of Pidyon Haben _____

Name of Cohen _____

Father's English Name _____

Father's Hebrew Name _____

Mother's English Name _____

Mother's Hebrew Name _____

Date of Bar/Bat Mitzvah _____

Place of Bar/Bat Mitzvah _____

Name of Torah/Haftarah Portion _____

Officiating Rabbi/Cantor _____

Date of Confirmation _____

Place of Confirmation _____

Date of Marriage _____

Place of Marriage _____

Name of Spouse/Partner _____

Name of Officiant _____

Education _____

Date of Death _____

Hebrew Calendar Date of Death _____

Place of Death _____

Place of Burial _____

Occupation _____

Notes:

being said, computer programs and technology change so quickly many new programs will appear by the time this book is printed. For that reason, included here are just a few of the current "bestsellers" to give you an idea of the type of programs that are available. The reader who wishes to purchase a computer genealogy program should check the Internet for new material. You should also look up the latest programs in a computer software magazine and you should definitely visit a few large computer stores before making a purchase.

No program for Jewish genealogy currently exists. However, most genealogy programs can be easily customized to include Jewish information such as the individual's Hebrew name, the name of the person the individual was named after, yahrzeit date, immigration date, naturalization date, and other such information.

Here is a look at some computer programs currently on the market:

- Family Tree Maker. Version 4.0 for DOS/4.4 for Windows95/ PowerMac

  Very easy to use. Highly recommended for beginners.

  Broderbund, P.O. Box 6125, Novato, CA 94948-6125; (800) 548-1804; http://www.familytreemaker.com

- Reunion (for Macintosh) Version 5.0

  Best genealogy program for the Macintosh. Very powerful program, with graphic user interfaces. This has chart-making capabilities. Leister Productions, P.O. Box 289, Mechanicsburg, PA 17055; (717) 697-1378; E-mail: info@LeisterPro.com or http://www. leisterpro.com

- Generations. Version 4.2 for Windows95 (formerly "Reunion for Windows")

  Sierra, 3380 146th Place, SE, Suite 300, Bellevue, WA 98007, (425) 649-9800; http://www.sierra.com/titles/generations

- Ultimate Family Tree (formerly Roots V), (Windows and Macintosh) Palladium Interactive, Inc., http://www.uftree.com

Other information about computers and genealogy can be found in the following sources: soc.genealogy.computing; the Internet usenet newsgroup devoted to genealogical software issues; *Genealogical Computing,* a quarterly magazine published by Ancestry, Inc., P.O. Box 476, Salt Lake City, UT 84110; and JewishGen, http://www.jewishgen.org, one of the most important Jewish genealogy Web sites on the Internet. It is constantly being updated and improved. This would be a good first stop for checking out new genealogy software.

6

Getting Organized to Find Your Missing Links

 There are a number of details to consider when preparing to work on a family tree. Some of these include:

- What do I want to accomplish by tracing my family tree?
- Which family line will I trace?
- How far back would I like to go?
- Who in the chosen family line can help me?
- What materials do I need to get started?
- What other resources for help do I have?
- How will I organize my results?
- How much time am I willing to invest in this project?
- How much money am I prepared to spend?

In this chapter, we will look at how to develop a research plan for your genealogical expedition so that your experience will be as rewarding and satisfying as possible.

SELECTING A GOAL

You need a place to start so that you have an idea of where you're going. The first step in your research plan is to decide which branch of your family tree to work on and what you would like to accomplish in your research. For example, as a beginner, you may be very happy developing a three- or four-generation family tree with lots of personal details and photographs. More ambitious or experienced genealogists may choose a date in time to which they would like to be able to trace their lineage, or may decide to search beyond four generations.

Most of the time, for beginners, choosing the easiest family line to research is a good way to start. By selecting a goal that is easy to accomplish, you will be able to acquire basic research skills while having the satisfaction of actually achieving your objective and seeing your family tree grow before your eyes. You are ready to begin once you've decided which branch of your family tree you wish to develop and have given some consideration to the questions raised at the beginning of this chapter.

TIP FOR SUCCESS

Beginners sometimes become overwhelmed by the task they map out for themselves. To keep from being overwhelmed, set limited, easy-to-achieve goals for yourself. For example, you might decide to start by obtaining the life-cycle certificates (birth, marriage, death) of a particular generation.

Write down your goal, and when you achieve it, note the date. Take a little time to enjoy your success and share your results with your family. Sometimes, when you receive documents, the information contained may be different from things that you know to be true. For example, when I obtained my grandmother's naturalization papers, my mother's birth date was listed as 1918, three years before my grandparents were married! I knew that that wasn't correct, so I made a note to that effect in my records. From this experience, I learned that it's important to have more than one source of information, if possible, especially if there is no one left alive in the generation that you're researching.

When you reach your first goal, evaluate your situation. Do you want to continue, or stop where you are? Remember that no one is judging you. You can do as much or as little as you wish to do. If you decide to continue, set another realistic, limited goal, write it down, and proceed. Doing this will help you stay focused and on track.

YOUR BASIC RESEARCH MATERIALS

Books

In buying and reading this book, you have already started to obtain research materials. Research and resource materials should be gathered so that you don't have to run to the library continually. Throughout this book you will find descriptions of other books, magazines, and additional resources relating to Jewish genealogy and genealogy in general. There are two books, however, that should be on every Jewish genealogist's bookshelf. The first is the revised edition of Arthur Kurzweil's book, *From Generation to Generation,* published by Harper Perennial, 1996. This book is a wonderful read, even for those with no intention of tracing a family tree. One of the problems with this book is that it was written and revised before the cyberspace revolution. As noted earlier, knowledge of what is on the Internet is vital for today's genealogist.

Another important book is Dan Rottenberg's *Finding Our Fathers: A Guidebook to Jewish Genealogy,* published by Random House in 1977. Along with *From Generation to Generation,* this book helped give birth to modern Jewish genealogy as a serious focus of study. Many of the resources listed in these books are out of date. However, by reading these books, you will get a good feeling for the range of materials that it was possible to find even before the advent of cybergenealogy.

Office Materials

Your "office" materials should include:

- file boxes or a "dedicated" file drawer
- hanging files and manila files
- clear plastic storage boxes of different sizes
- a dedicated bookshelf for genealogy resource materials (This is important! It will save you hours of saying, "Did you see that book?")
- plenty of pens and sharpened pencils (they always go astray)
- a number of notebooks for note taking
- a ruler
- white archival tape for labeling things (available in art supply stores)
- large binder with archival acetate pocket inserts for filing delicate photos and documents (Never paste things into a scrapbook. Over time, the paste or glue will be absorbed by the paper and will cause the document to deteriorate.)
- a tape recorder, a dozen sixty-minute audio tapes, and extra batteries for the tape recorder
- video camera—if possible, with several blank tapes and a backup battery

If you're a computer genealogist, you'll also need:

- genealogy software
- several blank disks for backing up information
- the latest books on Judaism in cyberspace: *Judaism on the Web,* by Irving Green, published by MIS Press, 1997, organizes information by topic. *The Guide to the Jewish Internet,* by Michael Levin, published by No Starch Press, 1996, comes with software called "The Electronic Guide to the Internet," which is helpful for computer-literate people but not really necessary to use the book effectively.

TIP FOR SUCCESS

Take some time to collect your basic research materials. Go to your local general bookstore, Judaic bookstore, stationery store, and computer store to see what what's available that might be of help to you. Don't buy everything in one day. Making several trips will give you time to think about what you would really like to own now and what materials you can add as your research progresses.

SETTING UP YOUR RESEARCH CENTER

Thinking About Storage

"Conventional wisdom" suggests that you use traditional file folders and file drawers for organizing files. However, there are other options. Since some of the material may be fragile—i.e., photos, family heirlooms on cloth or paper, video or audio tape—you may want to use see-through plastic storage containers with snap-lock tops to store the material that you are not working with at the moment. These boxes should be clearly marked and stored in a place that is out of direct sunlight and that is free of the danger of mildew. These materials should also be protected from extremes of temperature. The bottom or top shelf of a closet is preferable to the garage, attic, or laundry room as a storage facility. Although these storage containers are supposedly airtight, why take a chance?

For the materials you will be working with on a day-to-day basis, a portable, lightweight plastic file box with a handle makes an ideal organizer. These boxes come in both letter and legal size and are very inexpensive. Some, but not all, come already equipped with both hanging file folders and with tabbed manila folders. Check before you leave the store to make sure that you have all the materials that you need to get organized.

Plastic file boxes are preferable to paper boxes, since they will prevent the stored documents from becoming water damaged if there should be a flood, and these boxes are somewhat more resistant to mold and mildew.

If you have many nonpaper materials to work with—audio, video, memorabilia—you may want to get a separate box for these, and segregate them from you paper files.

The benefit of a portable file box for storing in-progress materials is that you can move it easily from room to room. It's important to keep your files together so that they do not get misplaced.

Organizing Your Working Files

Even if most of your files are stored on your computer, you will want to create hard copies of your files. In addition, many of the documents you'll be receiving will be in a paper format.

There are a number of different ways to organize your files, and your file categories may change as your research progresses. In general, the more detailed your files, the easier it will be for you to retrieve the material you want. The way in which you organize your files will depend on your own special way of thinking about things. For example, some people think alphabetically. For these folks, an alphabetic file, where each hanging file represents a letter of the alphabet, will work best. In such a system, a hanging file with the designation of "D" might contain individual manila folders marked "Deeds" and "Death Certificates."

Another way of setting up your files would be by category, with each hanging folder given a general designation—i.e., Ketubot, Marriage licenses, Naming certificates. These hanging files would be filed in the box or drawer alphabetically. In each category, there would be separate files having to do with the main topic—i.e., in the Marriage license file, there would be individual manila folders for each relative on the branch of the tree you're investigating.

Still another way of organizing files is by the individual person. The hanging file is given an individual's name and the separate manila files each contain a specific document relating to that person—i.e., birth certificate, naming document, marriage certificate, death certificate.

TIP FOR SUCCESS

Organize, organize, organize! One of the most frustrating experiences is working on a project and then finding that a vital piece of information or a specific research tool can't be found. Try to create a workspace that will be used only for your project. If you can't isolate a specific workspace, try to clear a separate shelf on which to keep all your materials. A separate file drawer can also be used for this purpose. Always return your materials to their designated storage area after use. If you keep forgetting where you've put things, make a directory of where your most important materials and files are kept and post the directory where you can see it easily.

CREATING YOUR RESEARCH MAP

Before you can begin to hunt down information, you need to figure out what information you need. If you haven't already done so, create a pedigree chart of the family line you'll be researching using the information and charts in chapter 5. Wherever you do not have specific information, circle or highlight the information area. You now have an annotated pedigree chart. The "blanks" that need to be filled are what you need to research.

Using your annotated pedigree chart, create an Individual Research Page for each member of your family tree. Fill in all the information that you have for each family member on this form. You're now ready to begin your research.

Start with the generation closest to your own, since these records may be most easily accessible. Work your way back in time generation by generation. Use your annotated pedigree chart as a roadmap and fill in the information as you accumulate it.

TIP FOR SUCCESS

Color coding information areas is a good way to give yourself an "at a glance" picture of your research goals. For example, you might use a yellow highlighter to indicate the names of family members, and green for marriage information. If you like, you can use a color bar to color-code all the information you collect. This will help you locate various files and records quickly and easily.

Research page for (name of relative) _____

Relationship to researcher _____

Birth date _____ Place of birth _____

Birth certificate found   yes ____   no ____

Hebrew name _____

Secular date of death _____ Date of death on Hebrew calendar _____

Place of death _____

Death certificate found   yes ____   no ____

Burial site _____

Inscription on headstone/footstone _____

Marriage date _____ Place of marriage _____

Name of spouse _____

Ketubah found   yes ____   no ____

Civil marriage license found   yes ____   no ____

Divorced   yes ____   no ____

Copy of Get located   yes ____   no ____

Remarriage   yes ____   no ____

Marriage date _____ Place of marriage _____

Name of wife _____

Ketubah found   yes ____   no ____

Civil marriage license found   yes ____   no ____

Name/s, birth dates, and places of birth of children _____

Synagogue membership   yes ____   no ____

Name and location of synagogue _____

Family plaques in synagogue   yes ____   no ____

Occupation _____

If not born in United States:

Date of entry to U.S. _____

Immigration papers found   yes ____   no ____

Naturalization papers found   yes ____   no ____

Date of naturalization _____

Membership in landsmanshaften organization or Verein   yes ____ no ____

Name of organization _____ Is it still active?   yes ____   no ____

Notes:

Getting Your Family Involved

Genealogy is an activity in which people of all ages can participate. Teenagers and computer literate preteens can be of help to adults with "low-tech" computer skills. They can both input data into computer genealogy programs and can help with surfing the net for information. Younger children can be pressed into service sorting photographs, filing, and inserting materials into document books. Older relatives, who may not be able to get out to do library research, can help by making telephone connections as new leaves of the family tree appear. The more ways in which you can involve many generations of your family, the richer the experience of creating your family history will become. And by encouraging other family members to participate, you will be helping them to develop new skills and learn new things about themselves and their family.

TIP FOR SUCCESS

Inviting others to help is not the same as giving people "jobs to do." To encourage the most effective participation by all members of your family, ask them to join you in your search. Tell them about what you plan to do. Show them some of the materials you have assembled to help in your search. Describe some of the different tasks that will be involved in the work. Seek their suggestions. Ask each person you would like to include what he or she would like to do. No one who is uninterested should be pressured to participate.

As you begin to get results and share them with your family members, those who initially expressed disinterest may come forward and ask to help. If they do so and you welcome them, you will be helping them to share your wonderful adventure.

Get Yourself a Teacher

In the Pirket Avot, Joshua ben Perachya teaches us, "Get yourself a teacher; acquire a friend to study with you." (1:6) Similarly, it will be good for you to find some people to help you in your family search. It will also make your experience as a genealogist much more pleasant. Teachers and friends can also come in the form of helpful magazines, seminars, and other learning experiences. Here are some possibilities for helping you to find teachers and friends who can guide you on your search for your family roots. Consult the Resource chapter for contact information on all the resources listed below.

Join a Jewish genealogy society in your area. There are Jewish genealogy societies all across the United States. Your local Jewish genealogy society will be listed in the telephone book. You can also get a list of Jewish genealogy societies around the world by writing to the International Association of Jewish Genealogical Societies, P.O. Box 26, Cabin John, MD 20818-0026 or by going online to the page for the International Association of Jewish Genealogical Societies hosted by the JewishGen Web site—http://www.jewishgen.org/ajgs.

Subscribe to *Avotaynu*. *Avotaynu* is a very important source for Jewish genealogists. Besides publishing many different types of hard-to-find materials, it serves as a focus for Jewish genealogists around the world. Mailing address: P.O. Box 99, Bergenfield, NJ 07621; telephone: (201) 387-7200; fax: (201) 387-2855; E-mail: info@avotaynu.com. Web site: http://www.avotaynu.com.

Attend a summer seminar on Jewish genealogy. Your local Jewish genealogy society will have information about these programs. You can also find out about them through the JewishGen Web site.

Join a discussion group through JewishGen.

Check out the JewishGen Family Finder, which is a subpage of the main JewishGen Web site. The Family Finder helps you to locate other researchers with your genealogical interests and makes it possible for you to contact them.

TIP FOR SUCCESS
Genealogy is a pursuit that will expand your horizons and introduce you to many different people. Enjoy!

7

The Wild World of Genealogy in Cyberspace

When Arthur Kurzweil's seminal book on Jewish genealogy, *From Generation to Generation,* was reissued in a revised edition in paperback in 1996, only one and a half pages at the back of the book were devoted to using computers to study genealogy, and most of the section deals with computer programs to organize genealogical research. Kurzweil's final words on the subject are: "Don't get distracted by the technology when there is so much hard work that you have to do yourself."

Since that book was released in 1996, however, a revolution has occurred in the field of genealogy in general and Jewish genealogy in particular. The revolution has been not so much in the area of computer software, but in the extent to which the Internet has become an indispensable research tool. Today there are literally hundreds of genealogy Web sites, and thousands of Jewish genealogy Web pages, with more being added almost every day.

When the Internet was launched, it was a "place" that seemed only accessible to computer geniuses and to those who were "technologically" gifted. Today, the Internet is an easy place for just about everyone to access and navigate. Since "user friendly" is the guiding rule for cyberspace, a fifteen-minute introduction should make it possible for most people to access a very large amount of information on almost any subject.

Despite the prowess of the Internet, there is no substitute for being able to visit your ancestral hometown in the "old country." However, using the Internet to identify and gather records and to locate difficult-to-find sources of information will save you literally hundreds of hours, especially at the beginning of your research. In this chapter, we will look at the various resources currently available through the Internet and discuss the ways to reach them and use the information you gather most effectively.

It is important to note that Web site addresses change and that Web sites come and go. The following list of general references should not be considered authoritative. The best way to check currently available resources is to log onto the Internet and see what is being offered under the topic "Jewish genealogy." In the not-so-distant future, advances in technology and programming may change the way in which some of the information that follows will be accessed or posted. In this book we discuss the use of computer programs for organizing and storing genealogical data. The purpose of this chapter is to discuss the role of the Internet in genealogical research.

I'm a novice when it comes to computers. If you are computer literate, you know all about computers and Internet access, and you should probably skip to the section on Web sites. However, if you are relatively new to the world of computers and cyberspace, read on without fear. I've tried to explain things about computers and the Internet in the way that I wish someone had explained them to me, that is, in nontechnical, very simple language. Also, I've tried to stick to the basics. This subject is not difficult. Would a rabbi lie?

Speaking Cyberspace

Like any specialized field, the world of cyberspace has a language all its own. When you think about these words, most of them are self-explanatory, once you understand how computers and the world of cyberspace operate. However, there are some terms that only the "initiated" will understand. Here are a few basic words and phrases that will ease your way into the wonderful world of cyberspace.

Beginner's Vocabulary

.com　A suffix for a Web site address that designates a commercial enterprise.

Cyberspace　Cyberspace is a general term sometimes used as a synonym for the Internet and the World Wide Web.

Homepage　The first page of a Web site.

Internet　The Internet is like a huge mall with many different stores. However, instead of being located on a street in a city, it exists in an electronic universe.

Link　An easy way to get from one Web site to another. Usually a "link" leads you to a Web site that has information that is related to that offered by the Web site you're visiting. For example, one Jewish genealogy Web site will provide links to other Jewish genealogy Web sites.

Log on　To connect with the Internet.

Search engine　A search engine is a Web site that makes it possible to search for information by topic and other methods. You go to a search engine as you would any other Web site. (Some of the most popular search engines are discussed later in this chapter.)

Surfing the Web　Surfing the Web is analogous to "cruising the mall." It's an expression that suggests that one is window shopping rather than going to a specific location. It can also be used to refer to a broad search for specific information.

Web page　An individual section of a Web site.

Web site　A Web site is a specific destination on the World Wide Web or the Internet. A Web site is like an electronic magazine, often with many different pages of information.

World Wide Web (WWW)　The World Wide Web, or just "the Web," is another way of speaking of the Internet.

HOW TO GET ON THE INTERNET

Please note that if you're already familiar with the Internet and computers, you can skip this section and go to page 91.

In order to get on the Internet, it's necessary to have four basic ingredients:

- a computer with the necessary software to let you get to the Internet. This software is known as "browser software." Netscape Navigator and Microsoft Explorer are two of the most popular browsers.
- a telephone line
- a modem
- an Internet service account.

A Computer

Today, almost all, if not all computers, whether they are desk-top models or lap-tops, have the built-in capability for Internet connection. However, if you're buying a computer for the first time, it's a good idea to ask, just in case. Dedicated word processors, which are not technically computers, do not usually have Internet capability.

Computers for home use come in two different types—IBM compatible, which are manufactured under a wide variety of brand names like Gateway, Dell, and Compaq; and Macintosh computers, which are made by Macintosh. The difference between the two is in the type of programs they use to run a computer. Each type of computer has its fans and advocates. Either type can be used for running genealogy software and accessing the Internet. However, it's important to know, in the case of software, what type of machine you're using. Macintosh programming is for Macintosh computers exclusively. The packaging for software always alerts the buyer to the type of machine on which the software should run.

A Telephone Line

Internet access is currently accomplished through telephone lines. In order to get on the Internet, you need a phone line that is free at the time that you want to make the connection. The best possible situation is to have a dedicated phone line for your computer, one that is not used for any other purpose other than Internet connection. Also, it's best if this line has no features other than the ability to make and receive calls.

Some people set up a phone line to serve a computer and a fax machine. This is possible if you rarely get incoming faxes. Otherwise it's not practical, since someone calling that phone line or wanting to send a fax will get a busy signal while you're on line. When you use your phone line to access the Internet, use a local phone number so that your charges for phone use for your computer will be relatively low.

A Modem

A modem is a piece of equipment that may be built in or added to your computer. When you buy a computer, very often the modem is an add-on piece of equipment not covered in the base price. The modem makes it possible for your computer to link up with your phone line so that you can get on the Internet.

Modems come in different speeds. The speed component is the amount of time it takes for your computer and the Internet to connect. When we talk about time in relation to modems, we're talking in terms of seconds rather than minutes.

Some people raise the concern that, because a modem connects your phone to your computer and printer, a lightening strike near your home could potentially cause a power surge through your phone line that could damage your computer. For that reason, a surge protector is a good investment. In addition, some people take the precaution of disconnecting their modem, or even their computer, during a thunderstorm.

Internet Service Account

An Internet service account is a service that you pay for, usually on a monthly basis. This service makes it possible for your computer to access the Internet. Once on the Internet, it's possible to go to any Web site you wish.

There are many different Internet service companies. America Online, Microsoft Internet Explorer, and Erols are among the most popular Internet servers. There are also small local service providers. Most universities offer students and faculty Internet access through their own "in house" service.

Most computers come with at least one, if not more Internet service programs already built in. In order to activate your account, you choose the program you would like to use, follow the directions that appear on your screen, enter your credit card number, and your account is immediately activated.

HOW TO GET ONLINE

Every Internet access program is a little different. However, almost all follow a basic format:

1. Turn on your computer.
2. Double click onto the access program icon that will appear on your screen at the time that your computer completely wakes up—for example, the America Online icon.
3. A graphic will be displayed that asks you to put in your secret code name (which you decided on and entered when you set up your account) and to click the "sign on" graphic.
4. There is noise and a graphic usually comes up that shows you're being connected to the Internet.
5. Once you're connected, you're in cyberspace. To help you get to a specific Internet address, there will be a graphic that says something like "Internet connection." Some programs also have a blank space next to an icon that says "Keyword."
6. To go to a specific destination on the Internet, type the address you want to go to into the Internet connection box or the Keyword box and click the icon that says either "go" or "go to the Web." This will take you to the site you want to visit.

A Few Words About Internet Addresses

An Internet address usually, but not always, begins with a prefix http://www. The punctuation of an address is very important. The *http* is always followed by a colon (:) and two slashes (//). The *www* is always followed by a period.

The next part of the address is the actual place you are visiting. For example, if you want to go to one of the search engines like Yahoo, which is one of the most popular search engines, you would type the following: http://www.yahoo.com.

The suffix after the name of the place where you want to go is called a "domain." A domain tells you about the type of affiliation the Web site has. For example, *.com* signifies a commercial Web site, *.org*, as in the address http://www.jewishgen.org, usually signifies a not-for-profit organization. Schools use the suffix *.edu* and the government uses the suffix *.gov*. Some suffixes indicate the country of origin. For example, Israel uses the suffix *.il*, as in the address http://www.bh.org.il. This is the address for Beth Hatefutsoth, the Museum of the Jewish People in Tel Aviv. Sometimes, a Web site address will have a slash at the end of the address, as in http://www.avotaynu.com/.

It's unusual for a Web site address to end in a period. If you put in punctuation that is not part of a Web site address or leave out the proper punctuation, you'll get a message on your screen that tells you that the Web site can't be located. Before giving up, check all the punctuation carefully. The chances are that you have misplaced a period or a slash or turned a slash the wrong way.

A *search engine* is a Web site that makes it possible to search for information by topic and other methods. Some of the best search engines are Yahoo—http://www.yahoo.com, Webcrawler—http://www. webcrawler.com, Excite—http://www.excite.com, Alta Vista—http:// altavista.digital.com, and Maven—http://www.maven.co.il. You go to a search engine as you would any other Web site. Once there, you have an opportunity to search for your topic of interest through keywords that you supply or through various directories supplied by the search engine itself.

Now that you have an idea of what the world of cyberspace is like, let's look at some Jewish genealogy Web sites.

SHARING GENEALOGY INFORMATION

There are formal and informal ways of sharing genealogical information. Informal sharing takes place through phone calls, letters, E-mail notes, bulletin board postings, and conversations with those who share your particular interest.

Formal sharing of files is a very common practice. However, since there are many different computer programs in existence, and many different genealogy programs in existence, computer genealogists have been working since 1984 to find a common computer programming language for genealogists. The result of their efforts is a program called GEDCOM—Genealogical Data Communications.

GEDCOM exists in a number of different incarnations as programmers work toward making it a truly universal program for packaged genealogy programs and for the Internet. At the present time, there are a number of different versions floating around in cyberspace and in genealogy computer programs.

Without getting too technical, here's how GEDCOM works in theory.

1. You purchase a genealogy program that says that you can "import data from any other GEDCOM-compatible software." This means that the program itself can create a GEDCOM file for you to send to others and that you can receive and work with material submitted to you from some other source as long as it's sent in GEDCOM format.

2. If you want to submit your genealogical material to a database, you can convert it into a GEDCOM format in a few easy steps because the ability to do so is one of the options offered to you through the genealogy program that you purchased.

3. You can request that genealogy information be sent to you in GEDCOM format from a genealogy database so that you can review and work with the information on your own computer.

4. If, for some reason, you have trouble sending or receiving information in GEDCOM format, the computer manual that comes with the genealogy software package that you buy will tell you how to manipulate the incoming or outgoing data so that it can be either received and read or sent successfully.

GenServ is an international data bank of genealogical information. In order to get information from the database, you have to "join" by submitting your own genealogical information and paying a small yearly membership fee. GenServe is staffed by volunteers who are, in their own words, "addicted to genealogy." GenServe can be reached on the Internet at: http://www.genserv.com/ and by snail mail at: Cliff Manis— GenServ System, P. O. Box 33937, San Antonio, TX 78265-3937.

The amount of available cyber genealogy information in general and Jewish genealogy information in particular is staggering. The Web sites listed here represent "main points of entry" into this fascinating world. Besides providing the Web site addresses, I have included other ways to contact the organizations when this is possible. Some Web site organizations exist only in cyberspace! Most of these sites have numerous links to other, equally fascinating genealogy Web sites. There is literally something for everyone.

A Sampling of Jewish Genealogy Web Sites

Avotaynu—The International Review of Jewish Genealogy
http://www.avotaynu.com/

The word *avotaynu,* which is Hebrew, means "our fathers" or "our ancestors." Avotaynu, Inc. is the premier publishing company in the field of Jewish genealogical research. Its journal, *Avotaynu, The International Review of Jewish Genealogy,* is a must-read publication for persons doing Jewish genealogical research. The forty-five issues published between 1985 and 1996 include more than 2,300 articles—some 2 million words. In addition to the periodical, Avotaynu publishes a wide range of books, microfiche, and CDs. In addition, Avotaynu offers for sale books, maps, and videotapes published by other companies. All back issues of *Avotaynu* are available on CD-ROM as well as in printed form. Among the offerings available from Avotaynu are:

Library Resources for German-Jewish Genealogy. A concise directory of library sources and how to use them efficiently. The book gives details of scientific, university, and specialized German libraries that have material relevant to Jewish family research. It also explains how to access the most important online public access catalogues and how to use online ordering services.

Finding Your Jewish Roots in Galicia: A Resource Guide. This is the definitive work on Galician-Jewish genealogical research. This book organizes what is known about Galician Jewish record searching and other resources to assist genealogists in tracing their Jewish Galician roots. Such resources include archival collections of Jewish vital records and other records; geographic, visual, and language aides; books and documents related to the Holocaust, and articles about travel and research in specific towns by members of Gesher Galicia, the special interest group for Jewish genealogy.

Microfiche. Recognizing that some works are worth publishing but are not commercially viable in printed form, Avotaynu has published more than twenty works on microfiche, an inexpensive way of making information available to the public.

Beth Hatefutsoth—Museum of the Jewish People
http://www.bh.org.il/

Access to the unique Douglas E. Goldman Jewish Genealogy Center at Beth Hatefutsoth in Israel is available via the Internet. In the center, visitors can search a computerized database containing thousands of genealogies of Jewish families from all over the world and can also register their own family trees. More than 750,000 names have already been entered into the constantly expanding database. Visitors from all backgrounds can explore their ancestry, and record and preserve their own family trees for future generations, thus adding their own "branch" to the family tree of the Jewish people. One can place an online search order and receive the initial results by E-mail. Printouts will then be

sent to you by mail or fax. For more information, contact: Ms. Diana
Sommer, Director, the Douglas E. Goldman Jewish Genealogy Center,
Beth Hatefutsoth—E-mail: bhgnlgy@post.tau.ac.il; fax: (972) 3 646
2134; tel: (972) 3 646 2061/2.

FEEFHS—Federation of Eastern European Family History Societies   http://www.feefhs.org

This Web site offers information on the best genealogy search
engines, maps, and other information helpful to genealogists working
on Eastern European family connections. Among the areas covered are
Albania, Armenia, Latvia, Belarus, Bukovina, Bulgaria, Canada, Czechoslovakia, and Germany. The snail mail address is: Federation of East
European Family History Societies, P. O. Box 510898, Salt Lake City,
UT 84151-0898. To use this Web site, you just type in the key word—
a surname, full name, or place-name. As of the writing of this book, this
Web site offers 177 home pages of helpful organizations located in fourteen countries on four continents, five Canadian provinces and twenty-
seven U.S. states. It also offers important news in the world of genealogy.

JewishGen: The Home of Jewish Genealogy
http://www.jewishgen.org/

JewishGen is an excellent Web site for beginners. Easy to use and
navigate, it includes the JewishGen Discussion Group, the JewishGen
Family Finder (a database of over seventy thousand surnames and
towns), the comprehensive directory of InfoFiles, and a variety of databases like the ShtetlSeeker.

ShtetlSeeker, which can be reached directly at the address http://
www.jewishgen.org/ShtetlSeeker, helps you locate the shtetl (the small
town or village in Eastern Europe) where an ancestor lived. Very often
it's difficult to find these towns because of variations in spelling.
ShtetlSeeker provides optional spellings for the name of the town that
you provide. For example, when I asked for a search of the name
"Skwira," which appeared in this spelling on one of my grandmother's
documents, ShtetlSeeker found "Skvira," located 61.3 miles southwest
of Kiev, which I know is correct. ShtetlSeeker also gives you the lati-

tude and longitude for the place you're looking for and notes whether the name given to you is the native name or a variant.

JewishGen is staffed by volunteers and is supported by donations. It provides access to a number of different Jewish genealogical organizations, Web sites, and special interest groups. Among these are:

The Association of Jewish Genealogical Societies. This is the umbrella group for the more than sixty Jewish genealogical societies in the world. At its Web site, you can get the name and address of the society nearest to you. By joining a Jewish genealogical society, you will have access to people who can help you in your research as well as a number of books and databases of use in your research.

Regional Special Interest Groups. These are research and discussion groups interested in a particular region. Some of the current SIGs include: Galicia, Latvia, Lithuania, and Hungary.

The JewishGen InfoFile Index is a rich research and information source for both beginning and more advanced Jewish genealogists. There is a wide variety of topics and information covered including: books and periodicals, genealogical techniques, holocaust, immigration, Internet sources, libraries and archives, seminars, special interest groups, translation, travel, and vital records. Among the countries covered are: Argentina, Austria, Australia, Canada, Germany, Hungary, Israel, Lithuania, the Netherlands, Poland, Russian Empire, South Africa, United Kingdom, and the United States.

Stammbaum—Journal of German-Jewish Genealogy
http://www.jewgen.org/stammbaum/

Established in 1993, *Stammbaum* is an English-language publication specializing in German-Jewish genealogy. Besides covering information about Germany, it also covers areas of German historic and linguistic influence including Austria, Switzerland, Alsace, and Bohemia. *Stammbaum* is affiliated with the Leo Baeck Institute, which publishes this journal twice a year. Back issues are available. Snail mail address is:

Leo Baeck Institute, 129 East 73rd St., New York, NY 10021; telephone: (212) 744-6400; Internet address: http://www.lbi.org/; E-mail: frank@lbi.com.

The *Stammbaum* Web site is an excellent example of the crossover between the Internet and traditional published sources. On the Web site, one can find tables of contents of previous journals, a surname index, and a place-name index included in previous publications. Having this information can help the genealogist narrow the search and determine which back issues may be helpful. The Web site also lists the cost of subscriptions to the journal and provides the snail mail and the E-mail address for the Leo Baeck Institute. In addition, like many other Web sites, it provides links to other important Jewish genealogy Web sites.

Usenet   soc.genealogy.jewish—Jewish genealogy group
This usenet is a bulletin board that permits the genealogist to post inquiries about his or her own research and to scan posted messages. Other people may be looking for the same information that you are and this may turn up on a usenet bulletin board. In a moderated group, the messages submitted are monitored before being posted. This makes sure that the group will be free of postings that are not relevant to their interests.

YIVO Institute for Jewish Research
http://www.baruch.cuny.edu/yivo/
YIVO is dedicated to the study and preservation of the Eastern European Jewish heritage. Since its founding in 1925, YIVO has become the world's preeminent research institute and academic center for Eastern European Jewish Studies. YIVO is located in New York City. The Web site provides an overview of YIVO's extensive collections. Of special interest to Jewish genealogists are the memorial books, approximately seven hundred memorial volumes *(yisker-bikher; sifre-zikaron)* about the Jewish communities of Poland and neighboring countries published decades after World War II by mutual aid societies known as landsmanshaften. These collective compilations represent the most

extensive—and often the only—published accounts of Jewish life in cities and *shtetlekh* throughout Eastern Europe.

Also of interest is the YIVO Library, which has quite a bit of information regarding specific cities and towns in Eastern Europe, including encyclopedias, gazetteers, and reference books on the etymology and geographical distribution of Jewish family names. The library also owns many biographical directories and lexicons. These will be helpful if your ancestor was fairly well-known.

Then there is the YIVO archives, which boast a collection of thousands of photographs, indexed by town and searchable on videodisk, using a computer keyboard and mouse. The archives also has a special collection of old landsmanshaft records.

SEPHARDIC GENEALOGY

BSZNet—published by B'nei Shaare Zion Congregation

http://www.spacelab.net/~david/lgenealogy.htm

This Web site is a good jumping-off point for Sephardic genealogy sources. Among the links it offers are: Sephardim and Conversos—A JewishGen InfoFile, and The Sefard Forum for Sephardic Genealogy Research.

Sephardic Genealogy Web site Created by Jeff Malka

http://www.orthohelp.com/geneal/sefardim.htm

This is an extremely rich resource for Sephardic genealogical research. Among its offerings and links are: Sephardic Web sites; newslists; archival sources; and a search for Sephardic names.

Some of the countries covered include Holland, Egypt, Turkey, Greece, North Africa, France, the Caribbean, and South America. And a sampling of some of the topics dealt with are: Portuguese Jewish Community of Tunis; Sephardic Congregations Around the World; Judeo-Spanish Homepage; Jews of Cape Verde and of the Azores; Jewish Marriages in Amsterdam; Dutch Jewish Genealogy Homepage; Jews of Bombay; and library resources for Sephardic genealogy.

For Halocaust-related sites, see chapter 14.

LINKS TO PRINTED RESOURCES
AND SPECIALIZED INFORMATION

Generations Press   http://members.aol.com/townplans/

This is a publishing company specializing in immigrant research, Jewish genealogy, and historic map reproductions. The company offers almost 850 highly detailed maps of over six hundred cities and towns in Europe, the Middle East, North Africa, and the Americas. Most maps list street names, civic buildings, schools and universities, factories, places of worship and cemeteries by religious denomination, parks and other such features.

Cimorelli Immigration Manifests Online
http://www.cimorelli.com/vbclient/shipmenu.htm

This is a good place to search for the ship that brought your grandparents from Europe to America. It contains information from the *Morton Allan Directory* and other sources. Of special note is the SOUNDEX Converter and NARA Records service.

Cyndi's List of Genealogy Sites on the Internet
http://www.cyndislist.com

This is an excellent genealogy site that includes thousands of cross-referenced links for genealogy in over seventy different categories including ships, passenger lists, and immigration information. Although there is not a Jewish emphasis, there is good general genealogical information available here.

BLITZ   http://feefhs.org/blitz/blitzjgr.html

This is the Russian-Baltic information center for Jewish genealogy research in Russia. The information center provides genealogy searches as well as other research in different Russian archives and libraries.

SECOLO Italian Society for Jewish Genealogy
http://www.secolo.com/

SECOLO, the Italian Society for Jewish Genealogy, is a nonprofit genealogical and document-translation service. Its Web site is in both

Italian and English. SECOLO provides European genealogical research as well as translation services.

SURFING THE INTERNET FOR RELATIVES

The term "surfing the net" means to go online and search for information through the many different vehicles that are available in cyberspace.

Directories

There are a number of different directories that list people's names and E-mail or street addresses. One way of researching your family history on the Internet is to use these directories. When you find someone with the name you're seeking, write to him or her and ask if you could be related. Give a brief outline of the family line you're tracing. While this may not be the most "scientific" way to search for someone, you may actually be able to find people related to you in this way. You should use as many directories as you can find for this type of research. Here are some of the Web site directories you can visit:

Four11: http://www.Four11.com

LookUp!: http://www.lookup.com

Internet Address Finder: http://www.iaf.net

WhoWhere? People Search: http://www.whowhere.com

Yahoo White Pages: http://www.yahoo.com

America Online: http://www.aol.com/netfind/person.html

America Online: for Members—use membership directory

MIT mail server: This tracks people who have submitted articles to usenet. Send E-mail to mail-server@rtfm.mit.edu and in the body of the mail, include one line that says: send usenet-addresses/ fenstemacher.

Bulletin Boards

A bulletin board is just what it sounds like. On genealogy bulletin boards, people leave messages about the people you or they are searching for. Others who have information can contact you with their information. In addition, next to these bulletin boards are "file cabinets." It's possible to open the file cabinets and find information that may be of interest to you. A number of different genealogy sites have bulletin boards that you can explore and on which you can post your own information.

Throughout this book you will find other online resources that will help you in your research. In the next chapter, we will learn how vital records of many different types can be researched and requested on line and in many other ways.

8

How to Make the Most of Your Living Relatives

When most people think about constructing a genealogy, what comes to mind is complicated document searches, steamship records, and records that may never be retrieved. Interestingly, they never think of the resources that are close at hand and easily accessible—family members and family friends, family photographs, and existing written family records. In this chapter, we will explore the ways in which to collect information from these important, firsthand resources.

BE A PEOPLE PERSON—COLLECTING ORAL HISTORIES

Your living relatives are one of your most valuable genealogical resources. An Interview Resource Form will help you figure out who your family resources are for the purpose of collecting genealogical information. The sample form provided here illustrates how to complete an Interview Resource Form. After you've looked this over, complete an Interview Resource Form for your own family. You will find a blank form at the end of this chapter. Make sure to include the names of all your immediate relatives, living and deceased. Wherever possible, for female relatives who have married, add their maiden name if you know it. You should mention deceased relatives because they may have living relatives whom you might otherwise overlook.

SAMPLE INTERVIEW RESOURCE FORM

(Names, addresses, and phone numbers on this form have been changed to protect the privacy of the individuals concerned.)

Prepared by Lynn Davis, May 1998

Siblings:
Brother—Max Raven, 123 Spring Street, Roslyn, NY 11576, (516) 744-3222
Sister—self

Sibling's Children:
Andrew (minor)
Alison (minor)

Patrilineal and Matrilineal Family Members

Patrilineal

Father's Name: Ira Raven (deceased)
Father's Siblings:
Harry Raven—brother—23 East 68th Street, New York, NY 10021; (212) 249-0232
Harry's wife—Shirley Raven

Harry's Children:
Robert Raven—43 East 55th Street, New York, NY 10017; (212) 244-5678
Robert's Spouse—Susan Raven
Robert's Children—none
Ira's Father's Name: Irving Raven—deceased
Ira's Mother's Name: Sophie Sperling Raven—deceased

Matrilineal

Mother's Name:
Ivy Katz Raven—858 Fifth Avenue, New York, NY 10021; (212) 249-2543
Mother's Siblings: none
Ivy's Father's Name: Simon Katz—deceased
Ivy's Mother's Name: Rose Goldberg Katz—deceased
Simon's Siblings: All deceased
Rose's Siblings: All deceased

INTERVIEW RESOURCE FORM

Fill in as much information as possible.

Prepared by: _____   Date _____
                  Your name

Siblings

Brother

_____

Name   Address   Phone number

Sister

_____

Name   Address   Phone number

Sibling's Children (list address and phone number only if they are old enough to give you information not otherwise available. Otherwise, list name only for future reference.)

_____

Name   Address   Phone number

_____

Name   Address   Phone number

Patrilineal and Matrilineal Family Members (if no longer living, note as deceased).

Patrilineal

Father

_____

Name   Address   Phone number

Father's Sibling

Name	Address	Phone number

Sibling's Spouse

Name	Address	Phone number

Father's Sibling

Name	Address	Phone number

Sibling's Spouse

Name	Address	Phone number

Sibling's Children

Name	Address	Phone number

Name	Address	Phone number

Father's Father

Name	Address	Phone number

Father's Mother

Name	Address	Phone number

Matrilineal

Mother

Name	Address	Phone number

Mother's Sibling

Name	Address	Phone number

Sibling's Spouse

Name	Address	Phone number

Mother's Sibling

Name	Address	Phone number

Sibling's Spouse

Name	Address	Phone number

Sibling's Children

Name	Address	Phone number

Name	Address	Phone number

Mother's Father

Name	Address	Phone number

Mother's Mother

Name	Address	Phone number

CREATING AN INTERVIEW PLAN

Once you've got an at-a-glance overview of your living relatives, you'll need to decide where to start. Beginning genealogists may find it easiest to trace the family line that has the most living relatives. This is a good way to build solid research skills while having the satisfaction of compiling an accurate family tree.

Arthur Kurzweil suggests that a neophyte should interview all the oldest members of both sides of the family before making a choice as to which line to follow first. He makes the excellent point that the oldest members of each family are a fragile resource and may not be around when you're ready to interview them.

While this is solid advice, working with both sides of the family may be an overwhelming task for a beginner. It can be helpful to recall Rabbi Tarfon's advice that we are not responsible for every aspect of a task that we take on. If you find yourself feeling overwhelmed, remember you are not the only person responsible for preserving your family tree. Do what you can and what you feel motivated to do and don't worry about what you can't do or don't wish to do.

You can get started with an Interview Plan, a basic road map for the interview segment of your research. An Interview Plan helps you organize all your contact information and gives some order to your interview sequence. Even if you don't wish to interview all your oldest living relatives first, it's a good idea, once you've decided which side of your family you're going to research, to begin with the oldest relatives on your chosen side of the family. At the end of this chapter you will find an Interview Plan worksheet to help you organize your interview. Once you've filled it out, it's time to begin your interviews.

BREAKING THE ICE

Some people are very lucky. They have ongoing relationships with many people in their family sphere. Others may feel they need to reach out to relatives they haven't seen in years—if at all. If this is your situation, don't despair. Many genealogists find a warm welcome when they reach out to long-distant or even previously unknown relatives. Here are a few tips to help you break the ice:

- Remember that you and your request may surprise most of the people you will be calling. Work out a concise statement about what you're doing that you can use in any situation. For example: "I'm doing research so that I can create a family tree for our family."

- If the relative you are contacting doesn't know who you are, clearly identify yourself by referring to other relatives he or she will know—your parents, grandparents, aunts, uncles, cousins— whichever is most appropriate. Some examples: "I'm your sister Charlotte's niece," or "I'm your Uncle Herb's great-grandson."

- In speaking to someone you don't know in your matrilineal line, remember that the relative may not recognize your mother's or grandmother's married name. Use your mother's or grandmother's maiden name, if you know it, to identify yourself.
- Always be pleasant and thank the person for their help.
- Promise to make a copy of the finalized family tree available and make good on your promise.

THE INTERVIEW

Scheduling the Interview

In scheduling your interview, there are a few things to keep in mind.

Be courteous. You are asking your relative to share his or her life with you. You don't have a "right" to this information. Be respectful and aware that being the recipient of an oral history is a privilege. Try to let this sense of being given something very precious guide you in all that you do in your relationship with the relatives that you interview.

Set an appropriate time of day. Schedule the interview at a time that is not too early or too late in the day. Early interviews may be difficult for older relatives. Sometimes older people need extra time to get started in the morning. Late appointments may find older relatives tired or not at their most alert. Ask the person you would like to interview what time would be best for him or her.

Mealtime is not interview time. Interviewing someone over lunch or dinner may sound like fun, but a meal is not a good setting for an interview. At a meal, there's too much to distract both you and the person you're interviewing. It's important to focus on the interview and not on the soup that is too hot.

Schedule well in advance and confirm. Whenever possible, call or write to schedule your interview as far in advance as possible. Make sure to confirm the appointment a few days before your meeting. Be prepared to suggest some alternate dates and times.

Define your expectations. Make sure, when you arrange for your interview, that the person you are interviewing knows what you want to talk about and how much time will be needed. Get an agreement on the length of time to be devoted to the interview and an understanding on how the interview will be followed up—either in person or by phone.

Ask permission for audio/video taping. Older relatives may not feel comfortable with audio or videotape. If you would like to use these devices, ask permission to do so when you schedule your interview.

Seek permission before someone accompanies you to the interview. If you are planning to have someone helping you with the interview, you should ask your relative if this is okay. If your relative disapproves, do the interview alone.

Have the subject prepare for the interview. Ask your interviewee if he or she can find any family records, memorabilia, and heirlooms and have them ready for your interview.

Choose a quiet setting. If possible, the interview should take place in the home of the person you're interviewing. There are several reasons for this. Many people do their best "reminiscing" when they're in a familiar environment. Also, this setting should be relatively quiet, which will be relaxing for both of you. The person's home is a good place for the interview because when your subject says, "I think I have a copy of . . . ," he or she may then be able to retrieve that important document immediately.

Length of the interview. An interview that is too long will tire the both the interviewer and the interviewee. Plan about ninety minutes for the first interview. If you sense that the person you're interviewing is getting tired, cut the interview short and schedule a follow-up.

Follow up your interview. It's always a good idea to schedule either an in-person or phone follow-up interview the next day. Having started to think about their family history, many people will find that they remember other things after a good night's sleep.

Conducting the Interview

Be organized. Whether the interview is conducted in person or by phone, it's important that it be well organized. This is where your Interview Plan can help. Use it to make sure that you cover all the most important information first.

Your interview should be structured. To do this, you'll need an Interview Form (page 115). You should have one for each person you interview. You can use the form included in this book or create one of your own. Make sure to label each form with the name of the person and the date of the interview. Also, leave enough room for each answer. Write down everything that is said. Sometimes offhand remarks contain valuable clues for further research.

Be sensitive to emotional nuances. Just because you're excited about finding out about your ancestors doesn't mean that the people you're interviewing will have the same positive feelings. Reminiscing about family and the old country may bring up sad or difficult memories. It's important to be very sensitive to older relatives when interviewing them about situations that may be painful. Your expressions of understanding, caring, and sympathy will help put them at ease. However, if a relative refuses to talk about certain things, don't push. If you back off and pursue another topic, you may be able to get other important information.

Make maximum use of technology—and bring help. If your subject will permit you to do so, make audiotapes of every interview. Audio-taping an interview will help you decipher your written or keyboarded notes. If you can, videotape will also be extremely valuable, not only for what is said on the tape, but because you will be capturing "live" one of your ancestors for future generations. If you plan to use audio or video tape, it may be helpful to bring along a technical assistant. This will free you of the necessity of watching for the end of an audio tape or being concerned with the video camera.

The focus of this book is on genealogy. However, a related topic concerns the creation of family oral histories. This is a specific discipline within the field of genealogy. For more information about creating family oral histories, see the Bibliography at the back of this book.

After your interview, make sure to write a thank you note to your relative. While this may seem like a small detail, it will be greatly appreciated by the person who receives it. You should also try to keep in touch with

INTERVIEW TIPS

- On each audio and video tape, before the interview, record the name of the person being interviewed and their relationship to you.
- Label every tape with the interviewee's name and the date of the interview.
- Store the tape with a copy of the written questionnaire.
- Have the tape transcribed into a written document. You can do this yourself or have it done by a transcription service. (See the Appendix for the name of a transcription service that specializes in genealogy.)
- When asking your questions, speak slowly and clearly. Ask only one question at a time.
- Do not let the person you're interviewing "wander off." Keep your subject talking about the specific question.
- If something is not clear, make sure to ask a clarifying question immediately. Don't assume that you can figure it out later.
- Record the answers in black or blue ink. Make sure that you have several pens with you.
- Write clearly. Nothing is more frustrating than finding out later you can't read your own notes.

this relative and share your research as your project progresses. By doing these things, you will ensure your relative's goodwill and possibly interest him or her in your search.

YOUR FIRST INTERVIEW IN THREE EASY STEPS

An initial interview is as simple as one, two, three. Just follow these simple steps, which are the basis of the Interview Form at the end of this chapter.

Step One: Names, Dates, Relationships

Each person will have a piece of your family puzzle. The first step in your interview is to get as much factual information as possible. The purpose of step one is to help you find certain basic information for as many people and generations as your interview subject can provide. This information includes: English and Hebrew names; date and place of birth; date and place of marriage; date and place of death; place of interment; details of military service; names and birth order of siblings.

Even if you are only following one family line, if you have the opportunity, collect the information for as many branches of your family tree as possible. Other family members may be able to use this information later on. However, make sure that you get the information for the branch that you're following first.

Step Two: Details of Family Life

In step two of the interview, you want to obtain a more detailed look at the individuals you're discovering and what their lives were like. Each family will have its own stories and history. However, some categories to explore are: immigration; Jewish community affiliation; religious observance; and professional, educational, and lifestyle information.

Step Three: Collecting Documents, Photos, and Memorabilia

A wide range of possible documents, photographs, diaries, and other family memorabilia can help us trace our family background. The purpose of step three is to uncover these treasures, which are often overlooked. Although you may not have these documents yourself, other members of the family may have saved them. Besides asking the interviewee if he or she has such documents, it's a good idea to inquire if the interviewee could suggest other family members who might have or know of family papers and memorabilia.

Knowing what to ask for will make your search easier. Here are some suggestions:

- family photo albums, bibles, memoirs, genealogies, scrap books, and news clippings
- immigration and naturalization documents
- life-cycle documents—birth, naming, bar/bat mitzvah, marriage, death
- synagogue bulletins
- family circle records
- address books, letters, deeds, and financial records
- heirlooms.

LETTER WRITING—SNAIL MAIL AND E-MAIL

Sometimes it will not be possible to do an interview in person or over the phone. That's when you may need to correspond with relatives either by regular mail or E-mail. To get the best possible results, you should call the relative first and ask if he or she is willing to take a little time to fill in a family questionnaire for your genealogy project. Let your relative know when he or she will be receiving the information and also make it clear that you would like to have the information returned to you by a specific date. A two-week turnaround generally allows for sufficient time while making sure that the information doesn't get lost on someone's desk forever or until they "get around to it." If you're sending the material by mail, make sure to include a self-addressed, stamped envelope. Also, although most relatives will be cooperative, expect that you may have to mail your materials again to one or more of them. Sometimes things get misplaced.

The questionnaire you will send to your relative is different from the one that you use for your "in person" interviews. A sample questionnaire appears at the end of this chapter. Feel free to customize this questionnaire to meet the special circumstances of your family.

Your mailed interview package should contain a brief cover letter reminding your relative of your previous phone call, the purpose of the questionnaire, and the return date requested; the questionnaire (see sample); and a response envelope with sufficient postage, unless you are corresponding by E-mail.

When the completed questionnaire is returned to you, you should review it and call your relative to thank him or her for cooperating in the project. You may also need to clarify some of the answers.

FOLLOW-UP MAILING

Once you compile the information you receive through personal interviews and questionnaires and add it to your ascendant and descendent forms, you should mail these "works in progress" to everyone you've interviewed. Ask them to verify the information and to add anything that has been left out. This second mailing will help in filling in many of the blanks that may still appear. Also, it may encourage the members of your family to dig more deeply and may result in new information that the first round of interviews did not uncover. As with the first mailing, there should be a cover letter and stamped, self-addressed envelope for the subject's convenience, as well as a follow-up call.

Now that we've discussed how to interview your relatives, let's go to the next chapter and look at the many different types of family documents that can help you to fill in the missing clues in your family puzzle.

INTERVIEW WORKSHEET FOR IN-PERSON INTERVIEWS

Instructions

1. Fill out an Ascendant/Pedigree Form for the interviewee. (This form appears in chapter 5.)
2. Fill out this worksheet with the interviewee.
3. Each time the interviewee mentions a new relative's name, put that name on a separate Relative Form.
4. After interviewing your family member, review each Relative Form with him or her and fill in as much information for each individual as possible.

INTERVIEW FORM

Name of interviewer _____ Date of interview _____

Name of person being interviewed _____

Place of interview _____

BASIC INFORMATION

Complete Hebrew name (including parents' Hebrew names) _____

Name other than present English name (if changed at some point) _____

Date of birth _____ Place of birth _____

Birth certificate in family papers?   yes ___ no ___

Names of siblings in birth order _____

(Fill out a Relative Form for each sibling.)

Name of spouse _____ (Include female's maiden
    name; fill out a Relative Form for spouse.)

Date of marriage _____ Place of marriage _____

Name/type of officiant (i.e., rabbi, judge, city clerk) _____

Ketubah in family papers?   yes ___ no ___

Civil marriage license in family papers?   yes ___ no ___

If divorced, date and place of divorce _____

Copy of Get in family papers?   yes ___ no ___

Date and place of death of spouse _____

Place of interment _____

If remarried, date and place of marriage _____

Name of spouse (Fill out a Relative Form for spouse.) _____

English and Hebrew names of children _____

Birth dates and places of birth of children (Fill out a Relative Form for
    each child.)

Occupation of person being interviewed _____

Highest level of education achieved _____

DETAILS OF FAMILY LIFE

Immigration

Where did this branch of the family come from originally? _____

Did the family immigrate together? _____

Date you left the "old country?" _____

The original country to which they immigrated _____

Mode of travel to new homeland _____

The name of the ship you arrived on _____

Date of entry to U.S. _____

Date of naturalization _____

Are there immigration documents (immigration, naturalization) available?
_____

(If yes, make sure to get copies of these documents.)

Are there any family stories that exist in written or oral form? (If yes, make sure to obtain these.)

Did the family belong to a landsmanshaft organization or Verein?
  yes ___ no ___

If yes, name of organization _____

Is the organization still active?   yes ___ no ___ If yes, is there a contact address/phone number? _____

Are there any photographs from the "old country" or from the early years in their new country?   yes ___ no ___ (If yes, try to obtain these photographs.)

Were there relatives who were left behind?   yes ___ no ___

If yes, are they or their descendents known to the interviewee? If yes, list names here. _____
  (Fill out a Relative Form for each individual.)

Jewish Community Affiliation

Was the family affiliated with a synagogue or other type of Jewish communal organization in the "old country"?   yes ___ no ___

If yes, name of synagogue/organization and dates of affiliation. _____

If yes, is there still a family affiliation with this organization?

    yes ___ no ___

If yes, what is the nature of the affiliation? _____

Family plaques or other memorial in synagogue?   yes ___ no ___

Synagogue membership in the "new world"?   yes ___ no ___

If yes, dates of affiliation _____

Name and location of synagogue_____

Family plaques in synagogue?   yes ___ no ___

Religious Observance

Denominational affiliation if any (i.e., Reform, Conservative, Orthodox, Reconstructionist, Secular) _____

Did any of the family members marry someone who was not Jewish?

    yes ___ no ___

If yes, how was this received by the rest of the family? _____

_____

If there was intermarriage and there were children, in what religion were the children raised? _____

Did any of the family members convert to another religion?

    yes ___ no ___

If yes, explain _____

Professional, Educational and Lifestyle Information

What professions did the interviewee's father/mother pursue in the "old country"? _____

Who was the most financially successful member of the family? _____

_____

Explain _____

Interviewee's special achievements—i.e., publications, inventions, awards

_____

FAMILY DOCUMENTS, MEMORABILIA, AND HEIRLOOMS

1. Ask the interviewee if any of the following exist.

2. Ask who else in the family might have this type of information.

Family photo albums/scrapbooks _____
yes ___ no ___ Viewed by interviewer ___

Family Bibles   yes ___ no ___ Viewed by interviewer ___

Family genealogies   yes ___ no ___ Viewed by interviewer ___

Civil marriage certificate   yes ___ no ___ Viewed by interviewer ___

Ketubot (Jewish marriage certificates)   yes ___ no ___
Viewed by interviewer ___

Wedding invitations   yes ___ no ___ Viewed by interviewer ___

Birth certificates   yes ___ no ___ Viewed by interviewer ___

Birth announcements   yes ___ no ___ Viewed by interviewer ___

Bris certificates   yes   ___ no ___ Viewed by interviewer ___

Naming documents, including documents showing a change of name
yes ___ no ___ Viewed by interviewer ___

Bar/bat mitzvah announcements/invitations   yes ___ no ___
Viewed by interviewer ___

Confirmation announcements   yes ___ no ___
Viewed by interviewer ___

Synagogue bulletin   yes ___ no ___ Viewed by interviewer ___

Family circle records   yes ___ no ___ Viewed by interviewer ___

Death certificates   yes ___ no ___ Viewed by interviewer ___

Wimple   yes ___ no ___ Viewed by interviewer ___

Family memoirs and diaries   yes ___ no ___
Viewed by interviewer ___

Address books, letters, financial records, deeds   yes ___ no ___
Viewed by interviewer ___

RELATIVE FORM WORKSHEET

Name of relative _____

Information given by _____

Date _____

Instructions

1. Fill in an Ascendant Form for this person. _____

2. Fill in as much of the following information as possible. _____

BASIC INFORMATION

Complete Hebrew name (including parents' Hebrew names) _____

Name other than present English name (if changed at some point) _____

Date of birth _____ Place of birth _____

Birth certificate in family papers?   yes ___ no ___

Names of siblings in birth order _____
    (Fill out a Relative Form for each sibling.)

Name of spouse _____ (include female's maiden name)
    (Fill out a Relative Form for spouse.)

Date of marriage _____ Place of marriage _____

Name/type of officiant _____ (i.e., rabbi, judge, city clerk)

Ketubah in family papers?   yes ___ no ___

Civil marriage license in family papers?   yes ___ no ___

If divorced, date and place of divorce _____

Copy of Get in family papers?   yes ___ no ___

Date and place of death of spouse _____

Place of interment _____

If remarried, date and place of marriage _____

Name of spouse (Fill out a Relative Form for the spouse.) _____

English and Hebrew names of children _____

Birth dates and places of birth of children (Fill out a Relative Form for each child.) _____

Occupation of person being interviewed _____

Highest level of education achieved _____

DETAILS OF FAMILY LIFE

Immigration

Where did this branch of the family come from originally? _____

Did the family immigrate together? _____

Date they left the "old country"? _____

The original country to which they immigrated _____

Mode of travel to new homeland_____

The name of the ship arrived on _____

Date of entry to U.S. _____

Date of naturalization _____

Are there immigration documents (immigration, naturalization) available?
_____ (If yes, make sure to get copies of these documents.)

Are there any family stories that exist in written or oral form? (If yes, make sure to obtain these.)

Did the family belong to a landsmanshaften organization or Verein?
yes ___ no ___

If yes, name of organization _____

Is the organization still active? yes ___ no ___ If yes, is there a contact address/phone number? _____

Are there any photographs from the "old country" or from the early years in their new country? yes ___ no ___ (If yes, try to obtain these photographs.)

Were there relatives who were left behind? yes ___ no ___

If yes, are they or their descendents known to the interviewee? If yes, list names here. _____ (Fill out a Relative Form for each individual.)

Jewish Community Affiliation

Was the family affiliated with a synagogue or other type of Jewish communal organization in the "old country"   yes ___ no ___

If yes, name of synagogue/organization and dates of affiliation _____

If yes, is there still a family affiliation with this organization?

yes ___ no ___

If yes, what is the nature of the affiliation?

Family plaques or other memorial in synagogue?   yes ___ no ___

Synagogue membership in the "new world"?   yes ___ no ___

If yes, dates of affiliation _____

Name and location of synagogue   _____

Family plaques in synagogue   yes ___ no ___

Religious Observance

Denominational affiliation (i.e., Reform, Conservative, Orthodox, Reconstructionist, Secular) _____

Did any of the family members marry someone who was not Jewish?

yes ___ no ___

If yes, how was this received by the rest of the family? _____

If there was intermarriage and there were children, in what religion were the children raised?   _____

Did any of the family members convert to another religion?   yes ___ no ___

If yes, explain _____

Professional, Educational, and Lifestyle Information

What professions did the interviewee's father/mother pursue in the "old country"?   _____

Who was the most financially successful member of the family? _____

Explain _____

Interviewee's special achievements—i.e., publications, inventions, awards

FAMILY DOCUMENTS, MEMORABILIA, AND HEIRLOOMS

Family photo albums/scrapbooks   yes ___ no ___
    Viewed by interviewer ___
Family Bibles   yes ___ no ___ Viewed by interviewer ___
Family genealogies   yes ___ no ___ Viewed by interviewer ___
Civil marriage certificate   yes ___ no ___ Viewed by interviewer ___
Ketubot (Jewish marriage certificates)   yes ___ no ___
    Viewed by interviewer ___
Wedding invitations   yes ___ no ___ Viewed by interviewer ___
Birth certificates   yes ___ no ___ Viewed by interviewer ___
Birth announcements   yes ___ no ___ Viewed by interviewer ___
Bris certificates   yes ___ no ___ Viewed by interviewer ___
Naming documents, including documents showing a change of name
    yes ___ no ___ Viewed by interviewer ___
Bar/bat mitzvah announcements/invitations   yes ___ no ___
    Viewed by interviewer ___
Confirmation announcements   yes ___ no ___
    Viewed by interviewer ___
Synagogue bulletin   yes ___ no ___ Viewed by interviewer ___
Family circle records   yes ___ no ___ Viewed by interviewer ___
Death certificates   yes ___ no ___ Viewed by interviewer ___
Wimple   yes ___ no ___ Viewed by interviewer ___
Family memoirs and diaries   yes ___ no ___ Viewed by interviewer ___
Address books, letters, financial records, deeds   yes ___ no ___
    Viewed by interviewer ___
Heirlooms—i.e., kiddush cups, candlesticks, baby cups, wimple
    yes ___ no ___ Viewed by interviewer ___

INTERVIEW QUESTIONNAIRE TO MAIL TO RELATIVES

Dear _____ ,

Please fill in the information for as many of these questions as possible. After I receive this questionnaire from you, I'll be calling to ask some follow-up questions. Thank you for your help.

Sincerely,

_____

Personal Information

1. Your complete English name _____
2. Your complete Hebrew name (including parents' Hebrew names)

   _____
3. Did you ever have any other name? (For example, was either your first or last name ever changed?) _____
4. Do you have a copy of your birth certificate?   yes ___ no ___
5. What level of education did you achieve?   _____
6. What was your occupation? _____
7. Your father's name _____
8. Your father's birth date   _____
9. Where was your father born?   _____
10. What was your father's occupation?   _____
11. What level of education did your father achieve? _____
12. Please list the names of your father's siblings and their dates and places of birth _____
13. Your mother's name   _____
14. Your mother's birth date _____
15. Where was your mother born? _____
16. What was your mother's occupation?   _____
17. What level of education did your mother achieve? _____

18. Please list the names of your mother's siblings and their dates and places of birth _____

19. Please list the names of your own siblings and their date and place of birth _____

20. Name of your spouse _____

21. Occupation of spouse _____

22. What level of education did your spouse achieve? _____

23. Do you have a copy of your ketubah? yes ___ no ___

24. Do you have a copy of your civil marriage license? yes ___ no ___

25. Were you ever divorced? yes ___ no ___

26. If you were divorced, do you have a copy of your Get?
    yes ___ no ___

27. If your spouse is no longer living, what was the secular date of death?
    _____

28. If your spouse is no longer living, where is the place of burial? _____

29. If you were divorced or widowed, did you remarry?
    yes ___ no ___

30. If you remarried, please fill in the following:

31. Marriage date _____

32. Place of marriage _____

33. Name of spouse _____

34. Occupation of spouse _____

35. Level of education your spouse achieved _____

36. Name/s, birth dates, and places of birth of children from that marriage
    _____

37. Did you serve in the military? yes ___ no ___

38. If you served in the military, which service were you in? _____

39. What were the years during which you served in the military? _____

40. In what country did you serve in the military? _____

41. What rank did you achieve? _____

42. If your spouse served in the military, please supply the same information as in questions 29 to 33 for your spouse _____

_____

Immigration

1. What country did your family come from originally? _____

2. Did your entire family immigrate together? If not, please explain ___

_____

3. When did you immigrate? _____

4. What was the original country to which you immigrated? _____

5. How did you travel to America? _____

6. If you arrived by ship, what was the name of the ship you traveled on? _____

7. Are there any stories that exist in written or recorded oral form of this journey? yes ___ no ___

8. If yes, who has these materials? _____

9. Do you have copies of your immigration documents? _____

10. What was your date of entry to the U.S.? _____

11. At what port of entry did you arrive? (i.e., Ellis Island) _____

12. Did you become a naturalized citizen? _____

13. If yes, do you have your naturalization papers? yes ___ no ___

14. Date of naturalization _____

15. Are you, or were you, a member of a landsmanshaft organization or a Verein ? yes ___ no ___

16. If so, what is the name of organization? _____ Is it still active?
yes ___ no ___
If yes, do you have a phone number or name as a contact? _____

17. Are there any relatives who were left behind? yes ___ no ___

18. If there were relatives left behind, are you in contact with them or their descendents? yes ___ no ___

19. If yes, what are their names? _____

20. How are they related to you? _____

21. If you are still in touch with them, please supply any contact information you may have. _____

22. Is there a family burial plot in the United States? yes ___ no ___

23. If yes, where is this located? _____

24. If there are family members buried elsewhere in the United States, where are they buried? _____

25. Do you know of the burial location of relatives in the "old country"? yes ___ no ___

26. If yes, where are they buried? _____

Jewish Community Affiliation

1. Was your family affiliated with a synagogue or other type of Jewish communal organization in the "old country"? yes ___ no ___

2. If so, is there still a family affiliation with this organization? _____

3. If yes, what is the nature of the affiliation? _____

4. Did the family affiliate in the United States of America? yes ___ no ___

5. If yes, has this affiliation been maintained? yes ___ no ___

6. Are you affiliated with a synagogue or other type of Jewish communal organization? yes ___ no ___

7. If yes, what is the name of that of the synagogue or organization?

   _____

8. Where is it located? _____

9. Are there any family plaques in that synagogue? yes ___ no

10. If yes, please explain. _____

Religious Observance

1. What type of denominational affiliation did your family have in the United States? (i.e., Reform, Conservative, Orthodox, Reconstructionist, Secular) _____

2. Did any of the family members marry someone who was not Jewish?
   yes ___ no ___

3. If yes, how was this received by the rest of the family? _____

4. If there was intermarriage and there were children, in what religion were the children raised? _____

5. Did any of the family members convert to another religion?
   yes ___ no ___

6. If yes, please explain. _____

Professional Information

1. What professions did the various members of the family pursue in the "old country"? _____

2. What professions did the various members of the family pursue in their new homeland? _____

FAMILY DOCUMENTS, MEMORABILIA, AND HEIRLOOMS

Please indicate if you have any of the following in your possession.

Family photo albums/scrapbooks   yes ___ no ___

Family Bibles   yes ___ no ___

Family genealogies   yes ___ no ___

Civil marriage certificate   yes ___ no ___

Ketubot (Jewish marriage certificates)   yes ___ no ___

Wedding invitations   yes ___ no ___

Birth certificates   yes ___ no ___

Birth announcements   yes ___ no ___

Bris certificates   yes ___ no ___

Naming documents, including documents showing a change of name
   yes ___ no ___

Bar/bat mitzvah announcements/invitations   yes ___ no ___

Confirmation announcements   yes ___ no ___

Synagogue bulletin   yes ___ no ___

Family circle records   yes ___ no ___

Death certificates   yes ___ no ___

Family memoirs and diaries   yes ___ no ___

Address books, letters, financial records, deeds   yes ___ no ___

Heirlooms—i.e., kiddush cups, candlesticks, baby cups, wimple

    yes ___ no ___

FINAL QUESTIONS

1. Is there anyone else in the family whom I should speak to?
   yes ___ no ___

2. If yes, please provide that person's name and phone number or mailing address. _____

    _____

    _____

3. Comments—Please feel free to add any special information about our family that has not been covered by the questions above. Any details that you can add would be extremely helpful. _____

    _____

    _____

    _____

SAMPLE COVER LETTER FOR MAILING
AN INTERVIEW QUESTIONNAIRE

Date

Dear (name of relative):

I enjoyed speaking with you the other day. Thank you for your willingness to fill out the enclosed questionnaire. Your knowledge of our family's history will help a great deal in developing a well-documented family tree.

I look forward to receiving your completed questionnaire. As I mentioned on the phone, when my research is completed, I will be happy to send a copy of the tree to everyone in the family who would be interested in this information. I've made the questionnaire as simple to follow as possible. However, if you have any questions, please feel free to call me.

It would be very helpful if you could return the questionnaire within two weeks so that I can continue with the research. For your convenience, I have included a stamped, addressed envelope.

Again, thank you so much for your help and participation in this exciting family project.

Sincerely,

(your name)

9

Documenting Your Family—
The Jewish Life Cycle

There are many different types of documents, records, and memorabilia that can shed light on your family history. In this chapter, we'll discuss the various types of documents you should look for.

From a very early time in our history, Jews have kept genealogical and life-cycle records. The Bible itself records the birth of significant ancestors and traces the genealogical history of the most important families. As we follow the Jewish life cycle, we'll see that there are many different types of documents and heirlooms that may exist in your family linked to life-cycle events.

BIRTH

Civil Birth Certificates

When we come into the world, a record of our entrance in the form of a birth certificate is filed with the local department of vital statistics.

While the information on civil birth certificates, marriage licenses, divorce decrees, and death certificates can vary a great deal from city to city and even from one year to the next, they always provide some clues for the genealogist. Obtaining these documents should be an initial starting point for any research after initial family interviews.

Let's assume, however, that you have no living relatives and don't know anything even about your parents. Impossible situation? Don't despair! Believe it or not, you can still find out information about your family by beginning with your own birth certificate, which has a wealth of information on it. Depending on where you were born, you can expect to find at least some of the information below:

name of the baby
sex of the baby
number of babies in that birth
birth order of new baby
name and address of place where the baby was born
city and state where the baby was born
date of birth
blood type of baby
name of mother, possibly including mother's maiden name
marital status of the mother
home address of the mother
age of the mother
occupation of the mother
place—country, city, or state—of mother's birth
name of father
home address of the father
age of the father
place—country, city, or state—of father's birth
occupation of the father.

The information on your birth certificate gives you a number of different leads to follow up. If it lists your father's or mother's birth place, you can easily find their birth certificates, especially if they were born in the United States. These birth certificates will provide information about your maternal and paternal grandparents. The place where your parents lived when you were born may help you in tracking down their civil marriage license and possibly even a synagogue affiliation. There's a lot to build on once you have a birth certificate.

Jewish Names

Shortly after birth, most Jewish children are given at least one Hebrew or Yiddish name. Sometimes this name is referred to as your "Jewish" name. Until very recently in America, your English name was not necessarily your "Jewish" name. It was common practice for a child to be given an English language name and a different Hebrew or Yiddish name. Within the last decade or so, under the influence of Israeli practice where one's Hebrew name is also one's ritual "Jewish" name, traditional Jews and Jews with a strong attachment to Israel are giving their children Hebrew or Yiddish names as their only names. For example, Ya'akov (Hebrew for Jacob), who lives in Israel, is called Ya'akov all the time. Ya'akov, a traditional Jew living in America, may also be known only as Ya'akov, and not as "Jacob."

Your Jewish name is used for ritual purposes such as when you are called to the Torah and during your marriage ceremony. Your "Jewish" name is frequently inscribed on a memorial headstone in a cemetery.

Male children are usually named during the *brit milah* ceremony, also called a "bris." (*Brit* and *bris* are the same word. The difference in pronunciation reflects a difference between Sephardic (*brit*) and Ashkenazic (*bris*) Hebrew language traditions. This book uses the Sephardic form because that is the standard pronunciation for modern Hebrew in the state of Israel.)

Traditionally, girls were named in the synagogue sometime shortly after birth. Today, more and more families are celebrating a female infant's entry into a covenant with God with a ceremony called *"brit banot."* At a brit banot, held on the eighth day after birth, like a bris, the female baby is also given a Hebrew name.

An individual's Jewish name is composed of two different parts—his or her own Hebrew or Yiddish name and the Hebrew or Yiddish names of his or her father and mother. Jewish law requires that only the father's Hebrew or Yiddish name be recorded. Today, in most liberal Jewish communities, both the father's name and the mother's name are recorded as part of a child's Jewish name.

Before the founding of the state of Israel in 1948 and the legitimization of modern Hebrew as a living language, Yiddish was the lingua franca of the Ashkenazic community. Hebrew was considered a holy language to be used only for study and prayer. It was for this reason that Yiddish was often used for personal names. With the establishment of the state of Israel, the selection of Hebrew, rather than Yiddish, names came into more common practice. In the Ashkenazic tradition, children are named after relatives who have died. In the Sephardic tradition, children are named after living relatives.

Naming Documents

Although it is not required, very often there is some sort of written documentation to record the date of a brit milah for a boy. There may also be a naming document for a boy and for a girl. Since a naming document records the Hebrew or Yiddish (and often the English) names of both the child and his or her parents, naming documents give us access to two generations at once. Naming documents generally include some or all of the following information helpful to the genealogist.

- date of brit/naming—useful in the case of boys in establishing a previously unknown birth date since the brit is almost always done eight days after birth
- date of child's birth
- place of the ceremony—a brit is often done in the home or the synagogue
- name of officiant
- parents' names

Some naming documents are quite elaborate. A custom-made naming document may include family tree information as well as symbols that relate to the meaning of the child's name. More common are mass-produced documents. Sometimes only a letter on the *mohel* or rabbi's letterhead is given to the family. The mohel is the person who performs the ritual circumcision.

Adoption and Naming

When a Jewish couple adopts a child whose birth mother is not Jewish, Jewish law requires that the child be converted to Judaism. As part of the conversion, the child is given a Hebrew name. When adults convert to Judaism, the "parents" of the convert are listed as Abraham and Sarah on their naming and conversion documents. Abraham and Sarah are the first patriarch and matriarch of the Jewish people. In the case of infants who are converted for the sake of adoption, however, the parents listed on the naming document are actually the adoptive parents. This is done to save the child from any possible embarrassment or stigma and because, for a child, the waters of the *mikvah* are understood as being the "birth waters" of the adoptive female parent. A mikvah is a ritual bath which is used for a variety of purposes including conversion.

Birth Announcements

Another type of birth or naming document is the birth announcement. This is a simple announcement that gives the child's date of birth, weight, names of the parents, and, sometimes, the child's Hebrew name as well. In past generations, it was common to place an ad in the newspaper announcing the birth of a child. Copies of such announcements were often saved and may be available to you.

Heirlooms

The birth of a child brings great joy, and the creation or purchase of special gifts for the baby is a widespread custom. Sometimes these gifts hold clues for the genealogist. In Jewish families, there are a variety of different baby gifts that may yield information. Here are some things to look for.

Wimple   A wimple is a Torah binder made from a baby's blanket. In the eighteenth and nineteenth centuries especially, there was a tradition of using a wimple to tie the Torah during a young man's bar mitzvah, and also at the time when he was called to the Torah prior to his marriage. A wimple would often be beautifully decorated, usually with the name of the baby and his parents, his birth date, date of his bris, and possibly other family information. Although this custom was relatively unknown in the United States, it is now being revived.

Kiddush cup   A gift of a silver kiddush cup to be used at the bris might be engraved with the baby's name, birth date, and date of his bris.

Jewelry   Different types of jewelry may be given to a new baby, including bracelets and necklaces with the baby's Hebrew name. These are often "put away" for future use.

BAR/BAT MITZVAH

At the age of thirteen, a Jewish young man becomes a *bar mitzvah*—literally a "son of the commandment." At the age of twelve, a Jewish young woman becomes a *bat mitzvah*—literally a "daughter of the commandment." (In the Reform movement, a young woman often celebrates becoming a bat mitzvah at the age of thirteen.) These life-cycle events are usually celebrated in the synagogue with a religious ceremony and with a party of some type afterward. Very often, there are both documents and memorabilia associated with this event.

Bar/Bat Mitzvah Certificates

In the last couple of generations, it has become popular to present the bar/bat mitzvah with a certificate to honor this event. While it may not be possible to use this type of documentation to go back more than a generation or two, saving these documents within your own family will make it easier for future generations to document your family history.

Bar/Bat Mitzvah Invitations

Another form of documentation for the bar/bat mitzvah is the invitation that is sent to family and friends announcing the synagogue service to celebrate the event and the party to follow. Invitations will include the names of the parents, the child to be honored, and the synagogue where the event will take place. Very often, the child's Hebrew name is also included in the invitation.

Kippot—Yarmulkes

Many families have the tradition of creating special *kippot* (yarmulkes—headcoverings) for bar/bat mitzvah ceremonies. These kippot usually contain the name of the bar/bat mitzvah—sometimes both the English and the Hebrew name—the date of the occasion, the type of occasion, and may sometimes also include where the ceremony took place. Such kippot are often created for weddings as well.

Bibles/Prayer Books

Some synagogues have the custom of presenting the bar/bat mitzvah with a Hebrew Bible or prayer book (*siddur*). These are usually inscribed with the child's name, date of the bar/bat mitzvah, the name of the synagogue, and, sometimes, the rabbi's name.

Synagogue Plaques in Honor of a Bar/Bat Mitzvah

The name of the synagogue can prove helpful in uncovering previously unknown relatives. Very often, to celebrate a special event in a family's life, the family will dedicate a plaque of some sort in the synagogue in honor or in memory of a family member. If you know the name of the synagogue in which a family bar/bat mitzvah took place, you may be able to call the synagogue office to find out if a plaque exists for anyone in your family. Most synagogues keep a written record of such plaques.

A trip to the synagogue, if possible, might also be interesting and rewarding.

MARRIAGE

One of the most common Jewish life-cycle documents is the ketubah—the Jewish wedding contract. A traditional ketubah spells out the property to be set aside for the wife should her husband predecease her. According to Jewish law, a Jewish wedding may not take place without a signed ketubah.

In the past, a ketubah would be written only for a Jewish man and woman who were being married. However, today, some interfaith couples and same-sex Jewish couples choose to commission or buy "ketubahlike" documents, especially if they are being married by a rabbi and intend to establish a Jewish home. The information on these documents is similar to that of a traditional ketubah, both in Hebrew and in English.

The Ketubah

The use of a written ketubah—Jewish wedding contract—goes back over two thousand years. At times in Jewish history when a particular community was comfortably settled—the Italian Jewish community of the fifteenth century is one such example—the creation of Jewish life-cycle documents was raised to a fine art. In America and Israel today, we see a similar pattern. However, whether a ketubah or other life-cycle document is beautifully written and illustrated, or casually written on a piece of paper torn from a notebook, both are valuable for the wealth of family information that they yield.

The information that you find in a ketubah depends on where and when it was written. Many modern American ketubot—those written in this century—have both an English and a Hebrew or Aramaic section. In the English section, you will usually find the following:

secular date of the wedding
place where the wedding was performed—city, state, country

English first and surnames of the bride and groom

English first and surnames of the fathers of the bride and groom

English names of the witnesses

English name of the officiating rabbi

Some documents may include the names of the mothers of the bride and groom.

In the Hebrew or Aramaic section, you will always find the

date of the wedding according to the Jewish calendar

date of the wedding according to the secular calendar

place where the wedding was performed—city, state, country

Hebrew or Yiddish names of the bride and groom

Hebrew or Yiddish names of their fathers

date and the place where the wedding was performed

language indicating whether or not the bride was previously married

Hebrew names of the witnesses

traditional statement about the financial settlement for the bride.

In addition, in the Hebrew or Aramaic sections you may also find:

English surnames of the bride and groom transliterated into Hebrew letters

Hebrew names of the mothers

Hebrew name of the officiating rabbi

actual financial arrangements made for the bride and groom.

Except in the case of ketubot signed by a Reform rabbi, you can expect that the names of the two witnesses will be those of two Jewish men not related to either the bride or the groom. Reform rabbis, Reconstructionist rabbis, and some Conservative rabbis may permit women as well as men to sign the ketubah.

Ketubot that were especially commissioned for the wedding may contain a great deal of other family information including family trees, illustrations of relatives, places where the family lived or traveled, and other such details. Some ketubot even include portraits of family pets. For this reason, it's worth the effort to try to uncover these documents.

The ketubah is the property of the wife. If the ketubah is destroyed, according to Jewish law, the husband must move out of the house until he has replaced the ketubah. Beautiful ketubot are often framed and hung prominently in the home. Less elaborate ketubot are usually stored with other important family papers.

In most states—Florida is, at present, an exception—a religious wedding ceremony may not take place without a civil marriage license. Therefore, even if a ketubah is not available, a civil marriage license should be available.

Very often, especially with relatives who married before 1960, a request for a ketubah may be met with the response, "We never got one." This is unlikely if a rabbi married the couple and both parties of the couple were Jewish. However, prior to about 1970, for a variety of sociological reasons, and especially if a non-Orthodox rabbi married the couple, little emphasis was put on the "form" of the ketubah and a very simple "marriage certificate" was often used. These marriage certificates are actually a form of ketubah and will have information similar to that of a traditional ketubah. For this reason, even if your relative insists there was no ketubah, it may be worth pursuing the matter and to ask for a Jewish marriage certificate.

Civil Marriage License

A civil marriage license is usually purchased in the town or county where the wedding will take place, rather than where the couple will reside after the marriage. After the ceremony, the officiant signs the document and mails it back to the office that issued the license. This official copy is maintained on file as a public record. A certified copy is sent to the married couple for their own records. In addition, many rabbis keep a copy of the marriage licenses they sign. A copy of a marriage license can usually be obtained by mail with the payment of a small fee to the government bureau that issued it.

Civil marriage licenses generally provide the addresses of the bride and groom, whether or not either was previously married, the birth dates of the bride and groom, occupations of the bride and groom, names and (sometimes) addresses of the witnesses. There are no special requirements for witnesses for a civil license other than that they be of legal age. Not all states require witnesses to a civil license. The name and address of the officiant, whether a religious or civil official is also included.

Wedding Invitations

As noted in the section on bar/bat mitzvah, invitations to special life-cycle events can be helpful to the genealogist. Wedding invitations generally contain the names of both sets of parents as well as the names of the bride and the groom. Hebrew names may also be listed.

Wedding Programs and Benchers

Another document associated with a marriage ceremony is the wedding program. Wedding programs are as individual as the brides and grooms themselves. Some programs may actually list the guests in attendance and personal information about the bride and the groom not generally available. Although these are rare, it's always worth asking if such programs exist.

Religious families may also have produced a "bencher" for the wedding that may contain the names of the bride and groom in Hebrew, the date of the wedding, and other family information. A bencher is a prayer book that contains the special blessings that are said after a wedding meal.

DEATH

When someone dies, a great deal of paperwork is generated. This paperwork can be extremely helpful to a genealogist. Also, headstones, memorial plaques, and other memorial items help to preserve family history.

Death Certificates

Death certificates include a great deal of information. Since it is necessary to file death certificates with a wide variety of governmental and other agencies, most people order multiple copies. Therefore, it's not unusual for a copy to be kept as part of a family's important records. Death certificates are also filed with the local bureau of vital statistics. Most death certificates contain the following information:

cause of death (Since Jews do not believe in autopsies, an autopsy may not have been performed. If the cause of death is not known in some other way, the cause of death may be stated in very general terms.)

date of death (the secular date)

place of death

deceased's full name

name of deceased's parents, including mother's maiden name

name of spouse

name of funeral home

address at time of death

place of birth

number of years in the country

This information will offer many clues for the beginning genealogist.

Cemetery Records

In Jewish law, there is a strong prohibition against cremation because of the belief that when the Jewish Messiah comes, all Jews who have died will be resurrected and will be given eternal life. Resurrection requires a body, and a traditional Jew who loses a limb will have the limb buried so that the entire body can be whole at the time of resurrection. Cremation is seen as a rejection of the concept of the coming of the Messiah.

Although cremation is not permitted to observant Jews, organ donation is permitted and encouraged, since it is believed that one will not need organs in the time of the Messiah. In fact, it is considered a meritorious deed to be an organ donor, since donating an organ can help save a life, an extremely important act within Jewish law.

In recent times, some Jews have chosen cremation for a variety of personal reasons. However, the majority of Jews choose to be buried in a cemetery. This tradition is extremely helpful to the genealogist, since there are a number of different types of records that one can find at a cemetery.

All cemeteries keep records of those who are interred in their plots. These records generally include the name of deceased, name of next of kin, age at time of death, address at the time of death, name and address of the head of the burial society, and funeral home used for internment, if applicable.

Headstones and Monuments

In Genesis 35:20, it says, "Jacob set up a pillar on (Rachel's) grave." Until that time, the matriarchs and the patriarchs were buried above-ground in burial caves. This verse in Genesis is the basis of in-ground burial for Jews, and also for the tradition of marking a grave with a monument of some type.

Monuments and headstones vary a great deal depending on when they were erected, and on the cultural traditions of the Jewish community to which the deceased belonged. For example, Jews from Russia and Hungary often put photographs or engravings of the deceased on the monument, while this custom was unknown or discouraged in other cultures. Many headstones include both the Hebrew name and the English name of the deceased. The date of death is also included. Generally, either the age of the deceased or the date of birth is also given.

Jews have special conventions to indicate if the deceased was a Levi or a Kohen. A picture of two hands with the thumbs and index fingers joined in a triangle is the sign of a Kohen. This sign is taken from the hand position used when a Kohen blesses the congregation using a traditional blessing. A picture of a pitcher indicates one who is a Levi. The Levites were responsible for ritually washing the feet of the Kohanim in the Temple.

It should be noted that in order to create a marker for the gravesite, the monument company creates a "prototype" on paper which is sent to the family of the deceased for approval. Copies of these prototypes may be kept with other family papers and should be looked for, since they may yield information on Hebrew names.

Memorial Plaques and Books of Remembrance

Yahrzeit plaques are memorial plaques that are generally erected in synagogues and in Jewish organizations. They contain the name of the deceased and the date of death. Since these plaques are "made to last," even older synagogues are able to retain these important records. Questions about synagogue affiliation are important in helping to find such records. In addition, many synagogues keep written records relating to the plaques that may contain additional information. If a synagogue closes its doors, the memorial plaques may be sent to the family of the deceased. If it merges with another synagogue and moves its building, the memorial plaques are usually transferred to the new building.

Yahrzeit Calendars

Yahrzeit calendars are calendars sent by funeral homes to show the Hebrew date of a person's death. The Hebrew date is based on the rotation of the moon around the earth. The Jewish calendar is a lunar calendar. The secular date of death is based on the solar calendar. Although the two dates may sometimes coincide, in most instances they will be different. A yahrzeit calendar helps the mourner keep track of these variations year after year. Although not as popular today as they had been, yahrzeit calendars are valuable as sources of genealogical information. Besides listing the English name of the deceased, the secular date of death (including the year), and the place where the person is buried, some calendars also include the person's Hebrew name and names of other relatives. Yahrzeit calendars from the old country, especially Hungary/Austria and Germany prior to the war, were beautiful, elaborate documents. It's always worth asking if these records exist, especially if your family is from that area of the world.

In the next chapter, we will learn how to find other types of personal records.

10

Documenting Your Family— U.S. Government Records and More

In the last chapter, we discussed the various Jewish life-cycle documents that can provide important information for the genealogist. In this chapter, we are going to discuss how to find life-cycle and other personal records that are not in your family's files.

NATIONAL AND GOVERNMENT RECORDS

In the United States, there are a number of different government departments and agencies that provide research resources for genealogists.

When calling or writing to order a document, it will help if you know the approximate date of the particular record you want—i.e., the marriage date for a marriage certificate, date of death for a death certificate. Be pleasant and persistent. Many of these offices are thinly staffed and it may take awhile for you to get the information that you require.

The National Archives and Records Administration (NARA) in

Washington, D.C., provides information on how to find a wide variety of family records, including passenger arrival lists, U.S. military records, burial records of soldiers, pension records, land records, census information, and passport applications. The National Archives has an outstanding Web site, including a very good genealogy page. The National Archives homepage address is http://www.nara.gov/. The direct address for the genealogy page is http://www.nara.gov/genealogy/genindex.html. The National Archives also has regional offices. The regional Web site and snail mail addresses and thirteen regional records service facilities are listed on pages 146–147.

The NARA genealogy page has a great deal to offer genealogists. It's set up in a very user-friendly way. There you can find genealogical publications, general information leaflets, the Soundex machine (more about this later), catalogues of microfilm publications, NARA regional records information, listings of NARA-sponsored genealogy workshops and courses, naturalization records, post office records, and information about genealogical data in the National Archives Information Locator (NAIL), a pilot searchable database.

NARA offers a number of free publications from the Product Sales Section (NWPS). These can be requested by writing to: National Archives and Records Administration, Room G-7, 7th Street and Pennsylvania Avenue, NW, Washington, D.C. 20408; telephone: (202) 501-5235 or (800) 234-8861; fax: (202) 501-7170. Among their current publications are:

- GIL 5. *Using Records in the National Archives for Genealogical Research*
- GIL 7. *Military Service Records in the National Archives*
- GIL 30. *Information About the National Archives for Prospective Researchers*
- *Aids for Genealogical Research,* which describes publications by NARA and various commercial sources.

In addition to the free publications offered, NARA's bookstore has many publications for sale that are of interest to genealogists. Of special note is *The Guide to Genealogical Research in the National Archives.*

NARA has compiled microfilm catalogues related to subjects of high research interest to genealogists. The catalogues contain both detailed descriptions of the records and roll-by-roll listings for each microfilm publication. Each catalogue is also available for purchase in a print format. Among the topics covered in these catalogues are census records, military service records, immigrant and passenger arrivals, genealogical and biographical research, and federal court records.

Microfilm is available at the National Archives building in Washington, D.C.; at thirteen of the regional records services facilities; and through NARA's Microfilm Rental Program, although only certain titles are available for rental. It's important to note that many large libraries and genealogical societies have purchased all or some of NARA's microfilm sets.

NARA offers a wide variety of genealogical workshops and courses, with topics including an introduction to genealogy, and how to research census schedules, military service and pension records, and passenger lists. For information about workshops and courses in Washington, D.C., consult NARA's calendar of events. For regional workshops, contact the participating regional facilities. In addition, in an effort to help visitors to the national research center in Washington, D.C., the National Archives has started a program to train volunteer genealogy aides.

Regional Departments of the National Archives

The National Archives maintains regional archives centers across the country. Each regional archives has the complete U.S. census on microfilm (all states, 1790 to 1920); selected microfilmed records (such as military records and passenger lists); and local federal records (including federal court naturalizations) for that region. All National Archives records are available at the Family History Centers. The NARA branches and the areas they serve are:

New England Region, 380 Trapelo Road, Waltham, MA 02154, (617) 647-8100, archives@waltham.nara.gov. CT ME MA NH RI VT
Northeast Region (New York), 201 Varick Street, New York, NY 10014, (212) 337-1300, archives@newyork.nara.gov. NY NJ PR VI

Northeast Region (Pittsfield), 10 Conte Drive, Pittsfield, MA 01201-8230, (413) 445-6885, center@pittsfield.nara.gov. CT ME NH NY RI

Mid-Atlantic Region, 9th and Market Streets, Room 1350, Philadelphia, PA 19107, (215) 597-3000, archives@philarch. nara.gov. DE MD PA VA WV

Southeast Region, 1557 St. Joseph Avenue, East Point, GA 30344, (404) 763-7477, archives@atlanta.nara.gov. AL FL GA KY MS NC SC TN

Great Lakes Region, 7358 S. Pulaski Road, Chicago, IL 60629, (312) 581-7816, archives@chicago.nara.gov. IL IN MI MN OH WI

Central Plains Region, 2312 E. Bannister Road, Kansas City, MO 64131, (816) 926-6272, archives@kansascity.nara.gov. IA KS MO NE

Southwest Region, 501 West Felis Street, P.O. Box 6216, Fort Worth, TX 76115, (817) 334-5525, archives@ftworth.nara.gov. AR LA NM OK TX

Rocky Mountain Region, Building 48, Denver Federal Center, P.O. Box 25307, Denver, CO 80225, (303) 236-0817, archives@ denver.nara.gov. CO MT ND SD UT WY

Pacific Southwest Region, 24000 Avila Road, Laguana Niguel, CA 92677-6719, (714) 360-2641, archives@laguna.nara.gov. AZ, southern CA, and Clark County, NV

Pacific Sierra Region, 100 Commodore Drive, San Bruno, CA 94066, (415) 876-9009, archives@sanbruno.nara.gov. CA except southern CA, HI, NV except Clark County, American Samoa, and Guam

Pacific Northwest Region, 6125 Sand Point Way NE, Seattle, WA 98115, (206) 526-6507, archives@seattle.nara.gov. ID OR WA

Alaska Region, 654 W. 3rd Avenue Anchorage, AK 99501, (907) 271-2441, archives@alaska.nara.gov. AK

The U.S Census Bureau can provide information that will be helpful in building your family tree. The information provided by census reports varies from one decade to the next but generally all include citizenship and military records. The U.S. Census Bureau has a Web site but it does not list any information prior to 1990. The Web site for the Census Bureau is http://www.census.gov.

There is a seventy-two-year privacy rule for federal census records. For this reason, census information available to the general public begins with the 1790 census and ends with the 1920 census. The 1930 census will be released to the public in April 2002. Records of 1930 and later are restricted to the persons in the record or their heirs.

Census information is available at all local Federal Depository Libraries. Each of these centers has a librarian who can help you in your search for life-cycle records. Virtually every congressional district has a Federal Depository Library. To find the nearest one to you, you can check your local phone book, call the Government Publishing Office, or visit the Census Bureau Web site.

Census information varies by the census. Family History Centers, which are discussed on page 158, can give you census worksheets for various years. It's a good idea to check all the census years covering the person you are researching. There are a number of reasons for this:

1. The respondent in the household may vary in different census years, so different information may be available.

2. The same person may give different information to the same question, depending on how the question was asked.

3. The situation in the household may have changed.

Here's an overview of what you can expect to find in different census years:

- Years married—1900, 1910
- Number of children born to a woman—1900, 1910
- Number of children born to a woman and still living—1900, 1910
- Year of immigration—1900, 1910, 1920
- Citizenship status—1900, 1910, 1920 (*AL* means alien, *PA* means first papers filed, *NA* means naturalized)
- Year of naturalization—1920

More recent census information is available if you are the person named in a census or an heir or legal representative of the person you're researching. To get this information, you will need to know the exact address of the person and will have to provide death certificates or copies of court orders to prove your right to have the information. There is a special form needed to request this information, which can be requested from NARA.

Because of the difficulty of getting this information, other resources may be more fruitful to pursue. However, if you don't have information about one or both of your parents, this might be one place that could provide some leads. Another possibility is to ask an older relative to request the information for his or her parents. This could provide new leads to information about a generation that is no longer alive for you to interview.

The Social Security Administration and the Social Security Death Index. The "good news" is that, if you could gain access to Social Security Administration records for your genealogical research, the amount of information you could hope to find would be limited. The most that you could hope to obtain would be the person's name, his or her parents' names, his or her year of birth, the state where the Social Security card was issued, and possibly where the person died. That's the good news? Actually, yes. Because the "bad news" is that it is impossible to get this information unless you are the next of kin to someone who has died.

Social Security did not begin until 1935, so taking on the Social Security Administration has limited benefits. If you know the name of the person you are researching, finding birth, marriage, or death certificates will provide much more information than the Social Security Administration could give you.

Even if Social Security information seems like an important or only route to explore, all is not lost. A nongovernmental information source issues a database called the "Social Security Death Index" (SSDI). The Social Security Death Index is an index of 60 million U.S. residents who died between 1962 and 1996, had Social Security numbers, and whose deaths were reported to the Social Security Administration. The

SSDI begins in 1962 because that is when the Social Security Administration began keeping the database on computer.

The SSDI is available on CD-ROM at most Family History Centers, for use free of charge. You can purchase it for home use through genealogy resource vendors and it can be accessed online through the Ancestry Web site—http://www.ancestry.com/ssdi/advanced.htm. *If Social Security death benefits were paid,* you may be able to find some information about the person you're looking for through this index. Please note that death benefits are not always paid when someone dies. Therefore, just because a relative died after 1962, it is not a foregone conclusion that he or she will be listed in the SSDI.

The SSDI works as follows:

1. You enter a surname and get a listing of people who died, generally in the United States, plus some individuals with U.S. Social Security numbers who died overseas.

2. If you find the person for whom you are looking, you'll be able to discover their entire name; Social Security number; date of birth; date of death; state where the Social Security number was obtained; and, in many cases, the location (ZIP code) of last residence or where the survivor checks were mailed.

Many reputable published and cyberspace sources advise you to write to the Freedom of Information Officer at the SSA in Baltimore with the information gained from the SSDI. For seven dollars per name, you will purportedly receive a copy of the individual's application for a Social Security card. This is not correct. At the present time, there is no Freedom of Information Officer at the Social Security Administration in Baltimore. The Social Security Administration does not release such information, except, possibly, to the next of kin. Don't waste your time and money. As noted above, the information that might be accessed in this way is available from many other documents.

NATURALIZATION DOCUMENTS

There are two ways of becoming a citizen of the United States. One is to be born here. The other is to become a naturalized citizen. Although it is not necessary to become a naturalized citizen in order to reside here, many of our ancestors from the old country chose to become "real" Americans by going through the naturalization process. The precise regulations and details have changed over time, as has the documentation.

It is important to note that there was a difference in the naturalization process for men and women and children between 1855 and 1922. During this period, wives and children became citizens when the husband or father obtained citizenship. In addition, a woman became a citizen automatically if she married a native-born or naturalized citizen. After 1922, women had to file their own naturalization papers.

Today there are a variety of forms that will be available to future genealogists. For those of us looking for ancestors who immigrated to America before the World War II, there are two different documents of importance.

The *Declaration of Intention* was the first form to be filed. The following information can be found on the Declaration of Intention:

name of the filing party (If a name change has occurred, this will be noted.)

occupation

color

physical description

place of birth

date of birth

point of emigration

name of vessel

port of arrival in America

date of arrival in America

date of filing of Declaration of Intention

place of filing

marital status

name of wife, if married

place of residence in America.

Usually three years after the filing of the first petition, a *Petition for Naturalization* was filed. This form included additional information including the names, birth dates, and places of birth of any children and the names, occupations, and residences of two witnesses known to the applicant. In addition, this form served as a legal change-of-name document. For genealogists, the wealth of information on these two forms makes locating them for your relatives a very important undertaking.

The NARA Web site has an excellent page on naturalization, including the history of this process in the United States. You can access it from the NARA homepage or directly through the address http://www.nara.gov/genealogy/natural.html.

Even into the early part of this century, naturalization was not a standardized procedure and record keeping was left in the hands of the individual courts. While record keeping and standardization have improved, early records are not centrally located. For this reason, the genealogist seeking these papers may have to do some legwork.

Naturalization records may be found in county courts, county or state archives, or regional archives.

Some naturalization records or indexes have been published, such as the *Index of Naturalizations, Ashtabula County, Ohio, 1875–1906,* published by the Ashtabula County Genealogical Society. When looking for naturalization records at the local level, county court employees may be unaware of where they can locate their own records. In such cases, the genealogist may have to be a detective. Many states have their own archives where these records are stored.

There is a commonly held misconception that naturalization records created in state or local courts are filed in the National Archives. This is not so. However, some county court naturalization records have been donated to the National Archives and are available as National Archives microfilm publications. A list of available records can be found on the NARA National Records page on the NARA Web site. Three National Archives microfilm publications also serve as indexes to some state and local court naturalizations in Connecticut, Illinois, Indiana, Iowa, Maine, Massachusetts, New Hampshire, New York, Rhode Island, and Vermont.

Naturalizations also took place in federal courts. These records, including the declarations of intent and petitions for naturalization, will usually be found in the National Archives regional records services facility serving the state in which the federal court is located. Some of these indexes and records have been microfilmed.

The Microfilm Reading Room (Room 400) in the National Archives Building, 700 Pennsylvania Avenue, NW, Washington, D.C., contains some microfilmed federal court naturalization indexes, declarations, and petitions. For listings of naturalization indexes and records available as National Archives microfilm publications in Room 400, see listings for:

Record Group 21, Records of U.S. District Courts

Record Group 85, Records of the Immigration and Naturalization Service

Donated Materials in the National Archives in Microfilm Resources for Research.

These listings can be found in *A Comprehensive Catalog of National Archives Microfilm Publications,* published by NARA in 1996, and can be purchased through NARA. It is also available online at the NARA Web site.

There are three ways to obtain naturalization papers:

1. *E-mail or write to the NARA branch* that covers the city, state, or region where your relative lived and ask for the Declaration of Intention and Petition for Naturalization for the person you are researching. Give them as much of the following information as you can: the name of the person you are researching, the address where the person was living when he or she was naturalized, the court in which the naturalization took place, the person's country of origin, the year or year range of naturalization, and the persons's birth date and occupation.

If you know the court in which the naturalization took place, include a check or money order made out to NARA for ten dollars. (This was the price as of October 1998. Prices may change. It is a good idea to check with NARA before sending any money.) If you don't know which court supervised the naturalization, do not send the check. NARA will send you an index card for you to verify that the individual they have traced is the right person. When you return the card with your approval, you should enclose your check at that time.

With your request, include your snail mail and E-mail addresses. Each branch responds differently. This procedure works very smoothly. I was able to get my maternal grandparents' naturalization records within a few weeks working through the regional NARA office in New York.

2. *Locate and contact the local court of naturalization* and request the papers for the person you are researching. As noted above, this may be a county, state, or federal court in your area. A call to one of these branches should guide you in the right direction.

3. *Use microfilms of naturalization indexes/Soundexes* at a Family History Center. Look in the catalogue under the location of the court where you think your relative was naturalized.

SOUNDEX

Soundex is a code that was developed in the 1930s to organize surnames into groups depending on how they sounded instead of how they were spelled. This was an important breakthrough for genealogists, because very often "foreign" names were not transliterated into English according to a uniform standard, even by members of the same family or even the same individual. For example, my grandmother's maiden name was Pockreshevsky. That's the way she spelled it in English. Her brother David spelled it Pakrashevsky on his Declaration of Intention and Pakrashevski on his Petition for Naturalization. His son spelled his name Pokraschewsky. Before Soundex, in order to find an individual, one would have to look up all the possible variations of the spelling of the name—a huge task and not one that guaranteed success. With Soundex, all the variations of Pokreshevsky are listed together, making the search much easier.

Initially Soundex was used to organize some census information, naturalization information, and ship arrivals. Today, the Soundex code can be used to research NARA's census microfilm holdings from 1880 to 1920. In addition, some immigrant and passenger arrival lists are coded in Soundex. Soundex is also used to facilitate family reunions. The International Soundex Reunion Registry, for example, is the world's largest reunion registry and is a free service. It was established to help families who were separated by birth or other life circumstances find one another. They can be reached by phone at (702) 882-7755 or through their Web site: http://www.plumsite.com/isrr.

Knowing a surname's Soundex code is an important first step in using NARA's census microfilm holdings (1880–1920) and immigrant and passenger arrival lists. Until recently, genealogists had to learn to work out the Soundex codes for themselves. Now, however, there are a number of ways to obtain this information, literally with the click of a button.

The Soundex machine on NARA's Web site does this instantly for you. You can find the Soundex machine at http://www.nara.gov/genealogy/soundex/soundex.html. You just type in the last name of the person you're looking for and the Soundex designation is produced for you. Another site where you can get a Soundex code is on the Surname to Soundex Converter Web site: http://www.geocities.com/Heartland/Hills/3916/soundex.html. The Soundex code for all my Pokrashevsky relatives is P262.

Once you have your Soundex code, you can go online to the Federal Population Census page to find the census you wish to consult (only 1880 to 1920 are Soundexed). Within each census you must find the state in which the person lived. Soundex codes are arranged alphabetically by the first letter of the surname.

OTHER GOVERNMENT REGULATED RECORDS THAT YOU MAY WANT TO SEARCH FOR

World War I Draft Registration Cards, 1917–1918

Men born between 1886 and 1897 (whether citizens or aliens) should have had a World War I Draft Registration Card. This card contains the person's exact name and place of birth. This information is available through the National Archives.

Passport Applications

A passport was optional for U.S. citizens traveling abroad until 1941, except during wartime. Records through 1925 are at the National Archives and can be researched at the National Archives and Records Administration, Archives 1, Reference Branch, 8th and Pennsylvania Ave. NW, Washington, D.C. 20408. You can also find this information on microfilm at Family History Libraries.

Passport records after 1925 are located at the U.S. State Department, Passport Office, Bureau of Consular Affairs. To obtain passport information after 1925, the person whose passport it is may apply by sending a typed or clearly printed notarized request, providing his or her full name, date, and place of birth, current address, and the reason for the request. Provide the estimated date of issuance and any passport information that will help the department institute a full search. For an authenticated copy of your own passport records, please submit a check or money order for twenty dollars (made payable to the Department of State). Mail your request to: U.S. State Department, Passport Office, Bureau of Consular Affairs, Research and Liaison Branch, 1111 19th Street NW, Suite 200, Washington, D.C. 20524.

The Passport Office has a general Web site, http://travel.state. gov/, and a special page for passports, http://travel.state.gov/ passport_records.html. While a copy of your own passport may not be helpful, it may be possible for you to persuade older members of your family to request their own passport information and passport information for their deceased next of kin. Like census information, passport information can shed light on a generation that is no longer with us. Passport application information normally includes the person's full name, date of birth, place of birth, and home address.

Probate Records

Wills and other legal documents can yield a great deal of family information. Wills are filed on the county level. Some states have online information available by searching the keyword probate. Addresses of all U.S. county courthouses can be found in *Ancestry's Red Book: American State, County, and Town Sources,* by Alice Eichholz (editor), William Dollarhide, revised edition, 1992, and *County Courthouse Book* (second edition), by E. P. Bentley, 1995, and the *United States County Courthouse Address Book,* by Leland K. Meitzler (editor), 1991. One or all of these books should be available in major libraries and, as of this writing, are available for sale through Amazon.com and vendors of genealogical books.

So far, we've been discussing agencies and resources that are national or governmental in scope. However, there are many local and regional sources for documents that can be helpful to a genealogist.

LOCAL DIRECTORIES

City directories are similar to phone books. Although not all cities published directories, many cities will have this information. City directories often list not only a person's name but their occupation, address, and name of their spouse. Some cities have directories that go back to the 1800s. A city's central library is the best resource center for this type of document research.

Telephone directories, also available at large libraries, can be excellent resources for finding names and addresses of people related to you. Many large libraries have phone directory collections from all over the world. Phone directory information can be found on the Internet, although it is not always complete or accurate.

LOCAL DEPARTMENTS OF VITAL STATISTICS

If you know where the relative you are researching lived, you can contact the local records office directly. Most areas have a Department of Vital Statistics or a county clerks office that keeps track of birth, marriage, and death records, property deeds, wills, legally executed name changes, and other such important information. These records are usually housed in the local city hall. Most offices charge a fee for providing a copy of the document you are seeking.

It's important to know that if you have a computer, much of the initial legwork for locating the office that you need to contact can be done online through a Vital Records Web site. Most states and many counties have their own Web sites that are focused on vital records and genealogy. Logging on to a search engine like Yahoo and using the keyword "vital records" can access these sites. Another excellent resource is the Vital Records Information Web site that can be reached at http://www. inlink.com/~nomi/vitalrec/staterec.html. This Web site offers both regional and national information and features addresses and costs for obtaining vital records from all states. It also has links to each state, genealogy resources, state and local historical societies, and information about foreign records.

RESEARCHING RECORDS OUTSIDE THE UNITED STATES

If you are trying to research genealogical information from countries outside the United States, access to a computer is vital. Through a general search engine like Yahoo, you can call up the governmental and specific genealogy Web sites for virtually any country in the world and at least some of the information will be in English.

In accessing government information around the world, you may need to be a little creative. Some countries are more organized and accessible than others. However, in general, the Internet makes initial research in foreign countries much easier and less costly than was previously possible. We will discuss Internet resources in the next chapter.

FAMILY HISTORY CENTERS

You have probably heard that the Mormons are "into" genealogy. However, finding information about what the Mormons have to offer is not quite that simple until you know that the genealogy resource centers that the Church of Jesus Christ of Latter Day Saints maintain are called Family History Centers.

Most of the Family History Centers are located in the local LDS (Latter Day Saints) meetinghouses and are open to the public during specific times of the day and week. The address of local centers is available by calling Family History Support at (800) 346-6044, from 8:00 A.M. to 5:00 P.M. Mountain Time, Monday to Saturday, and through the LDS Web site—http://www.deseretbook.com/famhis/. It's important to note that although this church has a reputation for being a zealous proselytizer, the church does not proselytize people using the Family History Centers.

Why is genealogy so important to members of this church? According to information on their Web site, Mormons believe that the spirit is eternal and continues to live on after death. Members of the church also believe that, since the spirit is eternal, the family unit can also continue after the death of its individual members. This is facilitated through specific religious rituals. In order to perform these rituals on behalf of deceased family members, members of the church must first identify their ancestors.

The church has gathered genealogical records from all over the world to make this identification possible. These records are available at the Family History Library in Salt Lake City, Utah, and at Family History Centers throughout the world.

The larger goal of the church is to determine the genealogy of everyone in the world for the purpose of posthumous conversion. Recently it was discovered that the church was posthumously converting Jews who had died in the Holocaust. This issue was raised with them through the proper channels and, as of this date, they are no longer pursuing this course of action.

The library has collected millions of microfilms, thousands of microfiche and books, and many other records. Most of the microfilms have been acquired through an extensive microfilming program that began in 1938 and is still ongoing. Copies of microfilms are available for use at the Family History Library and at Family History Centers.

Of special interest to Jewish genealogists is the Family History Center's microfilm collection of nineteenth-century Jewish records from Poland, Germany, and Hungary. Listings of these records (over five thousand reels microfilmed as of 1985) were published in *Avotaynu* and *The Encyclopedia of Jewish Genealogy*. New records are microfilmed and added to the collection every year. They have recently begun micro-

filming in the former Soviet Union. Five to six thousand reels of microfilm are added to the collection each month. Therefore, rechecking their
catalogue on a regular basis is a good idea if you are doing research on
family members in these countries.

The Eastern European microfilmed records available through the
Family History Centers include:

Bulgaria: civil registrations

Estonia: all Jewish vital records

Germany: over 2,100 microfilms of Jewish records, through the
1880s; ongoing filming in Leipzig and Berlin

Hungary: over 800 microfilms of Jewish records, through the 1910s;
ongoing filming

Poland: over 2,000 microfilms of Jewish vital records thru the 1890s

Slovakia: ongoing filming since 1991 (Levoca, Presov, Kosice, Bytce,
Banska Bystrica); Jewish records from eastern areas are available

Ukraine: filming began April 1994; projects in progress in Kiev and
L'viv

A series of research outlines is available at the Family History Center.
Each outline describes records of genealogical value, where they are
located, and how they can be used. Each outline also describes how to
find the most important records in the Family History Library Catalog.
In addition, a number of different publications are available free or for
a small charge to aid the genealogist in making the most successful use
of the records at a Family History Library. These publications include:

- *Library Services and Resources* (four pages; free). This is an annual
  overview of the Family History Library and the local Family History Centers.

- *A Guide to Research* (twenty-four pages; $0.40 U.S.). A simple
  explanation of the research process.

- *Using the Family History Library Catalog* (forty-four pages; $0.75
  U.S.). This booklet explains the Family History Library Catalog,
  which is a listing of the worldwide resources available to each center.

Almost all of the Family History Library's worldwide collection of microfilm can be loaned, for a limited time, for use at the Family History Centers. There is a small postage and handling fee. The majority of the microfilms are copies of handwritten, historical records in a variety of foreign languages. The records include copies of government birth and death records, church registers, census schedules, military files, and immigration lists.

The Family History Centers also have extensive computerized information other than that which is available on their Web site. Of interest to Jewish researchers might be the Family History Library Catalog, the Social Security Death Index, and the Military Index.

The staff members at the Family History Centers are very friendly and helpful. On a recent trip to the center in Manhattan, a number of people helped me to find the record of my paternal great-great-grandfather's birth. This was a major breakthrough in my "German" research. It should be noted, however, that the material on the center's computer is not always complete. Although I know my paternal great-grandparents' names and approximately where and when they were born, I was unable to locate those records. However, the records are being constantly updated and added to, so return trips are a good idea.

OTHER ORGANIZATIONS AND ARCHIVES

The following organizations preserve documents, letters, local histories, manuscripts, and other documents of Jewish interest. They don't do research for you, but they can tell you whether they have records for a specific organization or locality so that you'll know if a trip to their site may be productive.

There are also many local Jewish historical societies and archives, i.e., Boston, New York, the Southwest. For the most recent list of these organizations check the American Jewish Historical Society Web site: http://www.ajhs.org/jhs.htm.

American Jewish Historical Society   The society was founded in 1892 to document the Jewish experience in the Americas and has a collection of materials for Central and South America. In more recent times, the AJHS has concentrated on the North American Jewish experience. They also maintain a very informative Web site.

2 Thornton Road
Waltham, MA 02154
(781) 891-8110
http://www.ajhs.org

Leo Baeck Institute   The Leo Baeck Institute specializes in records and information related to German Jewry and German-speaking Jewry.

129 E. 73rd Street
New York, NY 10021
(212) 744-6400
http://www.lbi.org/

YIVO Institute   The YIVO Institute is a resource center for Eastern European Jewry in general with an excellent collection of materials in Yiddish.

555 W. 57th Street, 11th floor
New York, NY 10019
(212) 246-6080
http://www.baruch.cuny.edu/yivo/

The Center for Jewish History   Billed as the "Library of Congress and Smithsonian of the Jewish people," this new center, due to open in Manhattan in 1999, will bring the American Jewish Historical Society, the Leo Baeck Institute, the YIVO Institute, and the Yeshiva University Museum together under one roof. The new address for the Center for Jewish History is:

15 W. 16th Street
New York, NY 10011
http://www.cjh.org/index.html

The American Jewish Archives   The American Jewish Archives was founded in 1947. The organization's mission is to preserve a documentary heritage of the religious, organizational, economic, cultural, personal, social, and family life of American Jewry. The American Jewish

Archives focuses its work in four areas: Western Hemisphere Judaism, the Reform Jewish movement, Cincinnati Jewish history, and Hebrew Union College–Jewish Institute of Religion, its parent institution.

The collection includes archives, manuscripts, photographs, audio and video tapes, microfilm, and genealogical material. It is housed on the Cincinnati campus of Hebrew Union College–Jewish Institute of Religion. Its address is:

American Jewish Archives
Hebrew Union College–Jewish Institute of Religion
3101 Clifton Avenue
Cincinnati, OH 45220-2488
(513) 221-7444, Extension 403
E-mail:AJA@cn.huc.edu
http://server.huc.edu/aja/Archive.htm

FAMILY TREE OF THE JEWISH PEOPLE (FTJP)

The FTJP is a database of individuals on family trees submitted by Jewish genealogists. The information for individuals includes date of birth, place of birth, date of death, and place of death, parents' names, and spouse's name. This is available on CD-Rom. Most Jewish genealogical societies should have a copy of the most recent edition and may also have earlier editions.

This database was originally known as the Jewish Genealogical People Finder (JGPF), and was published on microfiche. It's available through Avotaynu, Inc. The first edition was released in July 1992. The third edition contains information on over 310,000 individuals, submitted by over two hundred Jewish genealogists, and was released in May 1995. The JGPF can not be accessed online, but there is a Web site that tells what information is available and about how to submit material for the next publication of JGPF. The address is http://www.jewishgen.org/infofiles/jgpf.txt.

Douglas E. Goldman Jewish Genealogy Center at Bet Hatefutsoth (Museum of the Diaspora) This is another organization that is collecting Jewish family trees. The Museum of the Diaspora on the campus of Tel Aviv University has a collection of more than 1,500 family trees listed in its database. This database can be accessed in person at the museum in Israel or by sending a written inquiry with a five dollar check to the address below. The center accepts family trees on diskette in GEDCOM format.

Douglas E. Goldman Jewish Genealogy Center
P.O. Box 39359
Tel Aviv 61392 Israel
Telephone 972 3 646 2062
Fax 972 3 646 2134
http://www.bh.org.il

Note: By the time this book is in print, an agreement between JGPF and Bet Hatefutsoth to merge their databases and make them available via JewishGen may have come to fruition. Check the JewishGen Web site for information on this fascinating possibility.

Knowing how to look up information in government and other archives can prove important for a genealogist. Family names are another source of important family information. In the next chapter, we will see how family personal and surnames add to our knowledge of our family history.

11

Uncovering the Clues Buried
in Family Names

There are many stories told about how Jews coming through Ellis Island ended up with unlikely new names. One well-known, probably apocryphal story concerns a young Jewish man who was so confused by his Ellis Island experience that, when asked by the Immigration official to state his name, he replied in Yiddish, "*Shayn Fergessen*"—I forget. And so his name was registered as Sean Fergussen.

Names in Judaism have always been understood to be extremely important. A name is not just a name. Every name should have a meaning related to the object or person to which the name is attached. In the Bible, for example, the first man is made out of earth. The Hebrew word for "earth" is *Adama*. Thus, the first man is named Adam to show that *Adama* gave birth to him. Similarly, Eve's name in Hebrew is Chava, which is a version of the Hebrew word for "life." The first woman is named Chava because she will bring the first human products of creation into life.

Names also reflect changes in one's status or one's life. When Jacob struggles with the angel by the banks of the Jabbok River (Genesis 32:25–30), he is lamed in the process. He is also given a new name—Yisrael—which means, "One who has struggled with God."

In addition to name changes that can occur because of particular circumstances, Jews understand that their lives are reflected in the variety of names that they may acquire as they live their lives. A famous rabbinic teaching instructs that each of us has three names: the name given by your parents, the name you call yourself, and the name given to you by others.

Personal and surnames can provide a number of different clues that can help us understand our family history. Among these clues are:

where our family came from or lived during a particular point in history

our family's religious origins

our family's financial situation at a particular point in time

historical events of importance to family members

time of the year that an ancestor was born

an ancestor's religious or political orientation

whether our family had Sephardic or Ashkenazic roots

the importance or unimportance of particular names within the family

the identification of a person of prominence within our family

conversion to Judaism of a member of the family

the circumstances of a person's birth

the occurrence of a potentially fatal illness in a person's life

the death of a family member at an early age

whether a family named children after a living or deceased relative

the migration of a family from one country to another.

Jews have a long-standing tradition of creating first names that tell something significant about the individual. These names often give us clues about the time in which he or she lived. One of the most easily identifiable clues is the language in which the name is given. For example, while Jews living in biblical times tended to use Hebrew names, when they came in touch with other, dominant civilizations, they tended to give their children names in the language of that culture. This continues to be so to this day, although the existence of the state of Israel has had an impact on how Jews in the Diaspora name their children. Hebrew names as "secular" names are gaining popularity outside of Israel.

In this chapter, we will look at the development of Jewish personal and surnames and see how these names reveal important information about our family history.

EARLY JEWISH SURNAMES

The use of surnames (last names) in the Jewish community is of very recent origin. Until 1787, when the Austrian Empire legislated the use of surnames for Jews, Jewish surnames were relatively unknown. For one thing, Jews tended to live in homogeneous communities where one could identify individual males by their place of origin—as in the name Eliahu HaTishbi (Elijah the Tishibite), by their father's name—David ben Avraham (David son of Abraham), or by their profession—Saul the Goldsmith.

The social sphere of women was relatively limited throughout much of Jewish history. For this reason, a woman's surname was not considered to be particularly important. Even later on, when Jews took surnames, since a woman's surname changed with marriage, little consideration was given to her name. Only in the last several decades have women retained their maiden names or their professional names after marriage, or taken new surnames other than their husband's name.

The only significant surnames that have endured throughout Jewish history are those related to Temple service. Even after the destruction of the Temple in Jerusalem in 70 C.E., the Kohens and Levites continued their genealogical tradition by adding the suffix "haKohen"—the Kohen, and "haLevi"—the Levite—to their personal names. These suffixes link Jewish families directly to their ancestors who, over three thousand years ago, were obligated to serve in the Temple.

When Jews adopted surnames in Europe, many people who were Kohens and Levites used variations of these titles as surnames. Cohen, Kahn, Kaplan, Katz, and Kagen are related to the title Kohen, although not all Cohens, Kahns, Kaplans, Katzs, and Kagens are Kohens. One of the obligations of a Cohen was to bless the congregation. The Yiddish word for this is *dukhen*. For this reason, Cohens may also be found among those people called Duchan, Duchen, and Duchin.

A Kohen is a Kohen in other languages, but those of us with an Eastern European name orientation may not recognize them as such. The Russian name for a Kohen is Agranat. In Italy, a Kohen is called "Sacerdote," and French Kohens may have the name Lepretre. A folk tradition that both Kohanim and curly-headed people have hot tempers created the surname *Kraushaar* (curly haired) for Kohanim.

Levy and Levi were the common surnames used for the title "haLevi," although, again, not all people with these names are Levites. Other forms of this name are Levin, Levinsky, Levitt, and Segal. Segal is an abbreviation of the Hebrew term *segan leviah,* "member of the Levites." Some variations of Segal are Zoegell and Chagall.

In Germany, Hebrew names were not always acceptable and Germanic name forms were insisted upon. This created Hebrew-German crosses like Katzman, Levinthal, and Aronstein. (Aaron was the first Kohen.)

The tradition of a family being a Kohen or a Levite was most often passed down orally and testified to by the appropriate suffix ending of a male relative's name. The status of being a Kohen or Levite traveled through the male line, from father to son. All the sons of a father who is either a Kohen or a Levite inherit this status and claim it as their own when they reach the age of thirteen, the age of Jewish religious maturity.

As was mentioned before, not all Cohens or Levis are Kohens and Levites. These and other related surnames are a very late development in Jewish life. Some families may have adopted these names for a variety of reasons having nothing to do with their actual genealogical claim on this heritage. All Jews who do not have a tradition of being either a Levite or a Kohen belong to the group known as Israelites. Most Jews fall into this category.

The most definitive "proof" of Kohen or Levite status is to trace the Hebrew names of a patrilineal line through a number of generations, preferably to a time before the family had an official surname. If the suffix "haCohen" or "haLevi" continues to appear, one may be able to claim this status for oneself.

EARLY SEPHARDIC NAMING CUSTOMS

Although Jews in Central and Eastern Europe did not use surnames until the eighteenth century, Sephardic Jews adopted this practice in the tenth and eleventh centuries because of the growth of cities and the involvement of many Sephardic families in commerce. Some Sephardic families adopted the Arab custom of creating a surname by using a father's first name, with or without the prefix *Ibn*—"son of." It was also popular to use occupational names and place-names as surnames.

Other Sephardic Jews created surnames by translating the father's name from Hebrew to Spanish. Joseph Caro, the author of the Shulchan Aruch, the first truly comprehensive book of Jewish law, was probably descended from an ancestor whose Hebrew name was Habib, which means "dear one." Caro is the Spanish equivalent. Other Sephardic Jewish names include Maimon (*Asher* in Hebrew, meaning "fortunate"), Benveniste (the equivalent of the use of the word *Shalom* as a greeting, meaning "welcome"), and Franco, which was used by Sephardic families who were exempt from taxes because of their service to the king of Spain.

The rendering of Hebrew names into the secular language of the country in which Jews were living was a common custom throughout Europe, just as "Americanizing" foreign-sounding names is a common practice today. The Hebrew name *Yehezkel*—May God strengthen—was translated by Italian Jews into the name Forti. French Jews also followed the custom of translating their surnames into French.

Occupational names were also very common. Chazan is derived from the Hebrew word *hazan*, which means "cantor." *Chalfan* means "money changer." *Dayan* is the Hebrew word for a judge on a rabbinic court.

Place-names were also popular with Sephardic Jews and Jews in

France and Italy. Alcalay, Cardozo, Castro, Luria, Montefiore, Modena, and Finzi are all Jewish names derived from specific locations.

NAMING CUSTOMS OF EASTERN EUROPEAN JEWRY

Jews living in the Austrian Empire were compelled to take surnames in 1787. This trend spread throughout most of Europe during the first half of the nineteenth century. Government officials were deputized to assign names to each Jewish family. The ability to bestow a name on a family gave the officials great power. Officially, each family could choose its own name. However, local registering agents could refuse to register the name the family chose and might give the family an unpleasant name unless a more desirable name was "purchased." In addition, taxes were levied against individuals for the registering of names.

One of the ploys of government officials was to give "nonsense" names to Jews who couldn't afford to bribe them for better names. Very often, when a family with a "foreign name" can not find the linguistic derivation, this is a sign that an early family member may have been burdened with a nonsense name. This practice was not isolated to Eastern Europe, but was also practiced in other countries in Europe where Jews were forced to adopt surnames.

Desirable Jewish surnames were based on nature, geographic location, and occupation. For example, the name Steinberg means "stone hill." The name Schechter comes from the occupation of being a *schochet*—a kosher butcher. The name Schwartz means "black." Melamed means "teacher" in Hebrew. The German form of this name is Lehrer. The Slavic form is Uchitel.

Some occupational names were based on the tools used rather than on the occupation itself. For example, a tanner who works with leather might name himself Leder (leather.) A tailor might become Fingerhut (thimble), or Nadel (needle). A German hazan might be named Grossinger (main singer) or Schulsinger (synagogue singer).

Some Jews took names that described physical characteristics—Gross (big), Chorney (Slavic: black), Roth (red), Stark (strong) Gelber or Geller (yellow). Some Jews used their nicknames: Kluger (wise), Lustig (happy), or names relating to seasons and days of the week—Sommer (summer), Sonntag (Sunday).

Place-names (called toponyms) provided many Ashkenazic families with names. The slavic suffix *ski* would be added to the name of a town or village—for example, Warshawski (Warsaw). In Germany, the suffix used was *er*, as in Bamberger, Berliner, Posner, and Wilner—from Vilana. *V/W* shifts are very common in Eastern European Jewish names.

In Slavic languages the endings *vitch, wicz, ov, off, eff,* and *kin* are common suffixes that mean "descendent of." *Vici* is a common Romanian patronymic ending.

Some families used the Hebrew form of their names—Joseph ben Jacob, dropping the word *ben*—to become Joseph Jacob, or Jacobs. Another way in which the Hebrew form of a name was adapted was to translate the word *ben* into the word *son* or *sohn* and add it to the end of the father's name, creating names like Jacobson.

Other families used a woman's name—often the mother's—as the basis of their surname. Rivkin, for example, means "descendent of Rivka." Baskin is a combination of the Hebrew name Basya—Batya and the suffix *kin*. Sorkin is a combination of the Yiddish form of Sarah (Sura, Sora) and the suffix *kin*.

The suffix *sohn* is a common suffix in Austrian and German names. In America, it was often shortened to "son." The name Perelson is a combination of a woman's name—Perel—with the *son* ending.

Some names have one meaning for Jews and one meaning for non-Jews. According to Benzion Kaganoff's *Dictionary of Jewish Names and Their History,* the English occupational name Cooper referred to one who was a maker or seller of barrels. However, the Jewish names Cooper and Cooperman are derived from the German word *Kupfer,* which means "coppersmith."

Another popular way for choosing a name was to take a person's Hebrew first name and translate it into the secular language of the country in which they were living. For example, if a Frenchman's name was Chaim (life) his new surname might be Vital (French for "life"). In Italy, Manoah's surname (restful) might become Tranquillo.

Still another way of developing a surname was to take a symbol or biblical reference related to one's first name and translate it into another language. For example, in Genesis, Jacob blesses his sons on his deathbed and ascribes specific symbols to each of his son's names. These names—Joseph, Gad, Naphtali, Asher, and others were common Hebrew personal names. Of Naphtali, Jacob says that he is like a swift-footed hart. "Hart" in German is the word *Hirsh*—pronounced "Hirz" or "Herz" in northern Germany. In Hebrew, the word for "hart" is *tzvi*. A German Jew whose first name was Naphtali might take a surname Herz, becoming Naphtali Herz. A Tzvi might become "Tzvi Hirsh." Some variants of the name "Herz" are Hershchel, Cerf (French), Yellin (Slavic), and Jellinik. Similarly, since Benjamin, Jacob's youngest son, was compared to a wolf, a man named Benjamin might take the name Wolf or Wolpe as a surname. The Hebrew word for wolf is *ze'ev*. From this word we get the Jewish surnames Ziff, Zev, Wolk (Slavic), Lupo (Rumanian), and Lopez (Spanish).

Many Jewish families changed their names in America, using a literal translation as a link to their original family names. For example, many Steinbergs took the name Stonehill as a way of blending into American society. Long names, like Davidovitch, were shortened to "David." "Foreign-sounding" names like Pokreshevsky were Americanized to names like Parker.

EARLY JEWISH NAMES

After the fall of the First Temple in 586 B.C.E., many Jews were carried into exile in Babylonia. Up to this time, Hebrew, although not biblical, names seem to have been most prominent in Israel. During the Babylonian exile and even afterward, two different naming trends appeared. One new custom was to name children after biblical figures—Benjamin, Reuben, Abraham. These names signified a desire to connect with the biblical past. Over the millennia, the use of biblical names, not only in the Jewish world but in the non-Jewish world, often coincided with a religious revival or renewal. The Pilgrims, for example, for whom the Hebrew Bible was a basic source text, often named their children after Old Testament heroes and heroines.

The other trend that emerged during the Babylonian period was the use of Aramaic names and name forms and Babylonia/Persian names and name forms. For example, names ending in the letters *ai* signify Aramaic names. There are many of these in the latter books of the Hebrew Bible. Hillel's famous adversary, Shammai, bears an Aramaic form of the Hebrew name Shemaiah. The names of the two most prominent figures in the Purim story come directly from Babylonia. Mordecai means "one who is devoted to Marduk." Marduk was a god in the Babylonian pantheon. Esther is the Babylonian form for the name of the goddess Ishtar.

When the Jewish people came in contact with Alexander the Great and Greek culture, Greek names made their way into Jewish society. There is a tradition in some Jewish families that a first son should be named Alexander in memory of Alexander the Great. Alexander's rule was seen as relatively benevolent by many Jews of the time. Another name that is passed along in some Jewish families, especially those who lived in Persia for many generations, is the name Cyrus. Cyrus the Great permitted the Jews to rebuild the Temple and the city of Jerusalem and ended the Babylonian exile in 560 B.C.E.

During the Roman occupation of Israel and after the fall of the Second Temple, Latin names came into vogue among some segments of the Jewish community. Drusus and Justus are two Latin names found in the Jerusalem Talmud. Marcus, Julius, Justinus, and Rufus were also common names. In addition, the names of Roman gods, like Apollo, were used as personal names. While the use of most of these names in the Jewish community waned over time, some names have reoccurred. Julius Marx was better known as Groucho. And over the last twenty years in America, there has been a bumper crop of little boys named Justin. The names Julia and Julie are feminine forms of Julius.

Most American Jews are familiar with the custom of having an English name and a Jewish name. This custom, of using a name in the vernacular for secular life and a Hebrew name (and later a Yiddish name) for use in religious life, has its roots in Second Temple times. For example, Esther is also called "Hadassah" in the Megillat Esther. Shadrach's Hebrew name was Hananiah.

Another custom that arose at around this time was the coupling of a Hebrew and a non-Hebrew name. The Hasmonean kings, like Yannai-Alexander, all had names that were Hebrew/Greek links. One's Greek name was a translation of one's Hebrew name. For example, the Hebrew name Joshua would be linked to its Greek form, Jason. As was discussed earlier, a similar formula was used much later when Jews began to take surnames.

Another way in which Jews mixed cultures in their names during the Talmudic period was to use Hebrew names whose spelling reflected other cultural influences. The name Yitzhak, for example, might be spelled Isak, indicating a Greek influence. We see this even today. The Hebrew name Yosef is rendered into English as Joseph. The name Rivkah becomes Rebecca.

JEWISH NAMES DURING THE MIDDLE AGES

In the Middle Ages, Jews began to give their children names based on when they were born, mimicking a custom that was already widespread in the non-Jewish community. For example, a boy born on Passover would be given the name Pesach, which is the Hebrew term for Passover, or the name Nisan, for the month in which Passover falls. A girl born during Purim might be named Malka (queen) because Esther became the Queen of Shushan.

Another popular naming convention at this time was to give a child a name related to the messiah or to messianic hopes. Names like Moshiah (messiah), Menachem Tzion ("comforter of Zion," an allusion to the effect of the coming of the messiah), and Zemach ("branch," referring to the idea that the Messiah will come from a branch of King David's family) were all names that gained popularity. Zemach is still used today.

By the twelfth century, the use of non-Jewish names was so widespread in the Jewish community that the rabbis ruled that every Jewish boy must be given a *shem hakodesh*—a holy name—at his circumcision. This name, to be used at all ritual occasions, did not have to be a Hebrew name, however. While there was (and still is in many communities) a preference for a Hebrew name, Aramaic names, Greek names of long standing, and, later,

Yiddish names were also considered appropriate for this use. Among the Greek names that were and still are used for this purpose are Alexander, Sender (a derivative form of Alexander), Kalman (from Kalonymos, which means "beautiful name"), and Geronymos (the old man.)

In addition to these names, Ashkenazic Jews formed diminutives of Hebrew and Yiddish names. Many of these "nontraditional" names were passed on from one generation to another. Very often, the Hebrew or true Yiddish root of the original name would be forgotten, but the name derived from the original name was taken very seriously as a family name. The name Eliezer appears in a number of variations including the name Leeser. Ephraim becomes Froim and Froikin. The name Samuel comes down through time as Shmelke, Sanvil, and Zangwill. If a genealogist finds a personal name in the family history that doesn't make sense in any language, the probability is that this is a corrupted form of a normative Hebrew or Yiddish name.

There is a folkloric Jewish understanding that personal names have power. Therefore, the selection of a Jewish name is a matter of great importance. Because of this, a number of naming customs developed. For example, if a child was endangered during birth, he or she might well be given a name that would be seen as supporting his or her life. The Hebrew word for life, *chai*, became the name Chaim, for boys, and Chaya, for girls. A child who became ill early in life might be given the name Alte (a girl) or Alter (for a boy). This Yiddish word means "old." By giving a child such a name, it suggests to God that the child should be permitted to live a long and full life.

JEWISH NAMES IN MODERN TIMES

Interestingly, in some Jewish circles today, there exists a bias against certain names, even though they are both biblical and Hebrew names. For example, in these communities, no biblical names that appear prior to those of Abraham and Sarah are permitted. Even the name Avram is frowned on. This is because Avram was Abraham's name before Abraham made his covenant with God. It was the making of the covenant, and the change of Avram's name to Avraham with the addition of the

Hebrew letter *hay* (*H* in English) which was a marker of the first patriarch's altered status. The *hay* is one of the letters used in God's most holy name, which is never pronounced. Its addition to Abram's name signifies his new relationship to the Holy One.

Before the covenant, Avram was not "Jewish" according to those who follow this custom. Therefore, while Avraham/Abraham is an acceptable name, Avram is not. The thinking goes that Jewish children should not be named after non-Jews, even if the name is found in the Torah.

A strongly held Jewish naming tradition is that of not giving the child the name of a person who died at an early age. There is a superstitious fear that giving the child such a name will "doom" him or her to a similar fate. Related to this custom is the idea that when you name a child after a relative who is deceased, you endow the child with the positive aspects of the person for whom he or she is named. In addition, naming a child after a deceased relative is seen as a way of welcoming that person's soul back to earth.

Another naming custom that is very entrenched in certain parts of the Jewish world is the tradition of changing the name of a person who became critically ill or adding an additional name. The name chosen, either as a new name or as an added name, is usually a name like Chaim or Alte. The idea here is twofold: By bestowing a name related to long life or health, it suggests to God that the decree of possible impending death be reversed. The other idea is that because the person's name has been changed, the Angel of Death will be fooled when he or she comes looking for the person who is ill. Since the person named in the Angel's "death warrant" cannot be found, the Angel will be compelled to go away "empty handed."

The changing of a critically ill person's name can be done in a number of different ways. Usually it is done as part of a Torah service. However, it can also be done with appropriate witnesses at the bedside of the person who is ill. The changing of a person's name is often linked to the giving of tzedakah (a donation to charity) by either the person who is ill or by a close member of the family on behalf of the person who is ill. The giving of tzedakah demonstrates to God that even at a time of deep personal distress, the person giving the tzedakah is able to

think about the needs of others. In traditional terms, this deed demonstrates that the giver is worthy of God's special concern.

While this theology may be very problematic for more liberal Jewish
thinkers, the actual act of giving tzedakah can be very empowering for
someone who is ill, or for someone who is caring for someone who is
critically ill. The ability and willingness to put aside your own concerns
when you are dealing with issues of life and death reminds the doer that
he or she can still act upon the world in a positive way and that there is
more to life than the world of the sickroom.

Today there are two simultaneous naming revolutions occurring in
the American Jewish community. The first can be seen among
liberal/traditional Jews and Zionist-oriented Jews. In these communities it is now quite common for a child to have only one name, and that
name is usually a Hebrew name. While biblical Hebrew names like
Yitzhak and Sarah continue to be popular, more secular, "Israeli" names
like Lior and Tamara are increasingly used. The use of these names
reveals a coming of age of liberal religious American Jews, who no
longer feel that they need to hide their Jewish identity, the identity of
their children, or their support for the state of Israel.

The other naming trend is taking place in the Reform and unaffiliated
Jewish world. Here, English names that were associated with being particularly Jewish two or three generations ago are making a big comeback. The nursery schools are now populated with three year olds
named Max, Sophie, Samuel, and Rose.

It still throws me when I hear someone shouting, "Sophie, where are
you?" I look around, expecting to see my great aunt. Instead, Sophie is
a moppet who barely reaches my thigh! The popularization of these
names in the American Jewish community today reveals a strong desire
to link with Jewish tradition and a willingness to be publicly identified
as Jewish.

SEPHARDIC AND ASHKENAZIC NAMING TRADITIONS

There's an idea in the Jewish community that a marriage between an
Ashkenazic Jew and a Sephardic Jew is an intermarriage. The reason

for this thinking is that there are many conflicts between Ashkenazic and Sephardic traditions. These traditions are so well established that the printed edition of the Shulchan Aruch, the "source book" for all of modern Jewish law, contains an interlinear commentary for the use of Ashkenazic Jews written by Rabbi Moses Isserles, a contemporary of Joseph Caro. Joseph Caro, who lived in Sfat in northern Israel, is the Sephardic author of the Shulchan Aruch. In the Shulchan Aruch, when Caro states something that differs from Ashkenazic tradition, there's a note that usually says something like, "But here [here meaning Ashkenazic Jews] we do it this way. . . ." Both ways of observance are seen as valid for their particular communities.

Passover is a holiday that demonstrates these differences very clearly. During Passover, Ashkenazic Jews avoid eating any food that can swell with the addition of water. Therefore, rice, corn, legumes, and even green beans are on the interdict list for that holiday. Sephardic Jews, on the other hand, while not eating bread, do eat rice, corn, legumes, and green beans. How does a properly brought up Ashkenazic spouse keep Pesach according to his or her tradition, when the other spouse insists that it's perfectly all right to eat everything that the other feels is prohibited?

This problem is minor, however, when compared to the complexities that erupt when a baby appears, because Ashkenazic and Sephardic Jews have diametrically opposed naming traditions. Ashkenazic Jews always name a child after a relative who has died before the birth of the child. In addition, great care is taken not to give a child inadvertently the name of another relative who is living. For example, if an aunt's Hebrew name is Sarah, even though the intention of the parents might be to name the child Sarah after a relative who is deceased, the parents will usually not name the baby Sarah.

Sephardic families also consider naming children after relatives a way to honor those relatives. However, there is no taboo against naming a child after a living relative. The names of grandparents have first priority. A firstborn son is usually named after the paternal grandfather. A second male child is usually named after the maternal grandfather. The first daughter is generally named after the paternal grandmother and the second daughter is named after the maternal grandmother. If the couple has more children, they alternate between the paternal and maternal uncles and aunts.

If a grandparent (paternal or maternal) or sibling is deceased, however, in some cases his or her name will take precedence over the living relative. On the other hand, some Spanish exiles named children after their own parents.

It is believed that the idea of naming a child after a deceased relative began in the Jewish community sometime after the fall of the First Temple. During this time, Jews had contacts with Egyptians through a variety of circumstances including military service on the Elephantine Island, which is located in the Nile. The tradition of naming a child after a deceased relative was practiced in Egypt. It's not clear exactly how this tradition changed in the Sephardic community. However, one possibility is that the idea of naming a child after a living relative was borrowed from the Catholic societies in which Sephardic Jews lived in later times.

SPELLING OF NAMES

Prior to the twentieth century, the spelling of names, and, indeed, of words themselves, was very fluid. One name, Sarah, for example, might be spelled as Sarah, Sara, Sura, or Sora, to give just a few examples. For this reason, it's important for a genealogist to be alert to the possibility that a family surname or first name may have a variety of spellings even within a single generation. Sephardic names also display this lack of standardization. For example, the names Aben, Ibn, Aven, and Ben all mean "the son of."

In naming, especially in relation to Hebrew names, certain consonant and vowel switches are very standard. For example, the name of our first patriarch is pronounced "Avraham" in Hebrew. However, when rendered into other languages, the *v* becomes a *b*, giving us the name Abraham in English. In Spanish-speaking countries, an additional switch between the vowels *a* and *i* give us the name Ibrahim.

Another way in which Hebrew names are changed has to do with the desire of non-Hebrew speakers to soften the guttural sounds so characteristic of the Hebrew language. A name like Chana, which, in Hebrew has a guttural sound at the beginning (like Chanukah) becomes Anna or Hannah in languages that do not have guttural sounds. The name Chaim becomes Hayim or, with the addition of *m* and *n* consonantal confusion, Hyman.

RESOURCES

The subject of Hebrew names is fascinating and complicated. Complicated, because of the many different languages involved and the fact that standardization was not necessarily a priority. However, one need not be a linguistics expert to learn enough to have a useful base of knowledge for genealogical research. There are a number of books that are available that can shed some light on this fascinating topic, with new material coming out all the time. Not all of these books are currently in print. However, most large libraries will have them, as well as many genealogy libraries. Some of these books may also be available through Avotaynu and bookstores that specialize in genealogy.

> *A Dictionary of Jewish Names and Their History,* by Benzion C. Kaganoff (Jason Aronson, 1996); ISBN 1568219539.

> *A Dictionary of Jewish Surnames from the Kingdom of Poland,* by Alexander Beider (Avotaynu, 1996); ISBN 0962637394.

> *A Dictionary of Jewish Surnames From the Russian Empire,* by Alexander Beider (Avotaynu, 1993); ISBN 0962637335.

> *Jewish Surnames in Prague (Fifteenth–Eighteenth Centuries),* by Alexander Beider (Avotaynu, 1994); ISBN 0962637351.

> *Jewish Family Names and Their Origins: An Etymological Dictionary,* by Heinrich W. Guggenheimer and Eva H. Guggenheimer (Ktav, 1992); ISBN 0881252972.

> *Russian–Jewish Given Names,* by Boris Feldblyum (Avotaynu, 1998); ISBN 1886223076.

> *Jewish Personal Names: Their Origin, Derivation, and Diminutive Forms,* edited by Chaim Freedman (Avotaynu, 1992); ISBN 0962637327.

Jewish and Hebrew Onomastics: A Bibliography, by Robert Singerman (Garland, 1977); ISBN 0824098811. This is a subject-organized list of nearly 1,200 books and articles on various aspects of Jewish names.

The New Name Dictionary: Modern English and Hebrew Names, by Alfred J. Kolatch (Jonathan David, 1989); ISBN 0824603311.

Russian-Jewish Given Names by Boris Feldblyum (Avotaynu, 1998); ISBN 1886223076.

Preserving family names through the generations is one way of sending a message about a family's values, ideas, and priorities into the future. In chapter 17, we'll look at a variety of ways in which a genealogist can also become a time traveler, collecting information from the past and delivering it to future generations.

12

Uncovering Further Links to the Old Country

 One of the most chilling questions all young children ask is, "Where do I come from?" This question immediately brings up images of storks, cabbage patches, and other folkloric responses. For Jews, however, the question, "Where do I come from," raises thoughts of desert travel, midnight treks through darkened woods, expulsion from our homes, and, almost always, a terrifying story of escape in the nick of time and tales of those who did not escape.

With such a background, it's no wonder that many Jews know little or nothing of their ancestors. When one does ask the question "Where do I come from?" of older relatives, the question is often deflected or answered in a very general way. "We came from Poland."

For the beginning genealogist, this type of response can prove very frustrating. There are a number of ways, however, to uncover more information from the few clues that you may already have. Understanding the patterns of Jewish immigration to the United States can provide some starting points. If you know that some relatives came "from Poland," you can probably pinpoint the dates with some accuracy based on your knowledge of the generation to which they belonged and an understanding of how and why Jews from Eastern Europe immigrated to the United States.

EARLY JEWISH IMMIGRATION TO COLONIAL AMERICA

There were a few individual Jews in the colonies as early as 1620, but the first "real" Jewish settlers were Portuguese Jews, who came to New York in 1654 fleeing the Inquisition in South America. These people were descendents of the Sephardic Jews who had left Spain at the end of the fifteenth century for Portugal, Holland, North Africa, South America, and the Ottoman Empire. It was Sephardic Jews who first settled America and who continued to immigrate to the United States and to flourish throughout the nineteenth century.

EARLY NINETEENTH-CENTURY EUROPEAN IMMIGRATION TO THE UNITED STATES

In the nineteenth century in Western and Central Europe, Jews were on a political roller coaster. During the end of the eighteenth century, European Jews slowly began to win political equality and civil rights throughout Europe. However, after the defeat of Napoleon in 1815, many of these rights were rescinded. General political unrest in Central and Western Europe over the next fifteen to twenty years further eroded the ability of Jews to make a living in their homelands.

Beginning around 1830, Jews from Central Europe, and especially Bavaria, began to immigrate to the United States. They were part of a mass migration of German Jews and non-Jews and Irish gentiles who were seeking a better life in a new land that promised more opportunity than existed in the old country.

In the 1830s, approximately 600,000 people immigrated to the United States. In the 1840s, over a million and a half people came to the United States. In the 1850s, immigration doubled to nearly 3 million people.

Between 1820 and 1860, approximately 100,000 Jews immigrated to the United States from Europe. During that period, the Jewish population of the United States increased from about 6,000 to approximately 150,000 Jews. Many of the Jews from German-speaking countries prospered in their adopted homeland and had a strong identification with American values. Most were literate in both Hebrew and German and had middle-class mores.

RUSSIAN AND GERMAN IMMIGRATION AFTER THE AMERICAN CIVIL WAR

Between the end of the Civil War and the beginning of World War I, more than 35 million people immigrated to the United States. This large movement of people was spurred by overpopulation and a resulting lack of opportunities in Europe and in Russia. Two million of these new immigrants were Jews, many from Russia. They represented approximately fifteen percent of European Jewry.

Jews had special reasons for wanting to leave Europe, and especially Russia, even before the American Civil War. Anti-Semitism limited the ability of poor Jews to improve their position in life. Obtaining an advanced education was almost impossible for most Jews. Pogroms, especially in Russia and the Ukraine, were a frequent and scary fact of life. In addition, the czar's solution to his "Jewish problem" was to conscript forcibly young Jewish men into the army for long periods of time—sometimes twenty-five years or more. While middle- and upper-class Jews were sometimes able to "buy" an army replacement for a son, this was rarely possible for poor Jews.

Pogroms in 1881–1882 stimulated Russian Jewish immigration to the United States. Poor Jews from Austria-Hungary and Romania also emigrated at this time for economic reasons. Most of the Jews who immigrated to the United States from Russia and the Pale of Settlement at the end of the nineteenth century were poor and often illiterate. As a refugee group, they were quite different from the Bavarian and German Jews who had come to the United States in the earlier part of the nineteenth century. The prosperous German-Jewish community created a number of different Jewish organizations to help settle their coreligionists and to "Americanize" them as quickly as possible.

JEWISH IMMIGRATION TO THE UNITED STATES IN THE TWENTIETH CENTURY

After World War I, life for Jews in Eastern Europe was precarious. Most European Jews lived in the Pale of Settlement and in Russia, Germany, Poland, and Austria-Hungary. The Pale of Settlement covered about 386,000 square miles and reached from the Baltic Sea to the Black Sea. The census of 1897 listed 4,899,300 Jews living within this area. This was about ninety-four percent of the total Russian Jewish population. The ten largest population areas were Warsaw, Odessa, Lodz, Vilna, Kishinev, Minsk, Bialystok, Berdichev, Yekaterinoslav, and Vitebsk.

The Pale of Settlement was rife with revolution, territorial disputes, and pogroms. Between 1919 and 1921, at least sixty thousand Jews were killed in this area. These events further stimulated Jewish emigration.

Hitler's rise to power triggered another wave of Jewish emigration from Eastern Europe in the 1930s. Between 1933 and 1941, when America entered World War II, more than two hundred thousand Jewish refugees fled to America from Austria-Hungary, Poland, and Germany. Unlike the wave of Eastern European immigrants at the end of the nineteenth century, many of these new immigrants had education, wealth, a professional skill or trade, or connections in the United States.

After World War II, a relatively small number of Holocaust survivors were permitted to immigrate to the United States, primarily for reunion with family members. After the establishment of the state of Israel, many survivors settled in the new Jewish homeland.

The Jews in the Soviet Union, the largest surviving Jewish population in Europe, were not permitted to emigrate until the late 1970s, when the "Refusenik" movement managed to clear the way for a small number of individuals. The fall of communism in Russia at the end of the 1980s further opened Russia's doors, and many Jews immigrated to the United States and Israel.

The late 1980s and the 1990s has also been a time of immigration to the United States for "Oriental" Jews—Jews from Islamic countries, especially Iraq and Iran.

Here is a simplified chronology of Jewish immigration to the United States:

1654–1800. Sephardic immigration from South America and Catholic countries

1815–1860. German/Bavarian immigration

1865–1914. Russian, Romanian, Austro-Hungarian immigration

1919–1924. Russian, Polish, Eastern European immigration

1933–1941. German, Polish, Czechoslavakian, Austro-Hungarian immigration

1950s. German, Polish immigration

1970s–1990s. Refugees from the former Soviet Union; refugees from Iraq, Iran, and other countries under Islamic control.

CONNECTING TO YOUR RELATIVES IN THE OLD COUNTRY

Today, there are a number of different ways to begin to link yourself to family members who did not leave the old country. One way is to make use of the many new databases that exist on the Internet. You would use a database to help you find specific information about a person or town you're researching.

Databases

JewishGen, an Internet site that was mentioned in chapter 7, hosts a wide number of databases for Jewish genealogical research. The Jewish-Gen databases described below can all be reached at http://www. jewishgen.org/databases. Among the databases offered are:

The JewishGen Family Finder (JGFF)   The JewishGen Family Finder database contains over 85,000 entries. It currently lists 30,000 surnames and 9,000 towns being researched by over 10,000 Jewish genealogists worldwide. These are indexed and cross-referenced by both surname and town name. If you are searching for information about a particular town or a particular surname, you can list your search on this database. In addition, you can search for people who are searching for a particular surname or town.

The Yizkor Book Project   Yizkor books are books containing information about a particular town or area compiled by synagogues, organizations, and communities. A common feature is a list of names of people in the community who have died. These books were created so that the names of the people and the history of the town would not be forgotten. Some Yizkor books contain maps, photographs, and even advertisements.

If you are looking for information about a specific area, locating a Yizkor book for that area could be very helpful. The Yizkor Book Project is a database that contains a listing of where these books are located. In addition, you can read translations of actual Yizkor book material.

The Phoenix Project—The Brest Ghetto Passport Archive   This database is a treasure trove for Holocaust researchers and for people who may have had relatives living in Brest.

The Brest Ghetto Passport Archive is the first stage of the Phoenix Project, a multiyear effort to computerize data on the Holocaust drawn primarily from newly opened archives in the former Soviet Union. The goal of this project is to recover as many names as possible of those Holocaust victims who perished in Nazi-occupied Soviet territory. Where possible, explanatory notes, background materials, eyewitness and survivor accounts, still photos, and video film will be included in the database. Every effort is being made to determine when and where the victims died.

The archive is composed of documents prepared by the Nazi authorities after the capture of Brest in the summer of 1941. All Jews living in the Brest Ghetto who were fourteen years of age or older were required to obtain identity papers, which included their names, ages, and the names and dates of birth of their parents. A photo of each person was taken. Everyone who received a passport was required to sign for it.

Over 12,000 people received these passports. The Brest Ghetto passports and a ledger recording the distribution of the passports were liberated by Soviet troops in 1944 and became part of the Russian

Holocaust Archives. By the time Brest was liberated, all the Jews living in the Brest Ghetto had been murdered. Only a few former Jewish inhabitants of Brest survived the Nazi occupation.

Grodno Gubernia 1912 Voters List   The names of over 26,000 men of Grodno Gubernia who were eligible to vote in the Russian parliamentary elections in 1912 are detailed in this database. If your family comes from this area, you may be able to trace family names and individuals.

HaMelitz **Lithuanian and Latvian Donors**   This database covers the period of 1893 to 1903. It contains the names of almost 20,000 Lithuanian and Latvian charity donors listed in the Hebrew periodical, *HaMelitz*. If you are looking for relatives who came from these areas, this database may help you make a genealogical connection.

Sugihara Database   As the Germans were advancing on Lithuania in 1940, all diplomats were told to leave their embassies in Kaunas. Only a Dutch consul and the Japanese diplomat Chiune Sugihara remained. Because of this, it was virtually impossible for Jews to obtain visas to leave the country. In July 1940, against orders from Tokyo, Sugihara and his wife spent four weeks writing out visas by hand. Sugihara visas saved almost 6,000 Lithuanian, Polish, German, and Russian Jews, most of whom spent the rest of the war in Kobe, Japan.

Jewish genealogists doing Holocaust research on relatives who passed through Lithuania, may find this database helpful. It lists the names of 2,139 Jews who received Sugihara visas.

Jewish Records Indexing—Poland   This is an index to over 200,000 nineteenth-century Jewish birth, marriage, and death records from eighty Polish towns. If you are looking for relatives in Poland, this is a good place to start.

The Jews of London (pre-1850)   This database contains the names and addresses of Jews in London in the first half of the nineteenth century. It was compiled primarily from London trade directories.

Welsh Census Returns—1851, 1891   This is a database containing information of Jewish residents of south Wales at the time of the 1851 and 1891 censuses.

Special Interest Groups

Special Interest Groups (SIGs) are made up of Jewish genealogists and others who are interested in doing research on a particular geographic region. Some special interest groups exist as offshoots of local Jewish genealogy societies. Others network through the Internet. Some SIGs have printed publications and others maintain discussion group mailing lists. The purpose of a special interest group is to help those with an interest in a particular geographic region exchange information and research tips, share resources, and exchange ideas.

JewishGen hosts a wide number of special-interest-group mailing lists. These groups span a wide variety of areas and interests. They include:

Hungarian SIG: The Hungarian Jewish Special Interest Group helps those with Jewish roots in the area known as "greater Hungary" or pre-Trianon Hungary and includes areas that at one time were predominantly Hungarian speaking.

Latvia SIG: A forum for researchers of Jewish families of Latvian descent.

Litvak SIG: Encourages preservation and computerization of primary sources of genealogical data for the descendents of the Lithuanian Jewish community.

Sefard SIG: A forum for researchers of Sephardic genealogies.

Volhynia SIG: A forum to share information and to bring together descendents of Volhynians and others with an interest in Volhynia (Ukraine).

Suwalk-Lomza SIG: Publisher of *Landsmen,* covering these two northeastern gubernias of Russian Poland, now in northeast Poland and southwest Lithuania.

Stammbaum-German SIG, Germany: Sponsored by the Leo Baeck Institute.

To subscribe to one or more of these special interest groups, and to see what new groups have been formed, you need to sign on to the JewishGen Web site at http://www.jewishgen.org.

Documents

The best way to find out about your ancestors is to talk to a living relative. However, as we discussed in an earlier chapter, it's important to try to get your relative to be specific about where your family came from. A general answer like "Prague" could mean the city itself or one of its suburbs. Make sure that you pursue this discussion to obtain an exact location.

For many people, asking a relative about the old country may not be possible. However, there are many different types of documents you can access that can give you this information. In chapter 10, we discussed how these records can be researched. What follows is an overview of the type of records to look for and the type of information that they can yield.

Naturalization records: On the Declaration of Intention and the actual Petition for Naturalization, the person's hometown is listed. However, if your relative did not become a naturalized citizen, these documents won't be available to you. In that case, you would try the next set of documents detailed here.

U.S. passenger arrival lists: After 1893, these documents contain a column for "Last Residence," which might be town, province, or country, depending upon the ship. Lists after 1906 always contain a "Birthplace" column, city, and country. For earlier immigrants, the Hamburg emigration lists contain town of origin.

U.S. life-cycle records: Birth, marriage, and death certificates. Some contain precise place of origin.

Social security application: An older relative may be able to obtain a parent's Application Form SS-5. This form asks for "Birthplace" and often the town name is filled in.

World War I draft registration cards, 1917–1918: This is for men born between 1886 and 1897, both citizens and aliens. The card gives the exact place of birth: city or town, state or province, and country.

Passport applications: Again, an older relative applying for a passport for his or her parent could be helpful.

Obituary notices: Obituary notices will often list the place of birth and other important information, including the names and places of residence of next of kin. Check the secular newspapers beginning on the day after the death for about a week. Sometimes the obituaries are not printed on a timely basis. Some Jewish newspapers also carry obituaries.

Alien registration: This was required of all noncitizens after 1941. Write to INS, Freedom of Information, Room 5304, 425 I Street NW, Washington, DC 20536; (202) 514-1554.

FINDING RECORDS IN THE OLD COUNTRY

There is no master list for vital records offices in Eastern Europe. The only way to find the address and phone numbers of an office you're interested in is to call information for that specific town.

In Eastern Europe especially, access to information can be difficult to obtain, especially for a beginner. Which is not to say that you shouldn't try. If you have gotten all the records you can get in the United States and want to go to this next challenging level of genealogy research, here are some tips to get you started:

1. Look for anyone in your local Jewish genealogy society who has had experience and success in doing research in your particular corner of the old country. A conversation with such a person can result in a number of good leads and helpful suggestions.

2. Check to see if there is a special interest group (SIG) for the town or country where you want to do your research. Some of the SIG's have information about doing research in the area they are concerned with.

3. Find a local genealogist "freelancer" in the area that you want to research. He or she will have a great deal of information about local records resources and can serve as your hands and feet. Your local Jewish genealogy society or SIG may be able to provide a few references.

4. Check current and back issues of *Avotaynu* for information about researching your country of interest. You may also find ads placed by researchers who specialize in document searches in your area of interest.

5. Check your local Family History Library. They may already have the documents that you want in their archives.

You Found Your Russian Great-Grandmother's Birth Certificate! It's in Russian!

At some point in your research, you are going to come up with a birth certificate, a Yizkor book, a letter, a photograph with strange writing on it, or something else in a language that you don't know. This is not cause for concern. There are many different services that you can take advantage of that will translate the documents or other information for you. Here are some options.

1. Check with your local Jewish genealogy society. There may be members who make their services available to other members. If not, the society will probably have a list of local translators whom you can contact.

2. If you are near a large university, the university may have professors and students who accept translation work in the language area you require.

3. If the material is in Russian and you live in an area that has experienced recent Russian immigration, check with a local synagogue or with a local resettlement organization to see if there are any recent émigrés who might be able to do a translation for you.

4. Check the JewishGen Web site. JewishGen maintains a list of translators and professional genealogists.

OTHER LINKS TO YOUR FAMILY'S ROOTS

Landsmanshaften

Landsmanshaften were organizations created by people from a specific geographic area—a village, a town, or city in the old country. These organizations helped immigrants adjust to their new country and often provided material help as well as emotional support and opportunities to socialize. An important function was to provide cemetery plots and burial at a reasonable cost for members. Although most of these organizations are no longer in operation, their records may offer important clues to details about your family members.

One of the ways to track down information about landsmanshaften is to visit the office of the cemetery where members of your family are buried. If they are buried in the plot of a landsmanshaft, the cemetery office can give you the name of the organization and tell you if it is still functioning. If it is still in business, there will be a contact person you can call. You can also obtain a copy of the organization's plot with the names of all those who are buried there.

Another term for these organizations is *Verein*—pronounced to rhyme with "wine."

Cemeteries

Cemeteries are an excellent source of genealogical information. If your family is buried in a plot that was purchased by a special interest group—a verein, landsmanshaft, fraternal organization, or synagogue—the name of that organization will be prominently displayed at the gravesite.

Moscow Jewish Heritage Center

The Jewish Heritage Society is an academic institution devoted to the general research of Jewish history in Eastern Europe. It is not concerned specifically with Jewish genealogy. However, its resources and programs may help to fill in parts of your puzzle in other ways. It's worth checking into. The center can be reached online at the following address: http://www.glasnet.ru/~heritage/start.htm. The street address: Novocheremushkinskaya Ulitsa, 1/14-3-12, Moscow 117449 Russia; telephones: 7-095-503-78-45, 7-095-316-99-30; E-mail: heritage@glas.apc.org.

The society recommends the following professional Russian genealogists and resources:

Jewish Genealogy Society in Moscow: jgsm51@glas.apc.org

Vladimir Palej, genealogist: vaadinfo@rosnet.rosmail.msk.su

Anton Valdin, genealogist: geneal@geneal.msk.ru

Dmitry Panov, genealogist: proband@glas.apc.org

PROFESSIONAL HELP

The wonderful thing about undertaking the project of creating a family history is that most people can accomplish a great deal with the investment of relatively little time and money. If you should run out of time or patience, there are well-trained professionals who can pick up the trail and accomplish a great deal on your behalf.

There are many genealogists who advertise their services. You can find their names through your local yellow pages, on the Internet, and through published resources such as this book. Professional genealogists are paid for their services, usually in relation to the amount of time that they put into the search. There are a number of things that you can do to keep the cost of the search within the range of your budget. Here are some suggestions:

1. Before you begin, ask the genealogist about the most suitable format for your passing along the information you have already collected. If you give him or her the information in a way that is easiest to work with, you will save the time of your genealogist reorganizing the files and documents you have worked so hard to compile. It's cheaper for you to do this.

2. Give all the information to the genealogist you are working with in a well-organized, typed, or neatly written document. Why pay for someone to try to decipher your handwriting?

3. Make sure that all the information that you give to the genealogist is accurate. If you are not sure about the accuracy of certain items, note this next to the specific item in question.

4. Be specific about exactly what you would like the genealogist to do. By limiting the parameters of your search, you can limit your costs. You may want to specify a search for a specific geographic area, a certain number of generations, or a specific relative or family line. As you begin to get results, you can always reevaluate your initial goals and expand the search if it seems that to do so would bring meaningful results.

5. Be clear about the cost of a project. It's best to decide what your budget is or what fee you can afford before hiring a professional. Find out how much research can be done within your budget. For example, if your budget is five hundred dollars, ask what results the genealogist feels are achievable within your budget range. Remember that out-of-pocket expenses are almost always additional.

   Your understanding of your financial obligations should include the way in which out-of-pocket expenses for travel, document fees, phone, fax, and other costs will be handled. Come to a clear agreement about when fees and out-of-pocket expenses should be paid and what results you expect to receive for your investment.

6. Set some type of limit on the amount of out-of-pocket expenses that you will pay for a particular project. One way to do this is to agree to a certain amount of money that you're willing to spend per month. Another way to control out-of-pocket expenses is first to approve each out-of-pocket expenditure over a certain amount of money. You should always require documentation for out-of-pocket expenses—receipts, notated phone bills, and expense reports.

7. Create a letter of agreement for you and the genealogist stating the parameters of the search, the cost per hour for the project, and your agreements on payment and out-of-pocket expenses. Both you and the genealogist should sign this letter and retain a copy. This letter will help forestall any misunderstandings at a later time. If changes are made to your working agreement, these revisions should be documented in another letter.

Professional genealogists are people with individual personalities, different styles of working, and their own idea of what constitutes reasonable compensation. In addition, many professional genealogists specialize in a particular type of search. It's important to find a person who meets your search needs, your own way of working and thinking about genealogy, and whose prices are affordable for you.

It's a good idea to interview a few different genealogists over the phone to get an idea of who's around and what their prices are. In addition, you should ask if they are personally affiliated with a Jewish genealogical society and if they specialize in Jewish genealogy. Many professional genealogists, but not all, are members of either the Association of Professional Genealogists (APG) or the Board for Certification of Genealogists (BCG). Each of these organizations has its own code of ethics. Members are expected to observe these rules of conduct.

In the Resource chapter is a list of some genealogists who work in the area of Jewish genealogy. For other names, you might want to look at the JewishGen Web site. For other recommendations, contact: Association of Professional Genealogists, 3421 M Street NW, Suite 236, Washington, DC 20007.

In the next chapter, we'll look at ways in which to make your genealogical research come alive.

13

Visiting Your Roots

No amount of collecting documents, photographs, and other people's reminiscences can substitute for a trip to the old country. Strolling along the streets where your ancestors walked can give you a new appreciation of your relatives, of the forces that shaped them, and of the texture of the life they lived before emigrating.

When I was growing up, I used to ask my grandmother if she and my grandfather ever thought of making a trip back to Russia to see the family and friends they had left behind. I remember my grandmother telling me, even though they were now American citizens, she and my grandfather were afraid that, once back in Russia, they would not be permitted to leave again. I remember that sentiment being shared by many of my grandparents' relatives and friends, especially those who came to the United States during the 1920s.

Even though I was a child of five or six at the time, my grandparents' fear of returning to their homeland for a visit aroused in me a burning desire to see this mysterious country. When I actually had the chance to visit my grandmother's shtetl near Kiev a few years ago, I was profoundly moved.

It was winter, a season I always think of as being distinctly Russian. I saw Russian crows and the shadows they cast and understood, for the first time, the many folk stories in which old women turn into crows, and crows into old women. By visiting my grandmother's shtetl and walking where she once walked, I came to understand so many things about her life, her fears, the things she embraced, and her view of the world. My only regret was that I had just a few short hours to explore the town. It was an experience I will never forget.

Visiting the old country is not easy, however, especially if one's roots are in Eastern Europe. A trip to that part of the world is quite different than one to England or Paris. There are many details that must be arranged beforehand, especially visas and, in some cases, letters of invitation. In addition, unlike most of Western Europe, where you can expect to find English speakers, English may not spoken in the country or village that you propose to visit. For this reason, expert help is strongly recommended if you plan to make such a trip.

Another thing to keep in mind: Many American tourists may not be used to the travel accommodations in Eastern Europe, even those in very good hotels. A spirit of adventure and the willingness to let go of preconceived or cherished notions about what makes a "good vacation" is necessary to truly enjoy your trip. Visiting your roots is not a vacation; rather, it's a journey back in time. If it's approached in this way, it will be an experience never to be forgotten.

When taking this type of trip, it's important to be careful about what you eat and drink. You should never drink any water that is not bottled or that you haven't seen boiled in front of you. Also, you may not be able to use either American currency or travelers checks in many places. Even credit cards may prove problematic. Unless you are a very experienced traveler, the best way to make this kind of trip is either with the assistance of a travel agency that specializes in Jewish tours to these areas, or with a native-speaking guide who can help clear the way for you.

A company that specializes in this type of trip is Routes to Roots, headed by prominent Jewish genealogist Miriam Weiner. Her company offers customized tours to towns in Poland, Ukraine, Moldova, and

Belarus. A full range of travel services, including trained guide/translators and driver/security personnel can be provided. In addition, an advance trip can be made to the places you want to visit to locate people who may remember your family, to search the Jewish cemetery for your family names, and to find appropriate accommodations.

Routes to Roots can be reached online at http://www.routestoroots. com or you can fax them at (201) 864-9222. Be sure to include your estimated travel dates, countries and towns of destination, number of people traveling, and your name, address, telephone/fax number, and E-mail address.

Another way to plan a trip to seek out your roots is to contact the consulate in New York or the embassy in Washington, D.C. of the country you plan to visit. These addresses and phone numbers are not widely available on the Internet through Web sites, but you can get this information by searching the yellow pages online. You can also obtain this information through regular directory assistance. Each consulate is set up a little differently, but if you explain to the operator the purpose of your call, eventually you will get to talk to someone who may be able to help you.

You can also get information about traveling to your ancestral hometown by phoning the national airline that serves that country. In addition, some countries, like Poland, have sophisticated Web sites where you can access information about travel agencies that specialize in trips to that country. Search the Web for these sites by the keyword "travel" and the name of the country that you want to visit. Keep in mind that these agencies may not be oriented toward Jewish travel.

To find Jewish travel agencies on the Web, go to a search engine and use the keywords "Jewish travel." Keep in mind that a general tour, even to your country of interest, may not give you time to make the special journey you have in mind. This is something to discuss with the tour company beforehand. Also, it's important to note that most tours that are advertised as "Jewish" are usually kosher. If this is not what you have in mind, you may be more comfortable on a tour sponsored by a different type of company.

To find Jewish travel agencies without going on the Web, you might want to check with your local branch of UJA-Federation. UJA (United Jewish Appeal) sponsors trips all over the world and has excellent travel contacts. You can reach UJA by mail, or you can go to their Web site: http://www.uja.org for information, or call the following numbers: National (212) 284-6500; Northeast Region (201) 489-2700; Southeast Region (954) 428-6677; Midwest Region (312) 427-1600; Western Region (818) 386-0100. To contact UJA by mail, write to UJA Federations of North America, Suite 11E, 111 Eighth Avenue, New York, NY 10011.

Another great contact is the Jewish Travel Network. It provides a wide variety of travel services including bed and breakfast listings, home exchanges, and business networking around the world for Jewish travelers. It can be reached on the Internet at http://www.jewish-travel-net.com; or by telephone: (650) 368-0880, or fax (650) 599-9066.

For additional information, there are a number of books available that deal with Jewish travel. These can be found through Amazon and Barnes and Noble and in many travel bookstores. In addition, there is an online Jewish travel magazine called *Jewish Travel* that has a Web page on Jewish travel books as well as some other, limited information. They can be reached at their address: http://www.jewishtravel.com.

Another place to look for help with your plans is *Moment* magazine. *Moment* usually carries a number of ads for companies that specialize in Jewish travel. In addition, from time to time, the magazine runs a travel section. You can reach *Moment* at their Web site: http://www.momentmag.com, or by mail or phone: 4740 41st Street, NW, Washington, DC 20016; (202) 364-3300.

PLACES OF PERSONAL AND JEWISH INTEREST TO VISIT IN THE OLD COUNTRY

If you're planning your own itinerary, there are a number of places that you will want to investigate. For visits to places like a synagogue, museum, or other Jewish landmark, it may be necessary to make an appointment in advance. These arrangements should be made as far in advance as possible and confirmed in writing.

If you plan to try to do some records or document research while visiting the old country, you might want to contact a local genealogist for help in arranging this part of your trip. This person may also be able to accompany you to the local records office and act as an intermediary and translator. If you have brought lipstick, fragrances, and American dollar bills with you, you may find that these will be helpful in greasing the wheels of Eastern European bureaucracy.

You may also want to bring a copy of a photograph taken before your family emigrated. Showing this photograph to Jewish people who might have known your family is a long shot, but you can never predict the results. As I explained earlier, when I was in Skvira, my grandmother's shtetl in the Ukraine, I showed a photograph of my grandmother's family—her grandparents, parents, and siblings—to a clerk at the "department store." The result was an invitation to the clerk's home for lunch so that I could meet her husband, the author of a book about the history of Skvira. Allowing for serendipity will make your trip a wonderful experience.

Here are some suggestions for places that could be interesting to visit on your trip.

Synagogue, or remains of the synagogue. In some towns, the building that was the synagogue is now something else. In Hungary, many synagogues have been restored, but are now used as community centers for concerts and other cultural events. In some cases, these buildings also house the town's Jewish museum or Jewish archives.

Mikvah or the remains of the mikvah

Matzah factory

Local Jewish Holocaust memorial. In Kiev, the central Holocaust Memorial in commemoration of the events of Baba Yar, in which a large percentage of the local Jewish population was slaughtered by German and Ukrainian soldiers and thrown into mass graves, is not a Jewish memorial. Actually, it says nothing about Jews, although there's an inscription in Yiddish. This memorial is in a large park.

If you want to visit the historical site of the Baba Yar massacre and the Jewish memorial there, you will need some cooperation from the local

Jewish community. The local Jewish agency representative or Israeli consulate can give you directions. The memorial is not centrally located and is somewhat difficult to find unless you know where you are going.

Excising Jews from Holocaust memorials was very common in Eastern Europe after the war. When such memorials were government subsidized, they tended to be nationalistic and supportive of communist values, which, by definition, repressed religious affiliation.

The monument at Bronnaya Gora, near Baranovichi, which is about halfway between Brest and Minsk in Belarus, is somewhat better than most of these memorials because it was erected after the fall of communism. It is inscribed in Belarusan and reads "More than 50,000 Soviet citizens and citizens of Eastern Europe primarily of Jewish nationality were brutally murdered by the Fascists during the Great Patriotic War, 1941–1945." From a Jewish perspective, the term "Great Patriotic War," rather than "Holocaust," or even "World War II," rings a somewhat uncomfortable note.

Sometimes a town's Jewish Holocaust memorial is located in the Jewish cemetery. I found such a memorial in the Jewish cemetery in Skvira.

Local Jewish museum. There are now quite a few of these in Eastern Europe. Often they are housed in a local synagogue or in a building that had been a synagogue. In Budapest, the Dohany Street Synagogue, also called the Great Synagogue, is in the process of being restored as both a spiritual center and a museum. At the back of the building is a moving memorial to Hungary's Holocaust victims, the Weeping Willow Memorial Tree. Each leaf on the tree is engraved with the names of Holocaust victims. It is dedicated to the 600,000 Hungarian Jews who died in the Holocaust and to those who died saving the lives of others.

Some museums are well endowed and have many Jewish artifacts. Others have very little. A Jewish friend of mine in Poland, who became the Jewish leader in his town, told me that in order to create an exhibit about Shabbat for their local museum, he handmade an havdalah candle because none could be purchased locally and no one living in the town owned one. An havdalah candle is a multiwicked, braided candle that is used in the service that is performed at the end of Shabbat. The ceremony, called *havdalah,* which means "to separate," divides the sacred time of the Sabbath and the nonsacred work week.

Present Jewish community center. In many cases, the community center is run by the Jewish Agency, an arm of the Israeli government that is responsible for a wide variety of activities, including education in the Diaspora and the preparation of individuals to immigrate to Israel.

Neighborhood where the Jewish community lived at the time that your ancestors were in residence.

Jewish cemetery. Jewish cemeteries abroad are very different from American cemeteries. Most of the gravesites are maintained, or not maintained, by family members. Although there may be an office and an office worker available, most of the time it is difficult to get information from this source. A local expert can help you a great deal here. Also, be prepared to tip the cemetery attendant liberally for any help that he or she may give you. It may help to indicate your willingness to be generous before making your specific request.

In fairness to the people who hold these jobs, this is not a well-paying occupation. The woman who was responsible for the Jewish cemetery in Skvira had her feet wrapped in rags. It was the middle of winter.

Present Jewish neighborhood, if one exists.

Present-day Jewish schools, restaurants, and businesses. If you see older people, you might ask if they knew your family.

Local hall of records, to do onsite research with the assistance of your guide/translator of a local Jewish genealogist.

The house/street where your ancestors lived. You may be able to find such a place if you can locate the birth certificate of a relative that was born in that town. People were born at home in the "old days" and the address or a location of the house may be on the birth certificate.

CONNECTING WITH THE EUROPEAN JEWISH COMMUNITY

If you decide to plan a trip to the country your ancestors came from, you might enjoy meeting Jews who still live there or in the area. Such meetings can greatly enhance your understanding of your family's homeland. In addition, you may be fortunate in meeting people who knew your family or who know descendents of your relatives with whom you have not yet been in touch. You may even find some relatives.

Another possibility is to arrange to spend Shabbat or part of a Jewish holiday with a Jewish family in the area, or to worship with the local Jewish community. Doing so will give you a real feeling for the lives of the Jewish people who live in that area. In addition, you may be able to get a sense of what Jewish life was like when your relatives lived there. Meeting real people and sharing their lives, even for only a few hours, will greatly enhance the quality and texture of your experience. You will certainly meet new friends and perhaps even reestablish some roots for yourself in the old country.

One way to make contact with the Jewish community is through a local rabbi. As a member of the Jewish community, you have the right to call, write, or fax and say, "I'm going to be in your area on this date and I would like to spend some time with the Jewish community." Most rabbis will respond positively to your request and will try to work something out. It's best to make this connection as far in advance as possible. Rabbis are not always easy to contact.

When you are making the arrangements for your visit with the rabbi, be sure to ask what the rabbi would like you to bring as a gift to the local Jewish community or to needy individuals. Some rabbis may be hesitant to make suggestions. However, persistence on your part should eventually elicit the information you want. Jewish books, audio tapes, and children's toys are always appreciated and appropriate. You should also plan to make a financial contribution to the rabbi's discretionary fund, if he or she has one, or to the local synagogue, if one exists. It's entirely proper to ask the rabbi if he or she has a discretionary fund. The amount of the donation should reflect your appreciation of the rabbi's efforts on your behalf.

How to find a rabbi? The World Union for Progressive Judaism has a list of names, phone, and fax numbers for rabbis with congregations outside the United States. This information appears later in this chapter. In addition, all the movements—Reform, Conservative, Reconstructionist, and Orthodox—have affiliated rabbinic organizations that maintain membership directories. A call to one of these organizations may help you find a rabbi in the area to which you're traveling. The names and contact information of these organizations appear in the resource list at the end of this book.

Another possibility is to contact your local UJA office. It may have contacts "on the ground" in the area where you're traveling who can arrange home visits and facilitate other meetings with the Jewish community in or near the town you're visiting. Yet another organization that may be able to aid you is the Jewish Agency in Israel.

The Jewish Agency maintains information and education centers all around the world. Their Web site, http://www.jaz.org.il/aliyah/index.html has a link to a page that contains information about the location of all these centers and how they can be reached. This Web page can also be reached directly at the address: http://www.jazo.org.il/aliyah/emi.html. The Jewish Agency also has offices throughout the United States that are listed on the Jewish Agency Web site. Below is a list of some of the Jewish Agency offices across the country.

Atlanta J.C.C., 1745 Peachtree Road, NE, Atlanta, GA 30309; (404) 873-1248

Israel Aliyah Center, 6600 Lincoln Ave., Lincolnwood, IL 60645; (708) 674-8861

Jewish Community Federation, 1750 Euclid Ave., Cleveland, OH 44415; (216) 566-9200

Allied Jewish Federation of Denver, 300 S. Dahlia St., Denver, CO 80222; (303) 321-3399

Israel Aliyah Center, 9647 Hillcroft, Suite 403, Houston, TX 77096; (713) 728-7686

Israel Aliyah Center, 6505 Wilshire Blvd., Los Angeles, CA 90048; (213) 655-7881

Israel Aliyah Center, 4200 Biscayne Blvd., Miami, FL 33137; (305) 573-2556

Israel Aliyah Center, 1360 N. Prospect Avenue, Milwaukee, WI 33137; (414) 271-8338

Israel Community Center, 4330 Cedar Lake Road S., Minneapolis, MN 55418; (612) 374-5242

Israel Program Center, 901 Route 10, Whippany, NJ 07981-1156; (201) 884-4800

Israel Aliyah Center, 110 E. 59th Street, New York, NY 10022; (212) 339-6000/6063

Israel Program Center, 401 Grand Avenue, 5th Floor, Oakland, CA 94610; (510) 839-2900

NEVER VISIT A PERSON'S HOME WITHOUT BRINGING A GIFT

How many times did you hear this when you were growing up? The roots of this tradition for Jews are not in Emily Post but in the Torah.

In Genesis 18:1, Abraham is visited by three messengers from God. He welcomes them into his tent, gives them water, prepares a lavish feast, and takes care of all their needs. As a reward for Abraham's hospitality, Sarah, who was previously barren and who is beyond child-bearing age, is blessed with a baby, Isaac. This story is the text upon which the mitzvah (the commandment) of hospitality and the rules for being a good guest are based.

Judaism is more than a religion. Judaism is a way of life. When a law creates difficulties, the "common people" usually find a way, although it may be "unofficial," to make the law work in combination with the realities of everyday life. While it's fine to say that one must wine and dine a visitor, the reality for most Jews throughout much of our history was that their means to entertain a guest might be limited. It's from this real-life situation that the custom of bringing your host a gift of food or drink or something else that might be in short supply probably originated. By bringing such a gift when you visit someone, you are able to reciprocate the blessing of hospitality with the gift of a deed of loving kindness, another mitzvah. With this in mind, when you plan a trip to visit the old country, you might want to think about what you can bring to your hosts, the local Jewish community.

In America, even Jews who are somewhat geographically isolated have access to any and all types of Judaica, Jewish books, audio tapes, and ritual objects. For Jews living in Eastern Europe and especially in parts of the former Soviet Union, the situation is very different. Not only do they have difficulty in obtaining things that American Jews take for granted, like kippot, prayer books, havdalah candles, and Chanukah menorahs, but they often lack basic health necessities like aspirin, antibiotic ointments, and over-the-counter medicines. Things that are common and inexpensive items for us like lipstick, stockings, deodorant, nice soaps, men's and women's fragrances, and even toothpaste are often in short supply and expensive when they can be found.

If you plan to take a trip to Eastern Europe or the Former Soviet Union, you might want to consider finding out what the needs of the local community are and then doing what you can to make a contribution of these things. The local office of the Jewish Agency can be helpful in guiding you in what is most needed. Another organization that may be helpful is the World Union for Progressive Judaism (WUPJ).

The World Union is the organizing body for Reform and liberal congregations outside of the United States. One of its priorities is to place Reform rabbis in congregations outside the United States. Because of this, WUPJ maintains a directory of Reform and liberal synagogues around the world. There are several of these communities in Eastern Europe and parts of the former Soviet Union.

To reach the World Union for help in connecting with a Jewish community abroad or for suggestions on what to take on your trip to a particular community, log on to their Web site at: http://rj.org/wupj. The World Union has offices in New York City with ARZA (American Reform Zionist Association) in the building of the Union of American Hebrew Congregations. Its address is 633 Third Avenue, New York, NY 10017-6778. The phone number is (212) 650-4090. In addition to its New York office, the World Union maintains headquarters in Jerusalem. That address is: 13 King David Street, Jerusalem, 94101, Israel. The E-mail address is: wupjis@netvision.net.

Another organization that does a great deal of work with Jews in Eastern Europe is the Union of Councils for Soviet Jews. This national organization supplies a wide variety of services to Jewish communities in all parts of the former Soviet Union. The union's national headquarters is in Washington, D.C. It can be reached at: 1819 H Street NW, No. 230, Washington, DC 20006; (202) 775-9770.

There are local "Action" centers around the United States that are affiliated with the national organization. A particularly active center where the people are very knowledgeable about what's happening abroad is Chicago Action for Soviet Jewry, 555 Pine Avenue, Suite 107, Highland Park, IL 60035; (708) 433-0144. If you want to do something good for the people you'll be meeting, give Chicago Action a call.

14

Genealogy and the Holocaust— A Reflection

 The history of the Jewish people is one of wandering, war, dislocation, persecution, and an abiding faith that someday the messiah will come and bring perfect and lasting peace to us and to all the world. Our history is also one of great achievement and "golden ages" of secular success and religious and secular learning. Jews have made unique contributions to the world. The Jewish people have overcome adversity and mind- and soul-numbing hardship with passion, power, love, and hope.

Throughout the millennia we have maintained our covenant with the Holy One whose name we never utter. Even in the aftermath of the Holocaust, we did not proclaim, as others did, that God was dead. Instead, some Jewish theologians posited that, during the Holocaust, God suffered and, overcome with grief, was unable to look at the suffering that human beings afflicted on one another.

The words *Never again* have a special resonance for Jews living in the second half of the twentieth century. They are not merely words of defiance. "Never again" compels personal commitment, a renewed covenant with God, and with the Jewish world. Each Jew who utters the words *never again* with an understanding of their meaning cannot help but begin to search for his or her special mission within the Jewish community and our world.

The response of the Jewish community to these words is as varied as the community itself. For some Jews, they are a call to repopulate the Jewish world by having many children. For other segments of the Jewish community, "never again" has led to efforts to embrace those Jews and Jewish families who, in the past, were not welcome—interfaith families, interracial families, gay and lesbian Jews, and the unconverted children of interfaith families. Still other segments of the Jewish world have devoted themselves to education and outreach to secular Jews. Some Jews put the words *never again* into action by dedicating themselves to working for Jewish and humanitarian causes.

For me, coming to terms with the words *never again* was an important motivating force in my spiritual journey. Those were words that led me to rabbinical school and to a "ministry" working with Jews in far-flung parts of the globe. Other colleagues have been inspired to work for change within the Jewish community, for improved religious and cultural education for our children and adults, and for equal access for and treatment of women in all phases of Jewish life.

What does this have to do with genealogy?

The rabbis teach us that saving one life is equivalent to saving the entire world. What does it mean to save a life? The most obvious meaning is saving someone from physical death. However, physical death is not the only kind of death with which Judaism is concerned. We also believe that as long as someone remembers a person who has died, in a very real way the "life" of the deceased is prolonged. When we say kaddish for someone who as died, either during the year of mourning, at the time of the deceased's yahrzeit or at a Yizkor service, we demonstrate that we still remember him or her, and so that person's essence continues to live with us.

When we undertake the sacred work of genealogy, we are literally "raising the dead." Through our efforts, we are restoring the memory of a relative to life. Whether we then take on the obligation to say kaddish for that person is immaterial. By adding an individual to our family tree, we are making sure that future generations will never forget that person's life.

For much of my life I believed that the Holocaust had not touched me personally through the loss of relatives. My German ancestors had come to America in the late 1880s. Some even immigrated earlier. My Russian ancestors came to America in the 1920s, and those who were left behind survived the war. It wasn't until I was in rabbinical school that I began to question this idea. I knew almost nothing about my German relatives except that some of them had immigrated to South America during the war and that there was a distant relative, Hans Summerfeld from South Africa, who once visited my father in the United States. I began to wonder. Were there cousins left behind somewhere?

Along with this question, I began to consider what I really knew about the Holocaust. For some reason, I always focused on Germany as a source of concern. But as I began to study the Holocaust I realized that its impact on Russia and especially on the Ukraine, was dramatic. Some of my maternal grandmother's family had stayed behind. And what about my maternal grandfather's extended family? Suddenly the Holocaust had a new meaning and a new urgency for me. What happened to those families? Did they survive the war? If they did, where were they now?

This new consciousness put genealogy in an entirely different light for me. I no longer felt that I was involved in a project that was just "interesting." I now felt that I was on a journey to "save a life." I wanted to find my Russian and German living relatives, if they existed. But I also felt an obligation to discover if, like so many Americans, I had relatives that I had lost in the Holocaust. If so, I wanted to redeem them, add them to my family tree, and say kaddish for them. So far I've not been able to find traces of my Russian and German relatives, but I'm committed to continuing my search.

Contrary to a widely held belief, many family records survived the Holocaust. In addition, German records of individuals who fell under their control have been preserved. And with the opening of many archives in the former Soviet Union, new information surfaces every day. We are also experiencing a time in history when there seems to be a growing willingness to study the Holocaust. As a result, the compiling and recording of Holocaust-related documents is a quickly growing undertaking for many organizations and individuals.

This is all good news for the Jewish genealogist. Combine this renewed interest in Holocaust documentation with the power of cyberspace, and we have a Holocaust information explosion. What follows is just the tip of the iceberg. Some of this information is directly related to the practice of genealogy. However, I've also included Web sites, museums, and organizations that offer general information about the Holocaust. Very often, when a genealogist does background historical research, unexpected genealogical clues appear.

HOLOCAUST-RELATED SITES ON THE INTERNET

United States Holocaust Memorial Museum
http://www.ushmm.org
This is the official Web site for the Unites States Holocaust Memorial Museum. Besides listing information of interest to those wishing to visit the museum, it provides a link to the museum's searchable resources and provides links to other important Holocaust-related organizations. For genealogists, one of the most important resources of the museum is the *Benjamin and Vladka Meed Registry of Jewish Holocaust Survivors*. These include:

The Shoah Museum in Belgium (in English)
http://www.cicb.be/shoah/welcome.html

The Topography of Terror Foundation, Berlin
http://www.dhm.de/ausstellungen/ns_gedenk
    This organization has published *Overview of Memorial Museums for the Victims of the Nazi-Regime in Germany*. The overview is published in English and German.

The Simon Wiesenthal Center   http://www.wiesenthal.com/
    This is an international center for Holocaust remembrance and the defense of human rights (in English).

Yad Vashem   http://www.yad-vashem.org.il

Yad Vashem is the national Holocaust memorial of Israel. Through this site, one has access to the Hall of Names. One can also do online requests or searches, and get information from the Yad Vashem archives.

The Concentration Camp Memorial of Mauthausen
http://www.mauthausen-memorial.gv.at

This site offers information about the memorial and a history of the concentration camp Mauthausen.

In 1981, the American Gathering of Jewish Holocaust Survivors established a national registry to document the lives of survivors who came to the United States after the Second World War. In April 1993, the registry was transferred to the United States Holocaust Memorial Museum in Washington, D.C. There are over 100,000 records now in the registry, which is located on the fifth floor of the museum, in the United States Holocaust Research Institute. The registry is open to the public seven days a week from 10:00 A.M. until 5:00 P.M. The goals of the registry are to include the names of all Holocaust survivors, to facilitate contacts between survivors, collect and display basic information about survivors, and assist survivors and their families in their attempts to trace missing relatives.

To request a registration form or other information, you can contact the Survivor's Registry by calling (202) 488-6130 or writing to the Survivor's Registry, United States Holocaust Memorial Museum, 100 Raoul Wallenberg Place, SW, Washington, DC 20024-2150.

Genealogists will also benefit from the museum's *Oral History and Yizkor Book Collection*, which is housed in the library. Many of these histories have only recently been published. The library has also developed a major collection of Yizkor books that preserve the memory of families and cultural life of many towns destroyed during the Holocaust.

The museum, through its Web site, also offers other information of interest and provides a link to the museum's searchable resources as well as other important Holocaust related organizations and their resources. Some of these include:

The Shoah Museum in Belgium (in English)

http://www.cicb.be/shoah/welcome.html

This site covers the deportation of Belgian Jews and their resistance. The museum and the Web site include information about Jewish life before the Holocaust, the history of the Holocuast, Belgium under the German occupation, and liberation. Personal testimonies are also presented.

The Topography of Terror Foundation, Berlin

http://www.dhm.de/ausstellungen/ns_gedenk

This organization has published *Overview of Memorial Museums for the Victims of the Nazi-Regime in Germany*. The overview is published in English and German.

The Simon Wiesenthal Center

http://www.wiesenthal.com/

9760 West Pico Blvd., Los Angeles, CA 90035; (800) 900-9036; E-mail: webmaster@wiesenthal.com

The Simon Wiesenthal Center is an international center for Holocaust remembrance and education and for the defense of human rights and the rights of the Jewish people. It hosts an active Web site with a wide variety of information pages about the Holocaust.

Yad Vashem

http://www.yad-vashem.org.il

P.O. Box 3477, 91034 Jerusalem, Israel 02-751611

Yad Vashem, Israel's Holocaust memorial museum, is the primary international organization for compiling information about the Holocaust. It has a museum, a library, an archive, and a special memorial called the "Hall of Names." Its library of over 100,000 volumes includes over one thousand Yizkor books. In addition, the archives contain original source material, much of which is organized by town.

The Hall of Names houses the Pages of Testimony. This is a manuscript collection of more than 3 million pages of information about victims written primarily by relatives of Holocaust victims and survivors. Each page of testimony contains the names of parents, spouse, and children; birth and death dates and places; and the name, address, and relationship of the person who submitted the information.

When visiting the Web site, one can also do online requests or searches and get information about submission of information to the Yad Vashem archives. It is also possible to do this when visiting the museum in person.

Survivors of the Shoah Visual History Foundation
http://www.vhf.org/
Shoan Foundation, P.O. Box 3168, Los Angeles, CA 90078-3168;
(818) 777-4673
This is Steven Spielberg's project of video-taping and archiving interviews of Holocaust survivors all over the world. Founded by Spielberg in 1994 as a nonprofit organization, interviews are catalogued and archived using breakthrough digital technology and will be made available online.

Cybrary of the Holocaust
http://remember.org/cylinks.html
This is an extremely rich Web site for those interested in Holocaust research, offering a great number of links as well as its own very interesting material. Of special interest to genealogists is the Resources for Children of Holocaust Survivors site at http://www.idot.aol.com/judy/Causes/cosh.htm. This extensive resource is for Children of Survivors, with numerous links and excellent references. "It is not about the legacy; it is about living with the legacy."

Association of Holocaust Organizations
http://www.ushmm.org/uia-bin/uia_list/sites.lst
This organization has over 120 members worldwide. A full listing of their members, with addresses and phone numbers, is available on its Web site, which is sponsored by the U.S. Holocaust Memorial Museum. For noncomputer folks, a copy of this list can be obtained by writing, faxing, or calling: Director, Holocaust Resource Center and Archives, Queensborough Community College, The City University of New York, Bayside, NY 11364; (718) 225-0378; fax: (718) 631-6306; E-mail: hrcaho@dorsai.org.

The following are member organizations with collections of both general interest and genealogical interest.

A Living Memorial to the Holocaust—Museum of Jewish Heritage
This new museum has a full-scale exhibit and is in the process of developing its archives and other resources.
1 Battery Park Plaza
New York, NY 10004
(212) 968-1800
Fax: (212) 968-1368

Allentown Jewish Archives/Holocaust Resource Center   This center, which has a library of over five hundred volumes, collects and transcribes oral testimonies from Holocaust survivors and has both education and outreach programs. They also collect and classify Holocaust-related memorabilia.
702 N. 22nd Street
Allentown, PA 18104
(215) 821-5500
Fax: (215) 821-8946

American Gathering of Jewish Holocaust Survivors
122 W. 30th Street
New York, NY 10001
(212) 239-4230
Fax: (212) 279-2926

Hidden Child Foundation/ADL
823 United Nations Plaza
New York, NY 10017
(212) 885-7901

Holocaust Documentation and Education Center, Inc.   This facility has an archives and resource center with over 1,200 video tapes, audio tapes, and books. They have an active program of video-taping survivors, liberators, rescuers, and other witnesses to the Holocaust.

Florida International University North Miami Campus
3000 N.E. 145th Street
North Miami, FL 33181
(305) 919-5690
Fax: (305) 919-5691
E-mail: xholocau@servak.fiu.edu

Holocaust Resource Center and Archives—Queensborough Community College This is an outstanding "little" museum and research facility. Its library contains 7,500 volumes and 535 videotapes, all of which have been catalogued. Their archive contains 235 catalogued audio tapes as well as artifacts and a photographic collection. Their microfilm and microfiche collection includes doctoral dissertations, the *New York Times*, the *London Times*, and the *Jewish Chronicle*.
222-05 56th Avenue
Bayside, NY 11364
(718) 225-1617
Fax: (718) 631-6306
E-mail: hrcaho@dorsai.org

Joseph Meyerhoff Library, Baltimore Hebrew University
5800 Park Heights Avenue
Baltimore, MD 21215
(410) 578-6936
Fax: (410) 578-6940

The Dallas Memorial Center for Holocaust Studies This museum offers a research library and has an ongoing program of video-taping Holocaust survivors and liberators.
7900 Northaven Road
Dallas, TX 75230
(214) 750-4654
Fax: (214) 750-4672

The Holocaust Center of Northern California This museum has a library of over 2,500 volumes; 250 posters; and 150 films and videos. Their archive contains 750 audio and video oral histories; 3,000 pamphlets; and 2,500 photographs, documents, and artifacts related to the Holocaust. They also have a Yizkor book for Kosow Lacki, Poland, and a translation of the Kobrin, Poland, Yizkor book.

639 14th Avenue
San Francisco, CA 94118
(415) 751-6040, 751-6041
Fax: (415) 751-6983

The Kharkov Holocaust Memorial Centre and Museum
P.O. Box 4756
Kharkov 31002
Ukraine
0572/436887

The Society for the History of Czech-Slovak Jews, Inc.
c/o Temple Shalom of West Essex
760 Pompton Avenue
Cedar Grove, NJ 07009
(201) 239-2333

World Federation of Bergen-Belsen Associations
P.O. Box 232
Lenox Hill Station
New York, NY 10021
(212) 752-3387

Avotaynu   Avotaynu has a number of different materials of special interest to genealogists doing Holocaust research, including:

Index to Memorial to the Jews Deported From France. This is an alphabetic list of 50,000 surnames that appear in *Memorial to Jews Deported From France.* The index shows the person's surname and convoy number. It's available on microfiche.

Gedenkbuch (Koblenz, 1986). This collection lists 128,000 German Jews who died in the Holocaust. The listing includes birth date, the place deported from, the place deported to, and sometimes the death date. This covers former West Germany only.

HIAS (Hebrew Immigrant Aid Society)   HIAS, which was founded in 1880 to help Jews who were emigrating, assisted more than 70,000 families of the Holocaust. HIAS maintains case files on the people they helped. They will perform searches for a moderate fee.
http://www.hias.org/
333 Seventh Avenue
New York, NY 10001-5004
(212) 967-4100
E-mail: info@hias.org.

Holocaust and War Victims Tracing and Information Center   This is the liaison for Americans who wish to send search requests to the International Tracing Service.
American Red Cross
4700 Mount Hope Drive
Baltimore, MD 21215-3231
(410) 764-5311
E-mail: afoxson@arc-cmc.org

Holocaust Yizkor Books   Holocaust Yizkor (memorial) books are published histories of individual Eastern European Jewish communities that memorialize the town and its Holocaust victims. There is usually a narrative section on the town's history, culture, institutions, and rabbis, and sometimes a list of Holocaust victims, survivors, or emigrants. Most memorial books are entirely in Hebrew and/or Yiddish. Some have sections in English or other languages. Holocaust Yizkor books have been published for over one thousand towns.

As of the writing of this book, the most complete published bibliography is in Arthur Kurzweil's *From Generation to Generation*. The list was compiled by Zachary M. Baker in 1993. JewishGen has a Yizkor Book SIG, which can be reached online at http://www.jewish gen.org/yizkor.

Most Holocaust Yizkor books were published in the 1950s and 1960s in very limited quantities. This makes them both difficult to find and expensive to purchase. There are eleven institutions with Yizkor book collections in their libraries. See the Resource section for contact information.

The following establishments sell Yizkor books:

J. Robinson & Co.
31 Nachlat Benjamin Street
P.O. Box 4308
Tel Aviv 65162, Israel

Moshe Schreiber
Mea Sharim Street 16
Jerusalem, Israel

Chaim E. Dzialowski
P.O. Box 6413
Jerusalem 90163, Israel

Pinat Ha-Sefer
P.O. Box 46646
Haifa 31464, Israel

International Tracing Service (ITS)   This service was set up by the International Red Cross after World War II. It maintains 40 million index cards, mostly of survivors. Genealogical requests do not get fast attention. Yad Vashem has the same records on microfilm. These are available for personal genealogical research.

Grosse Allee 5–9
34454 Arolsen, Germany

National Archives, Military Archives Division   This division of NARA in Washington has microfilms of many captured German records from World War II, including concentration camp records. General phone number: (301) 457-7000. Or see page 293 for their Web site address.

Search Bureau for Missing Relatives   This is a finder's service focusing on finding relatives in Israel.

P.O. Box 92
Jerusalem 91000, Israel
02-612471; 02-612472

The Shoah Museum in Belgium (in English)   One out of two Jews in Belgium died during the Holocaust. This museum is dedicated to teaching about the Holocaust, Belgian Jewry, and Belgian Jewish resistance during World War II.

http://www.cicb.be/shoah/welcome.html
Goswin de Stassarstraat 153
B-2800 Mechelen, Belgium
32 (0) 15 29 06 60
Fax: 32 (0) 15 29 08 76
E-mail: infos@cicb.be

HOLOCAUST MUSEUMS

Sometimes visiting a place can create understanding where other types of study cannot. For example, many Jews have the custom of taking food to the cemetery for an unveiling and eating it after the ceremony. I have strong memories of this being done in the early 1960s when I attended my grandfather's unveiling. Although this is rarely done today, in some Jewish communities the custom still survives. But what is the origin of this tradition?

I had tried to find a written explanation, but was unsuccessful. Then, on a trip to work with the Jewish community in Alma-Ata, Khazakstan, I visited a Jewish cemetery. Most of the family plots contained a wrought-iron table and chairs. Suddenly, everything clicked. Most Jewish cemeteries are outside the city limits. Although we had traveled to the cemetery in a car, private cars are a luxury in most parts of the former Soviet Union. To get to the cemetery, most people took the bus. What was a forty-five-minute journey for us could easily take two hours or more each way for most people. For a funeral, cars are generally provided and mourners are supposed to return to the home immediately afterward for the meal of consolation. But if you are going to visit the grave of a loved one at a time other than a funeral, naturally you would want to take food so that you could eat your lunch!

It's a very short jump from this habit, deeply ingrained in most of our ancestors, to the generalization that, when one goes to a cemetery in America for a reason other than a funeral, one should take something to eat and drink. Interestingly, this tradition has evolved into one in which those attending the unveiling go together afterward to a nearby restaurant. There are even some enterprising businesspeople who have built large diners with group seating areas within easy driving distance of Jewish cemeteries.

This is a roundabout way of suggesting that going to a Holocaust museum offers insights into the experiences of our collective ancestors that are not possible to access in any other way. It may also help one who is genealogically inclined to find new ideas about tracing his or her Holocaust-related roots. Holocaust museums, by and large, make the experience real for those of us who did not experience it directly.

One of the most powerful tools used by the U.S. Holocaust Museum is a "passport" that one is given before the tour. Each passport has a name, photograph, and brief biography of a person who personally experienced the Holocaust. This personalization of the Shoah—the giving of a particular name and face—makes the journey through the museum an unforgettable experience.

Here are some Holocaust museums that were all established to make sure that the world never forgets.

The Museum of Tolerance   This museum is sponsored by the Simon Wiesenthal Center. An information resource center and the Wiesenthal Library are also located here. The Information Resource Center has materials on the Holocaust, anti-Semitism, racism, and other related issues. The Library contains 30,000 books and periodicals. The Archives is a primary research depository for materials dealing with the Holocaust and pre–World War II Jewish life. The Archives has documents, letters, manuscripts, personal narratives, diaries, artifacts, ghetto and concentration camp postage and money, liberation and occupation memorabilia, photographs, magazines, newspapers, maps, posters, rare books, pamphlets, and original artwork. This material is available to researchers, media, students, and the public.

9760 West Pico Blvd.

Los Angeles, CA 90035

(310) 553-8403

The C.A.N.D.L.E.S. Holocaust Museum—Children of Auschwitz Nazi Deadly Lab Experiments Survivors   The purpose of this museum is to educate the public about the horrors of the Holocaust, experiments that were performed on twins, and to tell the story of the children who survived.

1532 S. Third Street
Terre Haute, IN 47802
(812) 234-7881 or (812) 235-2665
http://www.candles-museum.com/
E-mail: Candles@abcs.com

Tampa Bay Holocaust Memorial Museum and Educational Center The Tampa Bay Holocaust Memorial Museum and Educational Center is dedicated to fostering education, public awareness, and understanding of the Holocaust. The museum contains art, photographs, and historical artifacts relating to the Holocaust. An interactive multimedia exhibit defines the history and heritage of the victims. In this exhibit, visitors are offered the opportunity to study the moral, ethical, and social issues raised by the Holocaust.

55 Fifth Street
St. Petersburg, FL 33701
(813) 820-0100
http://www.tampabayholocaust.org/

Holocaust Museum Houston   The goal of Holocaust Museum Houston is to promote an awareness of the dangers of prejudice, hatred, and violence. Besides its exhibits and collections, Holocaust Museum Houston houses the Ethel and Al Herzstein Theater, an eighty-eight-seat theater.

5401 Caroline Street
Houston, TX 77004
(713) 942-8000
http://www.hmh.org/

Holocaust Memorial Center—Detroit, Michigan   The Holocaust Memorial Center is on the grounds of the Jewish Community Campus in West Bloomfield, Michigan. Its mission is to preserve the memory of the Jewish people, the communities, and the heritage that perished in the Holocaust and to help future generations direct their lives toward the maintenance of an open and free society. This site was named as Michigan's number one historical site.

1998 Holocaust Memorial Center
6602 West Maple Road
West Bloomfield, MI 48322
(248) 661-0840
Fax: (248)661-4204
http://holocaustcenter.org
E-mail: info@holocaustcenter.org

El Paso Holocaust Museum and Study Center   The El Paso Holo-caust Museum and Study Center presents exhibits that chronicle the events that occurred during the Holocaust. The museum's mission is to combat prejudice and bigotry through education and to remind the world of the value and dignity of human life. A referral service provides speakers, including individuals who are liberators or survivors.

401 Wallenberg Drive
El Paso, TX 79912
(915) 833-5656
http://www.huntel.com/~ht2/holocst.html

BOOKS

There are a number of books that are considered to be invaluable to genealogists doing work on Holocaust-related areas of their lives. Here are the most important ones.

How to Document Victims and Locate Survivors of the Holocaust, by Gary Mokotoff, Avotaynu, 1995. Touted as the best book on this subject.

Where Once We Walked: A Guide to the Jewish Communities Destroyed in the Holocaust, by Gary Mokotoff, 1991. Available from Avotaynu and large book stores.

Woww Companion: A Guide to the Communities Surrounding Central and Eastern European Towns, by Gary Mokotoff (compiler), Avotaynu, 1995.

Black Book of Localities Whose Jewish Population Was Exterminated by the Nazis. An alphabetical list of 32,000 communities in Central and Eastern Europe where Jews lived prior to the Holocaust. This list was published as a book by Yad Vashem, but it is now out of print. Some Jewish historical societies and genealogy societies may have a copy. Jewish libraries may also have this book. It is available from Avotaynu on microfiche.

The World Reacts to the Holocaust, David S. Wyman and Charles H. Rosenzveig (editors), Johns Hopkins University Press, 1996. Developed by the Holocaust Memorial. A country-by-country chronicle of the impact of the Holocaust on world history.

In closing this chapter, it should be mentioned that many towns and villages in Eastern Europe that have remnant Jewish populations have begun a concerted effort to memorialize citizens of these areas who died in the Holocaust. In the town of Szeged, Hungary, for example, the local Jewish community has created a memorial plaque listing the names of all the members of their community who died during World War II. So, if all other leads fail, a trip to your family's hometown in Eastern Europe might provide some information not otherwise available.

15

Genealogy Puzzle Solving

Jewish genealogy is challenging because throughout history Jewish communities have been subject to instability due to political factors, war, and persecution. In the last hundred years, a number of cataclysmic world events have affected the worldwide Jewish population—the Russian Revolution, World War I, World War II and the Holocaust, and the Jewish fight for a homeland in Israel do not even reflect a complete list. When there are wars, individuals often lose personal records, and community records can be lost or stolen due to a wide variety of circumstances.

In this chapter, we'll look into the methods of retrieving records that might seem, at first, to be irretrievable because of the Holocaust and for other reasons.

Before one can find records, one must identify the town where those records originated. This search can have some interesting twists and turns. Locating the town in the old country where one's family lived before emigrating requires a thorough understanding of the way in which maps are created by governments. You'll also need to know the many different techniques that researchers can use to uncover the information they seek.

THE WONDERFUL WORLD OF MAPS

Those of us who are used to AAA trip instructions and computer-generated maps may be unaware of how politics influences how maps are created. The making of a map is actually a highly political act, because the way in which map makers identify places expresses the "legitimacy" of that particular place on the globe. Maps describe the borders of countries—a common issue of dispute. The names of places and the language in which they are rendered on a map give or deny legitimacy to a place or region. Very often, changing social and political factors can affect place-names and the languages in which they are written.

In 1987, for example, the social and economic reforms referred to as "glasnost" and "perestroika" began a process in Russia that led, within a few years, to the dissolution of the Soviet Union. Several of the larger "national" territories like the Ukraine and Khazakstan claimed their independence and quickly moved to divest themselves of all signs of Russian "domination."

One of the first acts of these new governments was to proclaim their national language as the primary language of teaching, culture, and government. When I was in Khazakstan in 1994, I witnessed the effects of glasnost in Alma-Ata, then the capital city of the new republic. Prior to about 1992, the official language of Khazakstan had been Russian. However, the new government had proclaimed that Khazak would be the new official language.

New street signs with Khazak names were quickly printed and hung. However, all the maps that were available had been printed prior to the break with the Soviet Union and listed only the Russian names. Therefore a "foreigner" had little chance of finding a street address using a map, and even the local citizens were confused. Many continued to use the Russian names while others used the Russian and Khazak names interchangeably. This situation, which occurred just a few years ago, is analogous to the place-name and street name changes in the Pale of Settlement that took place over a period of a few hundred years as national borders shifted with military and political conquest.

When a government wishes to delegitimize a particular region, it may do one of several things to the country's "official" map:

- give the area a name other than the name given to it by "the locals"
- give the area a name that was previously used, but which was eliminated on more modern maps
- change the spelling of the name to conform to the language norms of the map maker (For example, a map of Israel printed in the United States would "Anglicize" the spelling of the name of the town of Tiveria—Hebrew spelling—as "Tiberius.")
- eliminate the name from the map
- seek to decrease the importance of the area by the size of type or the color used to designate the area
- decline to issue "new" maps that list the town or region.

An interesting modern application of the first technique listed here is the labeling of the land of Israel as "Palestine" on maps created in countries hostile to the Jewish state.

For a Jewish genealogist, especially one working on a genealogy based in Eastern Europe, a working knowledge of the history of the area will help untangle some of the "map" problems that will certainly arise. A good modern history of this area will be a useful addition to your research library.

It's important to remember that maps are not always quickly revised to represent changes in borders and place-names. Therefore, when researching a particular area, it may be helpful to look at maps that were created before and after the time period you are studying, besides looking at a map that is concurrent with the specific time period in question.

With these cautionary words in mind, we are now ready to begin our discussion of some of the more difficult, but not impossible, challenges for Jewish genealogists.

THE TOWN THAT NO LONGER EXISTS

Jewish life in Eastern Europe was decimated by the world wars fought in this century, by the Holocaust, and by the subsequent rise, rule, and fall of communism in Eastern Europe. Here are some of the challenges a Jewish genealogist may encounter in researching an Eastern European genealogy.

1. The name of the town you are looking for doesn't appear on a modern map.

2. There are several towns with similar names, but you don't know which is which.

3. You were told the town was in a particular country, but no such place exists.

4. You were told that your family was from a particular area, but there's no evidence that they lived there.

5. The town used to exist, but exists no longer in any form.

Let's deal with these one by one.

1. You can't find the name of the place on a current map. During the first half of this century, some Jewish towns were completely destroyed during a war, a revolution, or during the Holocaust. Some places were renamed. Others have the same name, but the English transliteration has changed in modern times. Here are several tips for making the most of maps.

Check the Shtetl Seeker page on the JewishGen Web site. With this service, you type in your best guess at the English spelling for the town you're researching, the country in which it was located, and as much specific information as you have—i.e., nearest large city. The Shtetl Seeker will give you the closest matches to the information you've supplied, including alternative spellings.

Check out English language maps that predate World War II, working your way back in time.

Try alternate transliterated spellings. Since transliteration is not always standard, your concept of the transliteration of the place-name might be different from the map maker's.

Try maps produced in the country you're researching. In some languages, you may be able to do this by yourself. However, getting the help of a native speaker of the language of the country you're researching could be helpful at this stage.

Begin with a modern map and work your way backward in time.

Locate a scholarly modern history of the area you are researching and check for the name of the town you're looking for. It may have been renamed since your relatives left.

2. There are several towns with similar names, but you don't know which is which. Very often, English speakers may confuse the name of a town because they don't know the language of the country in which the town is located. English transliterations can be very inaccurate since it may be difficult to differentiate between several transliterations that seem similar. A native speaker may be able to advise you in this instance. If you have any documents that list the name of the town in the original language, this will prove enormously helpful. You may find the town's name on birth certificates, ketubot, photographs, postcards, or even yahrzeit calendars from the old country.

If possible, use a map produced in the country you are researching. If you have any geographical details about the town you are interested in, this information will help the native speaker pinpoint your location more accurately. Also, try to find a locally produced map that was created at about the time your relatives lived in that area.

There are a number of books available—and more being produced every day—with compilations of maps from Eastern Europe. These can be found through Avotaynu and the JewishGen Web site. Your local genealogy society may also be able to help you find these materials.

3. You were told the town was in a particular country, but no such place exists in that country. If your family emigrated from Eastern Europe, it is very likely that the town your grandparents insist was in Poland is now in Russia or vice versa. Or that the town that was in Hungary is now in Austria. During the last century, the borders between Eastern European countries went through many changes. Very often, the name of the town remained the same, but the country in which it was located may have changed not once but several times. If you can't match the name of the town and the country, try the following:

Check current English and foreign language maps for all the countries that border the country you originally searched.

Try to locate both English language and native language maps for that time period and for several decades prior to that period for all the adjacent countries.

Check a current history of those countries to see if the place you are looking for went through a name change.

4. You were told that your family was from a particular area, but there's no evidence that they lived there. Sometimes people generalize about where they came from. For example, a person from Brooklyn on vacation outside the United States might say that he or she lives in "New York," thinking that "New York" would be more identifiable than one of the other boroughs to a person who is not familiar with the United States. Similarly, if all the recent Jewish immigrants from the Ukraine really came from Kiev, as most of them claim when asked to name their place of origin, the census of Jews living in that city in the last decade would increase astronomically.

The "truth," the actual name of a city, may only surface when you ask the direct question, "Did you actually live there," or when you indicate a familiarity with the geography outside the generalized place-name. This is a very important dynamic for a genealogist to be aware of. When you ask where a relative lived, keep in mind that the person you're interviewing may assume that a place you've never heard of won't be significant to you and may instead cite a well-known nearby city.

It is important for a genealogist to ask specific questions about place-names. Very often, if you are looking in a large city for relatives, they may have not lived there. Rather, they may have lived in a nearby suburb. A detailed suburban map of larger cities in the region you are investigating may prove helpful in locating your family's actual place of residence before emigration.

Another type of place-name confusion can come about because some place-names that have been related to you may have been more like nicknames than actual place-names. For example, many people who live in Manhattan will tell others, especially those who live in the other boroughs, that they themselves live in "the city." Everyone understands that they mean "Manhattan," but this would not be comprehensible, necessarily, to someone outside the New York area. Another name for New York, which includes the five boroughs, is "the Big Apple." Yet neither the terms "the city" nor "the Big Apple" can be found on any map.

If you're having trouble finding the name of a foreign town, you may be dealing with this nickname phenomenon. It's important to remember that older relatives may not realize that you do not know the "insider's" history of their homeland. For this reason, it's extremely important to ask detailed questions about place-names. Here are some suggestions:

- What was the name of the town in which you were born?
- Were you actually born there, or is that the name of a nearby town? (If the name given is the name of a nearby town, ask for the name of the town in which the the family actually lived.)
- Was that the exact name of the town?
- What was the official language spoken in your town?
- Was there any other type of name for the town? (Give the example of New York/Big Apple to clarify this question.)
- Was there a different name used by Jews for this city?
- What was the largest nearby city?
- What was the largest natural landmark—i.e., major body of water, mountains, desert.
- What country was the town in when you were born?
- Was the town in the same country when you left? Is it in the same country now?
- Did the town ever become part of a different country? If so, when did this happen?
- If the town became part of a different country, did the name of the town change?
- If the name of the town changed, what was the new name? In what language was the new name identified?
- Did the official language spoken in the town change?
- Can you write the name of the town in its original language—i.e., Polish, Russian?

- If the name of the town changed, can you write it in the new language?
- How would you write the old/new name in English?

6. The town used to exist, but exists no longer in any form. Just because the town no longer exists does not mean that all the records from that town can not be found. Many Jewish towns and villages disappeared during the Holocaust. However, as was discussed in the last chapter, there is a richness of resources available to those who would like to trace their heritage back to their seemingly "disappeared" Eastern European roots.

I'M ADOPTED

When a child is adopted by a Jewish parent or a Jewish couple, one of several things could have happened.

JEWISH BIRTH MOTHER

If the child had a Jewish birth mother, a bris is usually performed for a boy, and a Hebrew name is given to the child, or, for a girl, a naming ceremony takes place. The child's Hebrew name consists of the name chosen by the new parents and the names of the adoptive parents. The names of the adoptive parents are used to indicate that the adopted child is to be considered a member of the family as if it were a birth child.

For both a bris and a naming, a certificate is usually created. This certificate will list the date the ceremony took place, where it took place, the child's and the parents' English and Hebrew names, and the names of the officiating rabbi and witnesses. It may also list the child's date of birth. If the child is a boy who is adopted after infancy, there may be a *brit milah* (circumcision) certificate in existence that lists the Hebrew names of the child's birth parents as well as the date and place of this bris. This could be of help to an adopted male genealogist as a clue to the identity of his birth parents. If there is no male name on the bris certificate where the father's name should be, this is an indication that the birth father was not Jewish.

It should be noted that some couples opt to have a male child circumcised in the hospital. Circumcision is not the same as brit milah. Circumcision is a surgical procedure generally performed on the third day after birth. No religious rituals are associated with it.

Brit milah is performed on the eighth day after birth and requires the presence of a *mohel* (a Jewish person trained in the necessary religious and surgical procedures) or, in the absence of a mohel, a trained surgeon and a person with a knowledge of the appropriate prayers and ritual. If a circumcision is performed in a hospital, there will be no bris certificate. However, a child may later be named in a home ceremony or in a synagogue, and a naming certificate may then be created to mark this occasion.

NON-JEWISH BIRTH MOTHER

If the child did not have a Jewish birth mother, a conversion is generally performed as soon as possible after the adoption. The conversion consists of a bris and naming for a boy, a naming ceremony for a girl, and immersion in a mikvah for both. The water of the mikvah is considered to be "birth water," which substitutes for the birth water of the adoptive mother. As in the first example, both children's Hebrew names include the Hebrew names of their adoptive parents. The conversion is considered conditional until the age of bar or bat mitzvah, when the child is asked to formally accept or reject the conversion. Some Jewish legal experts suggest that, even if the child is not asked to accept or reject the conversion, as long as he or she does not state that he or she rejects Judaism, the conversion is considered to be binding.

As part of the conversion, a conversion certificate is created and given to the parents, although technically, the certificate belongs to the child. The conversion certificate lists the date of the conversion, the child's Hebrew and English names, the Hebrew and English names of his or her adoptive parents, and the names of the officiating rabbi and the required witnesses.

NON-JEWISH ADOPTION OF A JEWISH CHILD

Sometimes children with Jewish backgrounds are placed with non-Jewish families. This is an issue of great concern to the Jewish community. It is not unusual for someone who is adopted and considers himself or herself to be Christian, for example, to discover that he or she had Jewish birth parents or grandparents. This can be very confusing and sometimes upsetting. A person in this situation might find it helpful to seek out a local rabbi in order to discuss the many feelings that arise from such a discovery.

Many rabbis are very open to such conversations and counseling and will not "push" the person into making a religious choice for Judaism. There are also many "Ask the Rabbi" sites on the Internet that offer more anonymity for people who would like to discuss their feelings. Resources for reaching rabbis are listed at the end of this book.

Which Family Tree?

When it comes to tracing their family tree, Jewish adoptees have several options.

You're a branch of your adoptive family tree. According to Jewish law, adopted children are considered to be identical to birth children. Therefore, a person who is adopted into a Jewish family can legitimately choose to claim their adoptive family trees as their own.

A step-parent adopted you. This is a case in which you were raised with one of your birth parents and a person who married your birth parent and adopted you. In this situation, you can choose to trace either your biological line—both parents—or the line of your biological parent and the line of your adoptive parent. Or you might choose to trace the genealogy of all three parents.

Tracing the roots of your birth-parent family tree. Some people who were adopted may wish to find information about their birth parents and that family history. For those who choose this path, there is now a great deal of help available. See below for more information.

People whose birth mothers were not Jewish will most likely find it helpful to use resources that deal with other religious, racial, and cultural backgrounds. Even if one has a non-Jewish birth mother, however, it may help to know that very often children placed with Jewish

families have been placed with these families because they had a
Jewish birth father or some other Jewish relative.

Searching for Your Birth Family

Searching for your birth family can be a complicated process. Each state
has its own laws regarding the confidentiality of adoption files. Some
states are quite liberal, while others are very restrictive. However, today
there are many different ways in which one can approach searching for
birth-family members. The Internet can be of great help. The following
agencies and resources will be of help to adoptees who would like to
research their birth families.

GENERAL INTERNET SEARCH

For general information on searching on the Internet, employ several
different search engines and use the keywords "adoption," "search,"
and "reunion." This shotgun approach should turn up the most current Web sites for birth-family reunion. It should be noted that some
organizations that deal with adoption and/or reunion issues may express
attitudes that some adoptees or adoptive parents may find troubling for
a variety of reasons. For example, some sites may express very strongly
worded opinions about reuniting or not reuniting with birth parents or
birth children. Nonetheless, these sites may have valuable information
and should not be dismissed out of hand.

*Jewish Adoption Information Exchange—Stars of David Interna-
tional, Inc.*   Stars of David is a national, nonprofit information and
support network for Jewish and partly Jewish adoptive families of all
sizes, ages, and origins. It is a grass roots organization that provides
information on all aspects of adoption, including searching for one's
birth family. While it is not a reunion registry, the organization does provide information for people interested in connecting with their birth
families.

  Hot Line: (800) STAR-349
  http://www.starsofdavid.org/
  E-mail: StarsDavid@aol.com

Jewish Family Service Agencies   While there is no specific Jewish reunion organization, Stars of David suggests that people placed with Jewish families might check the Jewish agencies in the city or state in which the adoption took place. Information about these agencies can be found on the Stars of David Web site. Jews placed with non-Jewish families should check all non-Jewish agencies in the area where they were born.

ALMA Adoption Reunion Registry   ALMA, according to its promotional material, is the oldest, most comprehensive, and succcessful registry of its kind. It is a worldwide matching registry that maintains an international reunion registry data bank.
P.O. Box 727, Radio City Station
New York, NY 10101-0727
(212) 581-1568
http://www.almanet.com

BirthQuest!   BirthQuest! is an online international database dedicated to searching adoptees, birth parents, adoptive parents, and siblings. There is a modest registration fee, but as of the writing of this book, this fee is waved for registrants outside of the United States with no access to U.S. funds (except Canada) and those for whom the registration would cause financial hardship.
BirthQuest International
9206 Bengal Road
Baltimore, MD 21133
http://www.birthquest.org

American Adoption Congress   This is an international search organization that has a search referral hotline and which operates the International Soundex Reunion Registry. (See below.)
1000 Connecticut Avenue, NW, Suite 9
Washington, DC 20036
(800) 274-6736

International Soundex Reunion Registry   The International Soundex Reunion Registry is the world's largest reunion registry and is a free service. You get your registration form by sending a self-addressed stamped envelope to it.

I.S.R.R.
P.O. Box 2312
Carson City, NV 89702-2312
(702) 882-7755
http://www.plumsite.com/isrr/

Voices of Adoption Web site
http://www.ibar.com/voices/resources/search.html
This excellent Web site has very rich resource links. Included on this site are some of the following topics:

How to Start Searching	Hospitals
Where to Write for Vital Records	Finding Prison Inmates
Help for Foster Children	International Locators
Family History Center	A List of Adoption Laws
Adoptee Waiver of Conifdentiality	by State
International Soundex Reunion	Confidential Intermediary
Registry	Program

A confidential intermediary is a person who may search through records that are not open to the general public. Stars of David (see page 236) offers a general contact person for finding a Confidential Intermediary Program in the state where you are searching. Contact its Web site for more information.

Adoption Search Menu Page
http://azstarnet.com/~vizedom/nan.html
The purpose of this page is to aid those seeking a birth family relative. It provides a wealth of information and links on wide-ranging topics including T.I.E.S Homepage—Terminal Illness Emergency Search, computer searching services, adoptee-related WWW library, and books for searchers.

Cyndi's List of Genealogy Sites on the Internet
http://www.CyndisList.com

This Web site has a special section on adoption that includes the following information and services:

Adoptees Internet Mailing List

Adoptees Mailing List

The Adoptees Newsgroup Homepage

Adoptees Resources Homepage

Adoptee Searcher's Handbook

Online searchable database for searching adoptees, birth parents, adoptive parents, and siblings

Making a Family Tree for the Adoptee

The Seeker Magazine

Adult Adoptees Chat

Tapestry Books
http://www.tapestrybooks.com
Tapestry is a bookseller that specializes in books on adoption. A wide variety of information is available. Some suggested titles for searchers include:

How to Locate Anyone Anywhere—Without Leaving Home, by Ted L. Gunderson, Plume, revised edition, 1996.

Adoption Searchbook: Techniques for Tracing People, by Mary Jo Rillera, Pure, 3rd edition, 1990.

Search: A Handbook for Adoptees and Birthparents, by Jayne Askin, Onyx Press, 3rd ed, 1998.

Searcher's Handbook: A Guidebook for Adoptees, Birth Parents, and Others, by Norma Tillman, Diane Publishing Co., 1994.

Missing Links: The True Story of an Adoptee's Search for His Birth Parents, by Vincent J. Begley, Claycomb Press, 1991.

Where Are My Birth Parents?: A Guide for Teenage Adoptees, by Karen Gravelle, Walher & Co., reprint 1995.

THERE ARE NO LIVING RELATIVES

It may be that there are some people who, for complicated reasons, will never be able to find out any information prior to their own immediate generation, someone who has no information about his or birth parents or adoptive parents. This is a worst case scenario and one that affects a very small number of people. However, if you are in this position, you still might be able to unearth some family history by working with a professional genealogist. Professional genealogists can be located through local Jewish genealogy groups and on various genealogy Internet Web sites.

Another starting point, however, is your own birth certificate. In chapter 9, we discussed the information available on a birth certificate. Your birth certificate can have a wealth of information on it that may help you uncover clues to your family background. However, since birth certificate information is not standardized, depending on where you were born, you may have many beginning clues or just one or two. Here are some discoveries you can make using only your own birth certificate as a starting point.

YOUR FATHER'S NAME; YOUR MOTHER'S MAIDEN NAME

Search usenet and other search engines for people with your father's surname and your mother's maiden name. This type of search may uncover relatives you never knew you had.

AGE OF MOTHER; AGE OF FATHER

This information will give you a rough guess as to your mother's and father's years of birth. Knowing their birth years can help you in searching for their birth certificates and social security information. This information can also help you in figuring out when your parents were married. For example, if your mother was in her early twenties, the range of years for their marriage is relatively narrow. Even if she was much older and gave birth to you at the age of forty, it would be unusual if she had been married for much more than twenty years. If you begin with the year of your birth and work backward, you should be able to find their marriage records, assuming that you know where they were married.

PLACE OF BIRTH FOR MOTHER AND FATHER

More help for finding your parents' birth certificates. Also, the place of birth can provide a hint on the general location of family graves, especially those of grandparents and great-grandparents. If your parents were born in the United States, you can search the local phone directory in the year they were born for other people with the same surnames. This may help you discover other relatives.

Your grandparents' names will be listed on your parents' birth certificates. This will help you begin to look for life-cycle documents—birth, marriage, and death certificates—for that generation.

NUMBER OF OTHER CHILDREN LIVING AT TIME OF BIRTH OF NEW BABY

Is there a sibling around of whom you are unaware? This information will tell you if there were other children living at the time that you were born and may give their ages or birth dates. Although their names will not be listed, you may be able to uncover their birth certificates by looking for children born with your family's surname and searching the probable range of years in which they were born. You would determine this range based on your mother's age at the time you were born and her probable date of marriage or earliest probable childbearing year. You'll know that you've uncovered a sibling if you find a birth certificate for a child with your father's surname and your mother's maiden name.

Another way to seek siblings is to search usenet and other search engines for people with your father's surname and your mother's maiden name. You could also make use of the reunion registries mentioned earlier in this chapter.

Because some children die in childbirth or shortly afterward, you might find information about siblings by researching death certificates for people who died between your mother's earliest childbearing year and your date of birth.

The record searches suggested above assume that your siblings were born in the town in which you were born. This, of course, may not be the case. However, it's possible that other clues, your mother's or father's place of birth, will suggest other places to search for documents. For example, you may not know where your parents were married, but a good guess would be either your mother's or father's hometown. If you have your parents' place of birth on your birth certificate, this will be a valuable clue to finding other family records.

NAME AND ADDRESS OF PLACE WHERE YOU WERE BORN

If you were born in a hospital, that institution may have other records relating to your birth and to your family. It's worth checking out. This can also give you a clue about where to search for your parents' marriage license, which, as noted above, will give you information about your grandparents.

HOME ADDRESS OF YOUR PARENTS

If your parents lived in a multifamily dwelling, you can look up the names of the other tenants living there at the time you were born by using a reverse directory. A reverse directory lists addresses of buildings first, then the names of the tenants. By using a reverse directory, you can also find the names of the people living on your street at the time you were born. If you can track down any of these people, they may be able to give you information about your family.

There are different types of reverse directories. Some cities published "city directories." These were reverse directories that listed the addresses, names, and phone numbers, where available, of many people who lived in a particular area. Not all people were listed. Many places that published city directories dropped these in the 1930s as more modern phone directories became popular. More recently, the Cole's Publishing Company published reverse directories for specific cities. The city directories and the Cole's directories are available at large libraries, especially those that have genealogy divisions.

If your parents' home address is very different from where you were born, it may give you another clue about where to search for your parents' marriage license. This information may also lead you to synagogue records related to your family.

Synagogues in America tend to remain in the same place. If your parents were affiliated with a synagogue, the probability is that they were affiliated with the one in their area. A yellow pages directory for the year of your birth, which you should be able to find at a large library, can give you the name and address of area synagogues of that time. You can also check a current yellow pages directory for the area in which they lived.

Most synagogues have cemetery burial plots. While not all members made use of this membership "perk," finding a synagogue affiliation for your family may lead you to family cemetery plots and death certificates. Finding the cemetery where your relatives are buried is important because the head- or footstones of their graves may give you other genealogical information including birth dates, Hebrew names, Kohen or Levi status, and whether or not the individual had other siblings. For example, a headstone may read "Beloved wife, daughter, mother, and aunt." This would tell you that the person who died had a sibling and that the sibling had a child. These are important clues.

Another way of using a synagogue affiliation for genealogical research is to ask the executive director or temple president for the names and addresses of living members who were affiliated at the same time as your parents were affiliated. This may lead you to people who actually knew your parents and other relatives and who can give you information about them.

OCCUPATION OF FATHER AND MOTHER

Knowing your parents' occupations may lead you to information about membership in unions, and occupational and fraternal organizations. Many occupational organizations maintain cemetery plots. Discovering that a parent was a member in an occupational or fraternal organization may be another way for you to discover where your relatives are buried.

16

How Jewish Traditions and Customs Can Help You Trace Your Jewish Roots

 What makes a pair of candlesticks "Shabbat" candlesticks? What makes a wineglass a "kiddush cup"? Is there any significance to the order of the foods served for a family dinner? Does the custom of buying new clothes every fall have any religious significance?

Most genealogists spend a great deal of time looking for physical records of their family's background. However, it's important not to overlook other ways of linking ourselves to our family and religious traditions. There are many customs that exist within families that can give us important clues about their lives. There are also ritual and family heirlooms that hold keys to the past.

The purpose of this chapter is to discuss basic Jewish customs and traditions that may help a Jewish genealogist shed light on his or her background. This chapter may also be helpful to non-Jewish genealogists and to those non-Jews who may suspect that there is Jewish ancestry in their families.

A Case History

A beautiful young woman from Trinidad was sitting in my office and explaining why she wanted to convert to Judaism. Whenever a rabbi has a discussion with a potential convert, one of the first things we do is to discuss the person's family history and the religious observance of his or her family. I began to ask the usual questions, starting with her father's side of the family.

"Where was your father born?"

"Trinidad."

"Where was your grandfather born?"

"Trinidad."

"Where was your great-grandfather born?"

"France."

This raised a red flag for me. Why had the grandfather moved from France to Trinidad in the late nineteenth century?

"What was your great-grandfather's religion?"

"I don't know. We didn't know much about him and my father never talked about him."

Another red flag. If an ancestor deviated in some way from the accepted family tradition, very often his personal history will be erased in a family. The most frequent reason is that the forebear's religion was different from that of most members of the family. However, there may have been other issues such as the person's character or business dealings. This was suggestive, but not conclusive, that the potential convert had a religious tradition in her family other than that in which she was raised.

"In what religion were you raised?"

"Catholic."

"Describe some of the religious practices your family observed in the home."

"Every spring, around Easter time, we would have a big dinner and my father would read us the Ten Commandments. Then we would watch the movie on TV."

"Is this a custom for Catholics in Trinidad?"

"No. We were the only family that I know of who did this."

Another red flag. A Catholic family practicing a home-based religious ritual different than the practices of the broader community sometimes indicates a family that has a "hidden" religious tradition which they do not practice publicly. On occasion, but not always, this religion is Judaism. A family with an established tradition of reading the Ten Commandments around Easter time and then watching the story of the Exodus on television could very well be observing a form of the Passover seder. The possibility was growing that this woman had some Jewish ancestry, at least on the paternal side of her family.

"Were the children in your family named after living or dead relatives?"

"All of the children were named after relatives who had died. In our family, we never named children after living relatives."

"Was this the custom for Catholics in Trinidad?"

"No. Most Catholics in Trinidad name their children after a living relative."

A big clue! A family that follows the tradition of naming children only after relatives who have died is following a very ingrained naming tradition. Ashkenazic Jews only name their children after relatives who have died.

My comment to this young woman was that, based on the family history that she had given me of her father's side of the family, there were a number of clues that suggested that the paternal side of her family had some Jewish ancestry through her great-grandfather. While a possible tie to Judaism through her paternal line didn't change her status as a non-Jew, since most of the Jewish world recognizes Jewish descent only through the maternal line, it could explain her feeling that she was being "pulled" into Judaism.

A Jewish mystical idea suggests that a person with even one drop of

Jewish blood carries within him or her a *pintele yid*. The *pintele yid* is like a sliver of Jewish identity that lies dormant within an individual with Jewish ancestry. Even if an individual has no idea that he or she has Jewish background, under the right conditions, the *pintele yid* can be activated. When this happens, the person feels an internal "pull" toward Judaism. Sometimes this results in conversion to Judaism. I've seen this phenomenon so often that I believe in it, although it challenges my more rationalist tendencies. For those genealogists who would like to explore this phenomenon more fully, I offer the following.

The only "hard proof" to establish Jewish identity would be a document of public record that states the religion of the person's mother or that person's own religion, or a religious document, like a bris certificate or a ketubah. A receipt for dues in a synagogue would, in most cases, also be proof of Jewish identity. Since the Reform movement's policy regarding patrilineal descent went into effect (1983), dues paid to a Reform synagogue after that date would not be definitive proof of Jewish identity as defined by the broader Jewish community.

Ten Clues That Suggest Jewish Ancestry

1. Date of Emigration

As we've discussed earlier in this book, the patterns of Jewish emigration are quite clear and well documented. If a person's ancestor(s) emigrated from a country with a large Jewish population during a "Jewish emigration period," this is an important clue.

2. Family Personal and Surnames

Some family surnames are distinctively Jewish in the language of origin. See chapter 11, which is about Jewish names, for more complete information.

3. Naming Customs Within a Family

If one's family has a distinctive pattern for naming children differs from that of the surrounding religious or cultural group, that can be a clue to one's Jewish ancestry.

4. Food

Food is an important clue in determining cultural identity. "Old family recipes" can shed a great deal of information on a family's history. Gefilte fish and the way it is flavored, for example, can tell you where a Jewish family came from. Gefilte fish recipes that originated in Poland tend to be somewhat sweet. Lithuanian gefilte fish is peppery.

FOOD TABOOS—MEAT AND MILK

There are two Jewish dietary customs that tend to remain active in families with Jewish ancestry even after a memory of that ancestry has been lost. One custom is the prohibition of serving foods that combine meat and milk or serving meat and milk foods at the same meal.

In the Torah, Jews are instructed that they must not "boil a kid in its mother's milk." (Exodus 23:19, 34:26; Deuteronomy 14:21) The rabbis interpreted this text as a prohibition against combining meat and milk or milk-derived products, like cheese, in the same recipe. A prohibition also exists against serving milk and meat at the same meal, although milk and related products may be served at the beginning of a meat meal if certain steps are taken after these dishes are eaten. However, because of the complications of serving food in this way, milk and meat are almost never served at the same meal, especially in one's home.

Interestingly, the Ethiopian Jews, who had no contact with rabbinic Judaism until their immigration to Israel in the 1980s and 1990s, have the tradition of not separating meat and milk. They understood the prohibition in Deuteronomy to mean that one may not cook a kid in *its* mother's milk; however, cooking a kid in the milk of another animal that is not its mother is permitted. For most of the Jewish world, however, mixing meat and milk was and is a powerful taboo.

The other food taboo that has remained in many families is the prohibition of eating pork. (Leviticus 11:7–8) While there are many other animals, birds, and fish and aquatic creatures prohibited by the Torah, the abstention from eating pork has been understood by the non-Jewish world to be a Jewish dietary convention from very early times. During the Inquisition, a converted Jewish family that did not eat pork was often convicted of heresy on those grounds alone. In other parts of

Europe, the Catholic church, at the height of its missionary policy against the Jewish community, would try to entice or force Jews to eat pork. Because of this history, many Jews who are not religious in any other way refrain from eating pork as a way of maintaining a connection with their Jewish heritage.

For all these reasons, a non-Jewish family that maintains a tradition of not mixing meat and milk or not eating pork, may very well have Jewish ancestry.

FOOD TABOOS—BREAD

Another food taboo found in some "non-Jewish" families is refusing to eat bread during Passover or Easter. This may be a clue that the family has Jewish background. However, it should be noted that some fundamentalist Christian groups in America also observe Jewish rituals as a way of connecting to the Hebrew biblical basis of Christianity. For this reason, not eating bread in the spring, around the time of Easter or Passover, might be a clue, but it should not be considered definitive unless there are other indications of Jewish ancestry.

5. Fasting

There are no fasts mandated in the Torah. The understanding of the verses that explain how Yom Kippur will be observed state that "you will afflict your souls." (Leviticus 23:27) This was interpreted by the rabbis as a mandate to fast for the entire period of the holy day, which runs from one evening to the next. As a result, the tradition of fasting on Yom Kippur is considered to have its origin in the Torah.

Fasting and asceticism were not an important part of Judaism in its early formulation. However, over the millennia, various fasts have become part of traditional Jewish life. There are two fast days other than Yom Kippur that are well known. One is the Fast of Esther, which usually falls sometime in March, a month before Passover. This fast is related to the holiday of Purim. The fast related to Tisha B'Av, the ninth day of the Hebrew month of Av, which occurs in late July to mid-August, commemorates the fall of the First and Second Temples. Very traditional Jews abstain from eating meat for three weeks prior to Tisha B'Av.

Another traditional, well-known Jewish fasting custom concerns the fasting of the bride and groom on the day of their wedding. This fast reminds the couple of the important step they are about to take and helps them attain a higher level of spiritual preparedness for their wedding and the consummation of their marriage.

Families who observe fasts in the fall, in March, or midsummer that have no other explanation may well be descended from Jewish families who were observant of these Jewish fasting practices. In addition, families that maintain a tradition of having a bride or groom fast prior to the wedding may well have Jewish roots.

6. Clothing

Certain Jewish holidays had definite customs relating to clothing associated with them. One of these was Rosh Hashannah. It was considered good luck to have new clothing for the new year. There is also a tradition of saying a *bracha*—a blessing—when wearing new clothes for the first time. This blessing is the "Shehehiyanu," which thanks God for enabling us to reach this special season. The Shehehiyanu is also said in conjunction with other holidays and happy life-cycle events.

Another tradition was the wearing of cloth or nonleather shoes on Yom Kippur. It was believed that leather shoes were more comfortable than cloth shoes. Since, on Yom Kippur, we are supposed to focus on our spiritual rather than physical needs, we wear shoes that are not as comfortable as those we usually wear as a way of de-emphasizing our physical comfort.

Yet another Yom Kippur tradition is to dress in white clothing. Wearing white is thought to be a reflection of the spiritual purity we wish to attain through our confession and spiritual cleansing. White is also the color of the shroud that traditional Jews wear when they are buried. By wearing white on Yom Kippur, we acknowledge the fragility of our lives. It is also a way of helping us to focus on the need to purify our souls so that when we die, may it be many years, our souls will be pure and we will ascend quickly to heaven.

A family tradition of wearing white clothes in the fall (after Labor Day), of wearing nonleather shoes for a particular religious holiday, of making sure that everyone has new clothing in the fall (not only the schoolchildren) may indicate a family's Jewish roots.

7. Family Heirlooms, Objects, and Secrets

Family heirlooms or even the special use of certain household objects can hold important clues about a family's background. Pots, pans, dishware, and utensils can be sources of clues to a family's Jewish heritage. For example, a special pot or pan used only for meat or only for cooking dishes with milk or cheese or for cooking fish (other than a pot designed only for this purpose) would suggest a memory of a kosher kitchen tradition. This would also be true if certain dishes were used only for either meat or dairy.

Similarly, if inherited china is used only for certain types of foods, or for certain holidays, this custom might also indicate a Jewish food tradition. Dishes used only at a spring meal, for example, would suggest a memory of dishes that appeared only on the Passover table. This would also be true for silver, glassware, tablecloths and napkins, and pots and pans.

I once met a young woman who was going to a liberal Christian seminary to become a minister but who was very interested in Judaism. She told me that sometimes she felt the urge to convert. In discussing her family background, she told me that her grandparents, who came from Hungary, had kept a kosher kitchen, even though the family was Lutheran. When I asked her if she had ever asked her grandmother why she kept a kosher kitchen, the young woman told me that her grandmother said that they lived in a Jewish neighborhood in Hungary. She told her granddaughter that she kept a kosher home so that her neighbors could eat in her home.

It's very unlikely that the reason the grandmother offered her granddaughter for keeping a kosher kitchen is true. Very few religious Jewish people would eat in the home of a non-Jewish woman even if she kept kosher. It would take a tremendous effort for a non-Jewish woman to convince Jewish neighbors that her kitchen was kosher according to Jewish law. Furthermore, some sects of Judaism believe that food prepared by a non-Jew, even in a kosher kitchen, is not kosher.

On the other hand, it's unlikely that the grandmother was lying about keeping a kosher kitchen. Most likely the grandmother was Jewish but had decided to keep the knowledge of her Judaism a secret from her granddaughter. The family had immigrated to the United States from Hungary in the late 1930s—a time when many Hungarian Jews came to the United States. Some officially converted to Christianity, while others attended Christian churches without formal conversion.

The young woman telling me this story related that her grandparents refused to talk about their life in Hungary, and her mother, who was born here, knew as little as she did. Refusing to talk about the old country, especially when the old country is Eastern Europe, is another clue that there may be Jewish ancestry in one's family. Secretary of State Madeleine Albright is a famous example of this. Raised as a Christian, it was only recently that she learned of her Jewish heritage, and that her family had been directly affected by the Holocaust.

I asked this young woman if her family had brought anything from the old country. Very often, family heirlooms can provide clues about a family's background. She told me that her family seemed to have a great number of candlesticks in sets of two that her grandmother had brought from Hungary. While this is not a definitive clue, it did suggest a family's collection of Shabbat and holiday candlesticks. Very often these candlesticks would be handed down from one generation to another. I suggested that the young woman inspect them to see if they were engraved with any Jewish symbols or Hebrew writing. I also suggested that she look for wine cups in ceramic or silver, and other items that might be Judaica, and that she question her grandmother about these objects and their origins. When I last spoke with her, she had not yet been able to discuss this subject with her grandmother.

One wonders why the grandmother told her granddaughter the story of keeping a kosher kitchen in Hungary, especially in view of her reluctance to talk about the old country at all. Was it her way of transmitting the truth of the girl's heritage without having to commit herself or explain why this knowledge was kept from the granddaughter? In families that hide their Jewish roots, such incidents are very common. Sometimes a "confession," is made when a relative is on the point of death.

I remember reading a true story of a woman who, on her deathbed, whispered to her son, "We are Jews." The son, a good Catholic living in Mexico, went on to trace his family's roots back to Spain. He discovered that his family were "Conversos"—Jews who converted to Catholicism under pressure from the Inquisition, but who continued to practice Judaism in secret. Upon learning the truth of his heritage, this man began to study Judaism and ultimately rejoined the Jewish community.

Because of the difficulties of emigration and the need to travel "light," many families left family heirlooms behind. However, very often beloved books or family Bibles survived the trip to the New World. For this reason, even if they look worn and worthless, books should not be overlooked as a source of family information.

Some families have wedding Bibles that have been preserved within the family. Very often these Bibles contain the names not only of the bride and groom, but also of other family members. These names can be very helpful in constructing one's family tree. Siddurs—prayerbooks—were often given as bar mitzvah gifts and were often inscribed with the name of the recipient, the date, and the giver's name. Sometimes this was an individual, sometimes a synagogue. Such inscriptions can be valuable hard evidence of your ancestors' life and circumstances.

8. The Calendar

The Jewish calendar is a combined lunar and solar calendar. The months are calculated according to the movement of the moon. A lunar year contains approximately 354 days. The years are calculated in relation to the sun. The solar year is approximately 365 days. In order to keep the festivals in their proper seasons, an additional month of Adar, which falls in March or April, is added in seven years of a cycle of nineteen years. The length of the Jewish months alternates between twenty-nine and thirty days.

All of the biblical holy days, with the exception of Rosh Hashanah, fall in the middle of the month because the beginning of the month had to be confirmed by a sighting of the new moon. Then the word of this sighting had to be spread to all Jewish communities. Without access to even a telegraph in ancient times, this was a very difficult process involving both signal fires on the mountaintops and messengers sent to out-lying communities. In order to be sure that all the holidays would be celebrated properly, it was necessary for the communities to know on what day the month had begun. Setting the holidays in mid-month made it possible for communities to be alerted to the proper beginning of the month.

In addition, from a very early point in our history, communities outside the land of Israel added a second day of each important holiday that was equal in religious requirement to the first day. This was done to ensure that, if they celebrated the first day too early, the second day would be celebrated properly. Even after the development of the fixed calendar in the fourth century of the Common Era, the Diaspora communities continued the tradition of the second day of the holidays because its celebration was so well established. Rosh Hashanah is the only major holy day that falls on the first of the month. Because of concern for making sure that the proper first day is observed, all Jewish communities, including those in Israel, traditionally celebrated Rosh Hashannah for two days. Today, some liberal Diaspora communities only celebrate the first day of the holidays.

Certain life-cycle events, like weddings and funerals, are prohibited during certain parts of the Jewish year. This can provide clues to a family researcher.

SHABBAT

Shabbat begins at sunset on Friday evening and concludes on Saturday night after three stars appear in the sky, usually about an hour after sunset. Jews may not marry on the Sabbath. In the summer, when the Sabbath ends very late on Saturday night, most Jewish weddings begin quite late to give people enough time to travel to the ceremony. Since they can't leave until after Shabbat is over, most Jewish weddings during June, July, and August occur midweek or on Sunday. A family history of weddings that do not occur on Saturday or Friday night could provide a clue to the family's background.

Jewish funerals are never performed on Shabbat or on the first day of a major festival, even though there is a Jewish law that requires that a person who dies must be buried within twenty-four hours. This custom deviates dramatically from that of Christian burial customs, which often postpone a funeral for several days. The custom of speedy burial within a family, and of funerals delayed over a Saturday, would suggest a Jewish custom being observed. Avoidance of burial on dates that coincide with the first and last days of Sukkot, Pesach, and Shavuot, Rosh Hashanah and Yom Kippur, should also raise a red flag for further investigation.

PROHIBITED DAYS FOR WEDDINGS

There are certain periods in the Jewish year when weddings are not permitted. These are:

- the days of observance of Jewish holidays, including Shabbat.
- the intermediary days of Sukkot and Pesach. The days between Rosh Hashanah and Yom Kippur are not prohibited, but many communities discourage marriage during this time.
- the period between the end of Passover and Shavuot, with the exception of the thirty-third day of the counting of the Omer—Lag B'omer. In some communities, marriages are performed after this day until the advent of the festival of Shavuot.
- the three weeks between the seventeenth of Tammuz and the ninth of Av, including the ninth of Av, also known as Tisha B'Av. These are weeks of mourning for the loss of the Temple and are considered to be an inauspicious time for a wedding to take place. These weeks generally fall between mid-July and mid-August.

Avoidance of these times for weddings within a family may be indicative of a Jewish background.

9. Mourning Customs

Jewish mourning customs come to us from the Torah and the Hebrew Bible. Of all the customs observed by Jews, mourning customs are among the most carefully observed, even by secular Jews. For this reason, a family's customs related to the death of a relative can often be a "tip-off" to Jewish ancestry. The following list describes a wide range of distinctively Jewish customs related to death and mourning. I've modified my description of some of them to create a picture of how they might appear in a family that does not realize that these are Jewish customs.

burial within twenty-four hours

having someone sit with the body from the period of death until the funeral

closed casket

lighting of a seven-day candle in the home after the interment—the initial period of Jewish mourning is seven days, unless interrupted or cancelled by a particular holy day

throwing dirt into the grave

tearing of a piece of clothing or wearing a torn ribbon by a member of the immediate family—spouse, children, siblings; also, wearing of this piece of clothing or ribbon for a period of time

washing the hands outside the house when returning from the cemetery

leaving the front door unlocked during the period when guests are expected for a condolence call

prohibition against the sending of flowers as a memorial

donation to charity in memory of the deceased

serving a meal of boiled eggs, lentils, or dairy when returning from the cemetery; alternatively, preparing a meal in which only dairy or only meat dishes are served

the bereaved sit on the ground or lower to the ground than others

covering the mirrors in the home of the deceased

gathering for prayers in the morning and/or evening in the home of the deceased

women not using makeup during the mourning period; men refraining from shaving during the mourning period

wearing of cloth shoes during the mourning period

a strong bias against or prohibition of cremation

bias against an elaborate coffin

burial in a shroud or simple white garments

mourners remaining in the home for a period of a week

not seeing visitors on the Saturday after a death

walking around the outside of the house after a period of mourning

going to the cemetery to see the headstone a year after the burial

requiring ten men to be present for the burial or for seeing the headstone a year after burial

10. Chanukah and Christmas

The close proximity, in most years, of Chanukah and Christmas made it easy for Chanukah customs to be masked in family Christmas celebrations. Clues of Jewish ancestry at Christmastime would include:

lighting of eight or nine candles during Christmas either once or for a week or eight days

giving children coins as a gift, which is reflective of the custom to give children pennies so that they could play dreidel and wager during Chanukah

giving children spinning tops to play with—these toys could be substitutes for dreidels

making a point of eating foods fried in olive oil, especially foods with potatoes

eating a meal with dairy foods only. This is related to the story of Holofernes and Judith. She saved her city, Bethulia, which was besieged during the Maccabean War, by feeding this military leader dairy products to make him thirsty. Then she brought him wine and he drank himself into a stupor. While he slept, she cut off his head.

Judaism is a religion and a culture with over 3,500 years of customs and traditions. The more understanding a Jewish genealogist has of these customs, their origins, and their development, the more clues he or she may be able to find about his or her family history.

17

Creating and Preserving Genealogical Treasures for Future Generations

Imagine what it would be like to talk to your descendents a hundred and fifty years from now and tell them about your life, your dreams, your priorities, and your love for them. Or imagine what you would ask and tell your ancestors who lived a hundred and fifty years ago.

We very rarely think about how we might conduct such communications. And yet, as genealogists, we have a unique opportunity to do just that.

When we research and develop our family tree, we learn many things about the lives and times of our ancestors. By creating durable family albums and archives and contributing a copy of our research to Jewish institutions that collect these documents, we make it possible for our work to endure and to inform the lives of our descendents.

We can also reach into the future by creating and preserving a wide variety of life-cycle documents and heirlooms for our own generation and for the generations that immediately follow us. Another strategy is to become the archivist for one's own family. Finally, we can teach the skills of genealogy to our children and grandchildren so that they will value the work that we have done and be able to continue it into the future.

In this chapter, we'll look at the many ways in which we can create life-cycle documents and heirlooms that can send messages to our descendents. We will also discuss some techniques for creating family archives for future generations.

After you've been doing your research for a while, you may begin to discover that you have a lot of "stuff"—photos, various forms filled out, documents, notes, letters, video and audio tapes, and memorabilia. All these things are in boxes, files, drawers, on shelves—wherever you decided to store them. The challenge, at this stage, is to preserve these important documents and to turn your file of material into the life of your family.

PRESERVATION

All materials break down over time. Humidity, temperature fluctuations, light, handling, and a material's own built-in properties contribute to the deterioration of documents and objects. However, when treated properly, it's possible to extend the life of many valuable documents and artifacts for many, many years.

The key to preservation is understanding the nature of the particular material you're dealing with and giving it the best chance for survival by supplying ideal preservation conditions. Each type of document, artifact, or heirloom requires its own special handling. However, there are two primary commandments of document and heirloom preservation that apply to all preservation situations:

1. Thou shalt not do something to an item that cannot be undone.

2. When in doubt, leave it to the experts.

Here is a quick overview of the special needs of various types of items that you will most likely come across in your genealogical research.

Paper

Works on paper, such as documents, books, and prints, require very special treatment. The term used to refer to the techniques of preserving works on paper is "archival preservation." Products that can be safely used for document restoration and preservation are almost always labeled as such. Such products are designated as "archival" or "archivally sound." Most often, these terms refer to chemically stable or pH neutral papers, tapes, glues, and other materials used for preservation and restoration. Archivally sound materials help to extend the life of a document and, in many cases, may retard further deterioration.

Some Jewish documents, like ketubot, are frequently written on the skin of a kosher animal, as Torah scrolls are. Restoration and preservation of documents written on calfskin, sheepskin, or leather require special preservation techniques. Preservation of such documents is best left to the experts. A Jewish museum is the best place to go for referrals to people who specialize in this type of restoration.

Individual paper documents should be placed in individual acid-free Mylar folders and stored flat in archival boxes. Sheets of acid-free paper can be used between documents to protect them from rubbing against one another.

Try to handle the documents as little as possible. One of the most damaging elements to paper documents is dirt and oil transferred from one's hands. Using white cotton gloves, which can be purchased at most large drug stores, can help reduce this problem.

Documents should be kept in a place that is dry and which maintains a relatively stable temperature at all times. A room in which you feel comfortable—68 to 72 degrees—should be a good environment for most of your documents. Extremes of temperature and humidity can be very damaging to works on paper or those bound in leather.

Keep your documents away from light sources, especially natural light. Exposure to direct sunlight is damaging to all delicate materials. The best storage place for documents and other materials that you want to preserve is in a dry, dark place—a closet in the middle of a house is usually perfect.

Not all paper will age in the same way. All paper becomes more acidic over time. Until about the middle of the nineteenth century, most papers were made of rag or cloth stock. Sometime around 1860, paper mills started using ground wood with acids, bleach, and alum-rosin sizing. This created papers with a high acid content (low pH). They react with water and the atmosphere to produce self-destructive acidic compounds. The compounds shorten the fibers of the paper, causing them to become brittle and discolored. That's why the pages of many old books become yellowed and crumble over time.

Old paper and paper that is expected to have a short life—like the paper used for newspapers—is very unstable. For this reason, it's important to reduce or eliminate, as much as possible, any additional acid migrating into your documents from the surrounding atmosphere, improper handling, and from other high-acid objects stored nearby.

As you begin to create your own original documents, you will want to use acid-free paper, if possible, and to be aware of the special properties of the paper documents you may be collecting. For example, it is important to know that information printed on fax paper fades within a very short period of time. Therefore, if you receive faxes of family history material, it would be wise to Xerox them onto acid-free paper or onto the highest quality bond paper available. This will preserve your original source materials.

Besides using archival papers wherever possible, documents like immigration papers and birth certificates should be preserved by encapsulation. The most widely accepted encapsulation technique is to use Mylar-D and to thermally weld the edges. It is also possible to use Mylar envelopes with a special tape to seal in the document. Encapsulation provides a clean, dry atmosphere for the document you want to preserve. It should be noted that encapsulation, while it can help preserve many types of documents, does not stop acidification, although it may retard the rate of deterioration. If you have a very valuable document, you may want to have it tested for acidity and, if necessary, look into the possibility of stabilizing it.

It's important to be aware that encapsulation in Mylar-D is not the same as lamination. Lamination is not an archival technique. Quite the opposite. Lamination speeds up a paper's deterioration and is therefore not recommended for archival use. A document that is laminated cannot be removed from the laminate without damage to the document. On the other hand, a encapsulated document can be easily removed, if necessary.

Another way to encapsulize a document is to have it archivally framed. Archival framing uses only archival materials in the mounting of the document. The back of the frame is then sealed to prevent moisture and dust from getting in. This procedure is recommended, however, only for special documents, since the cost is quite high. Also, if you use this technique and plan to hang the document on a wall, you must make sure that it is out of both direct sunlight and lamplight. Most large cities have framing stores that specialize in archival framing. Museums can also offer references for framers who specialize in this technique.

If you have a document that is very fragile, you might consider having it photographed by a photo house that specializes in working with fragile documents or with works of art. By making a photographic copy and properly storing the negative, you can preserve a document that may not otherwise survive for very long. Another way to preserve newspaper clippings is to Xerox them onto archival paper.

Documents can also be scanned into a computer and stored on a disk using a variety of software designed specifically for this type of activity. Some genealogy software makes it possible to do this with both documents and photographs. The problem with this approach is that, while it stores the image, it does not preserve the actual document. This is a good way to back up your important document files, but it doesn't take the place of proper document preservation.

Some people like to store their documents in see-through plastic envelopes that can be put into binders. While this is both a good way of seeing your materials while you're working with them, and protecting them from too much handling, it's important to make sure that you use archival Mylar sleeves. Also, since these sleeves are not usually sealed, dust, moisture and other destructive elements can still infiltrate the document.

Occasionally, a family book—recipes, a bible with family-tree information, a handwritten manuscript, letters, or a journal will need restoration and preservation. There are many different ways to clean, restore, and preserve fragile materials. Unless you're an expert in this area, you should leave this to the professionals. Many books can be preserved and rebound so that their lives can be extended. Professional bookbinders can provide this service.

Most larger cities have companies or individuals who specialize in document and artifact restoration. You can usually find them listed in the yellow pages. Local art museums may have a restoration person on staff who can be helpful in a number of different ways, including providing local referrals for the type of restoration you require. Galleries that specialize in archival framing are another good restoration resource. There are also companies that advertise their services on the Internet. A list of some of these appears in the Resource section of this book.

Another way to preserve books, loose papers, photographs, and art work is to have archival portfolios, slipcases, binders, or special boxes made for you. These custom-made materials make it possible not only to preserve important papers and art, but also to display them in an attractive way.

Photographs

Photographs are another important genealogical resource. They need to be treated carefully in order to make sure that they survive from generation to generation. One way to preserve photographs is to encapsulate them. Another way is to frame each one in an archival frame. Photos can also be scanned into computer programs.

Fabric

Fabric heirlooms include wimples, baby blankets, prayer shawls, kippot, chuppah covers, tablecloths, clothing, challah covers, and afikomen bags. The type of fabric will determine the type of preservation needed for each item.

One of the most common questions I'm asked as a rabbi is if a tallit (prayer shawl) can be cleaned so that it can be worn by a bar or bat mitzvah. Older tallitot were usually made of silk, satin, or wool. In more recent years, rayon was also used. All of these fabrics can be dry cleaned, but it's important to take an antique item to a cleaner who is used to working with fragile fabrics. One should never wash a tallit or try to detach the tzitzith (fringes on the four corners) for cleaning.

Metal, Wood, and China Heirlooms

Heirlooms made of these materials are usually ritual objects— candlesticks, spice boxes, seder plates, and kiddush cups are the most common. Each type of material will need to be handled according to its special needs. A local museum is probably the best source of information for the preservation of these objects.

HOW TO CREATE AN ARCHIVAL SCRAPBOOK OR PHOTO ALBUM

An archival scrapbook or photo album will last many years into the future and preserve your family's history for generations to come. The ideal book or album is made out of 100 percent archival materials. While that may not always be possible, the more archival materials used for this project, the better the long-term results.

The book you use should have a protective cover, a hinge that permits the book to expand, and a size that is easy to handle and store. A multiring binder that permits you to add and remove archival Mylar pages is preferable to a bound paper scrapbook. Make sure that the rings close securely. In order to keep the size of the books manageable, you may want to have one book for each of your four grandparents and a separate book that includes you, your parents, and your descendents.

Make sure that the Mylar pages that you buy are actually archival products. Many "PVC-free" plastic sheets are not archival. Archival plastics include cellulose triacetate, DuPont Mylar polyester, polyethylene, and polypropylene. Archival pages are often available at good photo stores and can also be purchased from archival supply companies. It is always a good idea to ask whether the Mylar sheets you plan to buy are archival. Mylar sheets purchased from archival supply houses will be labeled as archival. Companies that sell library supplies may also have this type of product.

If you want to use a paper scrapbook, be very careful about all the materials you use. The pages should be white or off-white archival, acid-free eighty-pound weight or better. One hundred percent rag paper is usually archival. The brand names of some archival papers are Bainbridge, Lig-Free, Perma/Dur, Permalife, Strathmore, and True Core. You can find these papers in a paper specialty shop. In addition, many of these can be ordered through a printer.

Another possibility is to use a charcoal or artist's pad that is 100 percent cotton rag with sturdy-weight pages. These pads are bound. Use only the right-hand page to protect your documents from rubbing against and damaging one another. Leave the first and last page blank to provide extra protection.

You should attach your photographs, postcards, and other items with archival photo corners. Avoid albums with "magnetic pages." These pages emit harmful gases that can fade and discolor photographs. If you write on the back of photographs to identify them—not a bad idea—be sure to use an archival pen, *never* a ballpoint. Another possibility, and possibly a better idea, is to write the information on a piece of archival paper and attach it to the back of the photograph with archival tape. You can also write directly on archival tape—while it's still on the roll—and then tape it directly on the back of the photograph.

Mylar mounting corners for photographs are available from photographic supply stores and are an archival product. *Never use tape,* except for archival, acid-free tape. Scotch tape and other nonarchival tapes may cause yellowing. In addition, they often "ooze" and can cause items and pages to stick together.

Gluing documents into a book can cause the documents to deteriorate over time. In addition, many glues themselves deteriorate over time, causing the materials which have been glued into the scrapbook to fall out and possibly become damaged. If you need to use glue, make sure it's archival glue made for the type of material you are working with.

Handle With Care

When handling documents or other heirlooms that are fragile, here are a few tips to help you.

1. Make sure that the surface you work on is clean and dry. You might want to put a few sheets of archival paper on top of your work surface to make sure that your documents do not come in contact with a harmful surface or damaging material of any kind.

2. Wash and dry your hands thoroughly.

3. Wear white cotton archival gloves when you're working.

4. Use a good artificial light source. Do not rely on sunlight to light your work area. If you're dealing with very fragile materials, you might even want to close the curtains to make sure that no documents or photographs are unnecessarily exposed to the damaging rays of the sun.

5. Don't put any glasses or jars of liquid on your work surface. A careless motion of your hand could result in soda, glue, or other harmful liquids ruining your fragile documents or heirloom. It can happen in a second. It's better to be safe than sorry.

WHAT HAPPENS TO YOUR ARCHIVES?

How do you make sure that your family's documents and heirlooms are passed down from generation to generation?

Unfortunately, many people do not think about preserving their family documents and history until it's too late. It's only when "great-grandpa" dies and the rabbi asks, "What was his Hebrew name?" does a family realize that they do not even know where the documents—like a ketubah—are stored so that they can find out. If your heirs and descendents do not know that you have carefully preserved your family history, they may not think of looking for the documents, archives, and heirlooms that you've so carefully collected, created, and preserved. The key words here are "blab" and "display."

Getting the Word Out

Tell everyone in your family that you're interested in the family's history.

Make sure that a number of family members know that you have family genealogical information, papers, photographs, and other materials. Make multiple copies of the tree you've assembled and give it to all interested relatives.

Early on in your genealogical searches, identify two or three kindred genealogical souls in your family. Tell them where your files are kept, that you want them to have your files when you die, and that the disposition of the papers and heirlooms is in your will.

In your will, make sure to designate heirs for your genealogical archives.

As a clause in your will, require that recipients of your genealogical archives and one-of-a-kind heirlooms name their own heirs for inheriting the archives as a condition of their inheritance.

Make sure that your lawyer or a close family member is aware of where all your filed and other genealogical material is stored.

Keep a copy of your family tree, original documents, and other special papers in a safety deposit box in a bank or in a fireproof box in your home.

Make sure that a close relative and/or your lawyer knows about the existence of this box and has a key.

Encourage other members of your family to create and preserve their own special archival documents, family trees, and life-cycle heirlooms.

Keep a written record or description of each one-of-a-kind document or heirloom. Store these records with your will, or incorporate your description in the body of your will. I once saw a will that made a bequest of "the pearl-handled jug that my mother gave me that was always kept on the mantelpiece of the living room fireplace." This was the author's way of passing along an important piece of family history with the valued object itself.

Displaying Archival Material

Keep your heirlooms and one-of-a-kind and special life-cycle documents on display.

Take the opportunity, when possible, to discuss these treasures with family members so that they understand their significance and value.

Wherever possible, use archival and preservation methods to extend the life of your special documents and memorabilia.

Use heirloom objects in your life celebrations and in those of your family.

LIFE-CYCLE AND FAMILY-EXPERIENCE DOCUMENTS AND HEIRLOOMS

The Jewish life cycle places a special emphasis on ceremony and documentation of life-cycle ceremonies. Each life-cycle ceremony has documents and ritual objects associated with it. When you make an effort to create and preserve documents and ritual objects for each life-cycle event, you create links between yourself and future generations.

One type of heirloom is used in almost every life cycle and ritual occasion. This is the kiddush cup. Purchasing or commissioning a kiddush cup for significant life-cycle occasions—brit milah or naming, bar or bat mitzvah, wedding—is a wonderful way of creating an heirloom that will be used and that will be passed down through the generations. Each kiddush cup should be engraved or inscribed with the date and nature of the occasion and the person who is being honored, i.e., Max Schwartz and Sylvia Hersh, Wedding, May 10, 1946. If there is room, it's always a good idea to include the Hebrew name or names so that there will be a record of these passed down in the family.

Here are some other suggestions for creating documents and heirlooms that will send your family information into the future.

Birth

The birth or adoption of a new child gives the genealogist or archivist a great number of opportunities for creating wonderful commemorative documents and heirlooms. Here are some suggestions.

BASIC DOCUMENTS FOR A NEW BABY

- preprinted naming certificate filled in with the baby's English and Hebrew names and the English and Hebrew names of the parents (for boys and girls)
- brit milah certificate—if a boy
- baby's birth certificate, footprints, and fingerprints

INTERESTING OPTIONS FOR A NEW BABY

- Create an original naming or brit milah certificate incorporating the baby's family tree.
- Create an original birth announcement incorporating the baby's family tree or other information about the baby's family.
- Start a document file box for the baby. Label the box with the baby's name. In the box put a copy of all of the following, properly preserved: hospital records; birth certificate; parents' birth certificates; parents' civil marriage certificate; copy of parents' ketubah; copy of naming certificate; copy of bris certificate, if a boy; birth announcement; ascendant chart.

HEIRLOOM OPTIONS

- wimple, embroidered or painted, containing the baby's English and Hebrew name, birth date, and the name of the Torah portion of the week in which he or she was born
- quilt with genealogy and family information

Bar/Bat Mitzvah

There are many different options during a bar/bat mitzvah event to create meaningful documents and heirlooms. Here are some suggestions.

INVITATIONS

Most bar and bat mitzvah celebrations require the creation of an invitation. Although most invitations are somewhat standardized, it should be noted that they offer opportunities for creating life-cycle documents of some significance. Here are some suggestions for creating a bar/bat mitzvah invitation that will send a message into the future:

- Include the child's Hebrew name and the parents' Hebrew names in the invitation.
- Explain the meaning of the child's Hebrew name.
- Explain why the Hebrew name was chosen for the child and talk about the relative that he or she was named for.
- Include the child's genealogy in the invitation.
- Include all the Hebrew names that you know of for direct family members in the invitation—i.e., grandparents, parents, siblings.

BAR/BAT MITZVAH CERTIFICATE

Most synagogues provide some sort of bar/bat mitzvah certificate. Most of the time, the information on these is minimal. This is an opportunity for the family to create a unique bar/bat mitzvah certificate that will accurately record the information that the individual and later generations will find interesting. Here are some suggestions for what should be included:

- the date of the bar/bat mitzvah ceremony
- the place where the religious ceremony was held
- the child's Hebrew name (including the parents' Hebrew names) written in Hebrew and English transliteration
- the name of the Torah portion and Haftorah portion read
- the exact Torah and/or Haftorah verses read or chanted (in non-Orthodox synagogues, a bar/bat mitzvah usually reads only part of each portion)
- the name of the rabbi, cantor, or other officiants
- other things that the child did during the ceremony
- The English and Hebrew names of the people who were given aliyahs (called up to the Torah) during the Torah reading.

PRAYER BOOK OR BIBLE

Most congregations present a bar/bat mitzvah with an inscribed siddur or Hebrew Bible. Besides inscribing the book with the date of the bar/bat mitzvah, the Hebrew and English name of the child should be included, along with the information about the Torah and Haftorah portions read during the ceremony. A copy of the child's family tree might also be pasted into the back of the book.

Marriage

KETUBAH

Today, there are many different options for couples purchasing a ketubah—from inexpensive ketubot that can be purchased for a few dollars to limited edition "art prints" that can run into the hundreds of dollars. In addition, there are many talented artists who specialize in creating one-of-a-kind ketubot.

Whatever choice a couple makes about a ketubah, it's extremely important that the information provided to the person who is filling in the ketubah include both the bride's and the groom's mother's names. This is not the "traditional" way of filling out a ketubah, but there's no reason why the mothers' names can't be included. The reason that this is so important from a genealogical perspective is that the ketubah is one of the few documents that most Jewish couples manage to hang onto. If it records both parents' English and Hebrew names, it will provide future genealogists in your family with an accurate record of two generations of your family history.

If you choose to commission an artist to create a ketubah, the possibilities for capturing family history are limitless. Many couples today incorporate details like where they met, pictures of their family homes, family trees, even beloved pets.

Traditionally, a ketubah was only created for a Jewish man and woman at the time of marriage. Now, all different types of couples are commissioning ketubot. Anniversary ketubot, celebrating a significant wedding anniversary, are becoming increasingly popular. Some interfaith couples also choose to create a ketubah-like document for their weddings. Ketubot are also sometimes commissioned by Jewish same-sex couples for use in commitment ceremonies.

Traditional ketubot can be purchased in Judaica stores and some large Jewish museums. There are many artists who specialize in creating these new types of documents. They can be found by asking a local rabbi, talking to someone at a local Judaica store, looking in the ads of a local Jewish newspaper or national Jewish magazines, or checking the Internet under the keyword "ketubah."

CHUPPAH

A chuppah is the marriage canopy under which a bride and groom are married. Most couples opt for a "florist's chuppah"—a fixed structure that is covered with leaves, flowers, or both. A very traditional chuppah consists of four poles held by four relatives or friends topped with a large tallit. Some synagogues offer either fixed or movable poles with a more elaborate covering.

In recent years, several other options have emerged that are of interest to genealogists. One option is to commission a chuppah cover. Like the ketubah, commissioning a chuppah cover offers the couple the chance to create a lasting heirloom that can incorporate a wealth of family history. After the wedding, the chuppah cover is archivally framed and hung as a piece of art in the home.

Another interesting option is to involve family and friends who are invited to the wedding in the work of creating the chuppah cover. Each person is sent a square of material; several fabric pens; a stamped, return envelope; and instructions to create a picture and/or write a message of blessing or other words of help or advice to the bride and groom. These are returned several months before the wedding and are sewn together to create the chuppah cover. The bride and groom can also add their names, wedding date, and other family information to be incorporated into the cover. After the wedding, the cover is framed and hung in the couple's home.

End of Life

We spoke earlier of the important information that one can gain from a head- or footstone in a cemetery. Another way of communicating to future generations is through the creation of an ethical will.

ETHICAL WILL

An ethical will is a document written with the intention of passing along one's values to future generations. Creating an ethical will is a time-honored Jewish tradition. Right before his death, Moses addresses the Israelites and blesses them. (Deuteronomy 31:22–33:29) In this passage, he exhorts the Israelites to be faithful to God and to follow God's commandments.

Other biblical figures also tried to pass on their view of the world to their offspring. As King David was dying, he charged Solomon with keeping the Torah and the commandments and also reminded him of the friends and enemies of their family. The biblical book of Proverbs is ethical literature intended to instruct future generations. Later rabbinic literature, like the Pirket Avot (The Ethics of the Fathers), carried on this tradition. Many of the great scholars in the Jewish world also left letters of instruction to their children.

One of the most interesting ethical wills that has come down to us is that of Judah ibn Tibbon. Judah ibn Tibbon (approximately 1120–1190), was a Spanish Jew who immigrated to southern France. He was known as the "father of translators," because he translated important Jewish works from Arabic into Hebrew. His son, Samuel ibn Tibbon, who lived from approximately 1150 to 1230, translated Maimonides' *Guide for the Perplexed* from Arabic into Hebrew.

Judea ibn Tibbon's ethical will, written to his son, Samuel, can be found, along with many others, in Israel Abrahams' book, *Hebrew Ethical Wills*. In his ethical will, Judea ibn Tibbon urges his son to take care of the library he has created for him and to lend his books to those who are too poor to buy them for themselves. However, he cautions his son to lend his books only to people who will give them back. He also urges him to take care of his wife and to make sure that his home is clean, because filth breeds disease. He exhorts his son to study medicine and, when a doctor, to take fees from the rich, but to treat the poor for free.

Although neglected for some time, ethical wills are beginning to make a comeback in the Jewish world. If you're interested in learning more about ethical wills, the following books will help. The first is out of print, but can be found in most Jewish libraries or searched for through Amazon.com or used book dealers who specialize in Judaica.

> *Hebrew Ethical Wills,* by Israel Abrahams, Jewish Publication Society, 1976.
>
> *So That Your Values Live On: Ethical Wills and How to Prepare Them,* by Jack Riemer and Nathaniel Stampfer (editors), Jewish Lights Publishing, 1994.

EPHEMERA

Many of the things that we think of as being special to a person or a family are not necessarily documents or heirlooms. Rather, they are stories, songs, memories, recipes, and special family traditions. There are many different ways to preserve these special parts of your family's history.

Food and Family Gatherings

Family recipes and traditions are a rich source of family heritage. To capture these for future generations, create a special book of family memories. Include the following:

- recipes and photographs of the completed dishes
- menus for special occasions
- photographs of table settings, with an explanation of the event for which the table was set, people present, and menu served
- photographs of family members gathered for special occasions (don't forget to identify the family members)
- descriptions of special family traditions. (For example, some years ago, I acquired a reproduction of a colonial "birthday" plate. Now we use this plate to hold the birthday cake when we gather to celebrate a family birthday.)

Letters and Journals

Letters and journals tell one's story from an intimate point of view. Sometimes you don't want that story told. I remember the day, about fifteen years ago, when I decided it was time to do something about the hundreds of letters from old boyfriends that were stored in my mother's attic. I realized that there were things in those letters that I didn't want to be read by future generations. I gathered them together and burned them. The letters from my husband, written when we were in my teens, however, I carefully preserved. I trust that my descendents, when they read these, will understand that we were young when they were written.

Working with journals and letters is tricky. Rabbi Malcolm Stern's Ninth Commandment is "Thou shalt respect the sensitivities of the living in whatever you record but tell the truth about the dead." If you come across the journals or letters of someone who is no longer alive, you need to ask yourself two questions:

1. Is there anyone who is alive who would be hurt or upset by the publishing or use of these materials? And,
2. How will the publication or distribution of these materials expand the understanding of the individual or family in question?

It goes without saying that you may never use the journals or letters of a living person without his or her permission. Even in using your own letters and journals, it's important to read them carefully to make sure that no one else will be affected by their publication or distribution.

Music and Stories

Create a family journal that includes special family stories, things you liked to do as a family, and songs that you enjoy singing as a family. For example, whenever we went over the George Washington Bridge, which connects New York to New Jersey, my father always sang the "George Washington Bridge," song. I thought that "bridge" songs were limited to the "George," until someone told me recently that her father always sang the "Triborough Bridge" song!

While these songs are not major contributions to the corpus of American popular music, they usually have some special type of family history behind them. In my father's case, it was the fact that, as a Boy Scout, he and his troop took part in the opening of the George Washington Bridge

in 1931. He loved to tell us this story, and it was included in a wonderful book, *You Must Remember This, An Oral History of Manhattan
From the 1890s to World War II*, written by Jeff Kisseloff.

Recently, I wrote a story for my grandson, Lior, about a Russian song
my grandmother used to sing with me. After much hard work, I finally
was able to get the words transliterated and translated. I wrote down
the words and music, so this song will be passed down in my family.
The story and the song follow:

PAYDUYM DUNYA
For Lior Shalom Wolf David
by his grandmother, Rabbi Jo Lynn Marx David,
granddaughter of Bessie Steinberg, may her memory be for a blessing.

When I was a very little girl, my grandmother seated me on her lap
and taught me a song that her mother had taught her many years ago, in
Russia. The name of this song was "Payduym, Dunya," which means
"Dunya, Let's Go." Dunya is the name of the girl in the song.

I loved singing this song with my grandmother. It gave me the feeling
that we were sharing something very special from her childhood. Even
though I was a child, I sensed that when we sang "Payduym Dunya,"
my grandmother was remembering what her life was like when she was
a child and living in the little town called Skvira. "Payduym, Dunya"
was like a secret between the two of us. It evoked a land and a people
that I could only know through the feelings that I had when my grandmother and I sat and sang this song together. It was held in musical
amber during a time that is long gone, but could be recreated through
the simple words and melody of this special song.

In time, my brother became old enough to be able to repeat the lilting
Russian words and he too was initiated into the secret of "Payduym,
Dunya." Although we most often sang this song with my grandmother, as
we got older, we would also sing it ourselves, especially on family outings
in our car. Singing in the car was a very popular pastime in our family.

It was through the singing of "Payduym, Dunya" that my grandmother began to tell me stories about her childhood and how she and

my grandfather ran away from Russia and came to America. Some of my earliest memories are of her telling me about the food in Russia. Two specific foods were mentioned time and time again.

"The chocolate!" my grandmother would say. "It was so delicious!" Then she would give a little sigh.

When I was growing up, my grandmother always had wonderful chocolate in her home. It came in a special metal tin with the picture of a beautiful woman and a man in a uniform on the top of the tin. Each piece of chocolate was separately wrapped. The strawberry creams, my special favorites, were wrapped in light pink paper. I always imagined that the chocolate in the Russia of my grandmother's youth was like the chocolate that came in that tin.

Many years later, I had the chance to visit Russia and I made a point of buying a number of different types of chocolate while I was there. My grandmother had died many years before, so she couldn't tell me if the chocolate was like that of her childhood. However, it didn't taste very good to me, and I believe that she would have been disappointed. However, I had the chance to take a trip to another part of Russia later in the same year. Going there, I flew on a plane that sold Swiss chocolate that is unavailable here in the United States. I bought a bar. It was absolutely the best chocolate I've ever eaten. I like to think that the chocolate of my grandmother's girlhood was like the chocolate I ate on that airplane. It was thick, rich, subtle, sweet, soft on the tongue, and not too quick to melt. It was heaven.

The other taste of home that my grandmother would often talk about was as different as anything could be from chocolate. It was a dried fish called *kapchanka*. When my grandmother said that word, she would literally smack her lips and a soft look would come into her blue eyes. It's impossible to say the word *kapchanka* properly without a little lip smacking.

For many years, I thought that these remembrances of the foods of the old country were unique to my grandmother. However, when I began to study the Torah seriously many years later, I came across the passage in which the Israelites complain to Moses that they miss the food of their homeland. They say, "We remember the fish that we used to eat. . . , the cucumbers, the leeks, the onions and the garlic." This appears in the Book of Numbers, chapter 11, verse 5. I immediately saw and heard my grandmother saying, "The chocolate! The kapchanka!" This impression returns to me every time I read these lines in the Torah. Longing for the food of our homeland is part of the experience of being a wanderer or an immigrant. Even though our lives may be better in many ways in our adopted homeland, there will always be certain precious memories that have an everlasting hold on our heart.

My grandmother learned to read, write, and speak English very well, although she never lost her heavy Russian accent and sometimes she would misinterpret common English expressions. I remember one day when she told me that someone had "upset the apricot," meaning, of course, "upset the applecart." When we were singing "Payduym, Dunya," however, it was almost as if we were speaking Russian together.

I never knew the exact meaning of all the words in "Payduym, Dunya." I just knew that it was about a girl named Dunya who went out into the woods and had a pretty dress. I never asked my grandmother what the words meant exactly, because it didn't seem to matter to me at the time. It was only later, as an adult, that I began to wonder. And by then, my grandmother wasn't alive for me to ask her.

It was only recently that I found a Russian-speaking woman, Ita Shiryeyeva, from Alma-Ata, Khazakstan, who knew this song. Together, we reconstructed the words and the translation. It was important for me to do this for you. This is why.

When my grandmother and grandfather came here from Russia, they didn't bring any family heirlooms with them. Even the jewels that my great-grandfather had managed to smuggle out of Russia were lost at sea during a storm. The only thing from the old country that I have of my grandmother's is this song. It's my hope that you will teach this song and tell this story to your children, and they, to their children. I pray that, along with the song, the name and the memory of Bessie Pokroshevsky Steinberg will also be passed along and remembered. She was a very special woman, with a brave spirit and a loving heart. I know that she's looking down at you from heaven and kvelling because she has a wonderful great-great-grandson.

Payduym Dunya—A Russian Folk Song

The words

1. Payduym, payduym Dunya,
   Payduym, payduym Dunya,
   Payduym, Dunya, vo-di-sok, vo-di-sok,
   Payduym, Dunya, vo-di-sok, vo-di-sok.

   Let's go into the forest, Dunya.

2. Vorzmyum, vorzmyum, Dunya
   Vorzmyum, vorzmyum, Dunya
   Vorzmyum, Dunya, too-ya-sok, too-ya-sok,
   Vorzmyum, Dunya, too-ya-sok, too-ya-sok.

   Let's take a special basket, Dunya.

3. Nad-av-yorm, nad-av-yorm, Dunya
   Nad-av-yorm, nad-av-yorm, Dunya
   Nad-av-yorm, Dunya, cal-a-sok, cal-a-sok,
   Nad-av-yorm, Dunya, cal-a-sok, cal-a-sok.

   Let's pick grass, Dunya.

4. Sash-yorm, sash-yorm, Dunya,
   Sash-yorm, sash-yorm, Dunya,
   Sash-yorm, Dunya, sarda-fun, sarda-fun,
   Sash-yorm, Dunya, sarda-fun, sarda-fun.

   Let us sew a (new) dress, Dunya.

Vocabulary

Payduym—Let's go.
Dunya—A girl's name.
Vodisok—Into the forest.
Comment: The forests in
Russia are very beautiful.

Vorzmyum—Let's take.

Tooyasok—special basket.

Nadavyorm—Let's pick.

Calasok—Grass.
Comment: Some types of
long grass are put in vases
like flowers; sweet grasses
are used like potpouri, to
make a room smell nice.

Sashyorm—Let us sew.

Sardafun—a long, sleeveless
dress, like a jumper. The
women would wear this
dress with a long-sleeved
blouse underneath.

5. Nasi, nasi, Dunya,

Nasi, nasi, Dunya.
Nasi, Dunya, n'yem-a-rye, n'yem-a-rye,

Po-praznitkam na-dee-vye, na-dee-vye.

Nasi—Don't get (it)(the dress) dirty.

N'yemarye—Don't get spots on it.

Po praznitkam na dee vye—Put it on for festivals.

Don't get your dress dirty or spotted, Dunya.
Wear it for festivals.

A Reflection

In the course of doing this book, I've spoken with many people who have told me that they are not interested in genealogy, that they don't think that the past has anything to offer them. This attitude amazes me. It makes me wonder how they feel about their own lives. It makes me wonder if they think that their own lives are uninteresting and therefore won't be valued by future generations.

To me, each person's life experience is unique and valuable. I can't remember a time when I wasn't interested in people and their lives. To recapture at least some of the details of the lives of those whose genes we carry seems to me to be a sacred trust. To leave a record for those who come after me feels like a covenant with the future. I hope that you will find this book helpful in finding your place in the continuum of your family's history.

18

Resources

There are many different types of resources available to help genealogists at all stages of their work—from traditional books and periodicals to Web sites and CD-ROMs. This chapter is designed to help you access a wide range of services, books, and professionals.

BOOKS AND PERIODICALS

There is no end to the books that you can buy on the subject of genealogy in general and Jewish genealogy in particular. Most of the books listed here are available in large genealogy libraries, Jewish genealogy society libraries, and in large Jewish libraries.

Before buying a book, you should decide whether it is something that you will use over and over again, or if it is something that you can get at a local library whenever you need it. With that said, the following is a list of books and periodicals that are of special importance to Jewish genealogists. Avotaynu also maintains a list of suggested books on their Web site.

From Generation to Generation: How to Trace Your Jewish Genealogy and Family History, revised edition, Arthur Kurzweil, Harper/Perennial, 1996. This is an important "basic book" everyone should own.

Finding Our Fathers: A Guidebook to Jewish Genealogy, Dan Rottenberg, Random House, 1977; Reprints—Genealogical Publishing Co., Baltimore, 1986, 1995, 1998. This book contains a great deal of resource material and was one of the first major books on Jewish genealogy.

The International Review of Jewish Genealogy is a quarterly magazine. For a subscription, send check or money order to: Avotaynu; P.O. Box 900, Dept. W, Teaneck, NJ, 07666; or call 1-800-AVOTAYNU (U.S. and Canada); E-mail: info@avotaynu.com. This will help you keep up with the latest in Jewish genealogical research.

How to Document Victims and Locate Survivors of the Holocaust, Gary Mokotoff, Avotaynu, 1995. Audiotape. A "must" for genealogists doing Holocaust research.

A Guide to Jewish Genealogical Resources in Israel, Sallyann Admur Sack, revised edition, Avotaynu, 1995. A guide to collections in Israeli libraries and archives.

Sourcebook for Jewish Genealogies and Family Histories, David S. Zubatsky, and Irwin M. Berent, Avotaynu, 1996. Covers Jewish genealogies and family histories, both published and unpublished, for more than 10,000 family names.

Morton Allan Directory of European Passenger Steamship Arrivals. Ship arrival dates from 1890 to 1930. Available through Avotaynu. Available in most Jewish genealogical and general genealogy libraries. Also available through the Family History Centers on microfilm and at regional NARA offices.

They Came in Ships, John P. Colletta, Ancestry, Inc., 1989, 1993. A guide for beginners which includes step-by-step instructions on how to trace your ancestor's voyage to the New World.

Latter Day Leaders, Sages, and Scholars, Emanuel Rosenstein. Computer Center for Jewish Genealogy. An index of more than 5,500 rabbis, primarily those from Eastern Europe.

The Source: A Guidebook of American Genealogy, Loretto Dennis Szucs (editor), Sandra Hargreaves Luebking (editor), Sandra H. Webking, revised edition, Ancestry, Inc., 1997. A standard reference work.

Jewish Roots in Poland: Pages From the Past and Archival Inventories, Miriam Weiner and Michael Berenbaum; Polish State Archives, Miriam Weiner Routes to Roots, 1997. A vital book for genealogists doing research on Poland.

A Dictionary of Jewish Names and Their History, Benzion C. Kaganoff, Jason Aronson, 1996. An outstanding book, recently rereleased. Of special interest to genealogists looking for clues to their family history through their personal names and surnames.

Jewish Family Names and their Origins: An Etymological Dictionary, Heinrich W. and Eva H. Guggenheimer, Ktav, 1992.

Jewish and Hebrew Onomastics: A Bibliography, Robert Singerman, Garland, 1977. A subject-organized list of close to 1,200 books and articles dealing with various aspects of Jewish names.

The Complete Dictionary of English and Hebrew First Names, Alfred J. Kolatch, Jonathan David Publishers, 1984.

Following the Paper Trail: A Multilingual Translation Guide, Jonathan D. Shea and William F. Hoffman, Avotaynu, 1994. Available through Avotaynu. Covers thirteen European languages and contains translation information for vital records and other important documents.

American Naturalization Processes and Procedures, 1790–1985, John J. Newman, Indiana Historical Society, 1985. Provides a detailed look at this fascinating and complicated subject.

Documents of Our Ancestors: A Selection of Reproducible Genealogy Forms and Tips for Using Them, available through Avotaynu. Actual forms that are needed to request documents from various archives and organizations.

Compiled Genealogies. Avotaynu has available a number of books of compiled genealogies. These include:

- *Vilna Gaon: Eliyahu's Branches: The Desecendants of the Vilna Gaon and His Family.* This book lists 20,000 descendents of this important rabbi and scholar, 1997.
- *The Unbroken Chain,* Neil Rosenstein, 2nd ed. 1990. Lists 25,000 descendents of the founder of the Katzenellenbogen family.
- *The Book of Destiny: Toledot Charlap.* Charts the history of the Charlap family.

Genealogy Is More Than Charts: 100's of Activities to Enhance Your Family History, Lorna Duane Smith, Apronstrings Publishing, 1992. A family activity book organized around genealogy and preserving family history.

BOOK, MAGAZINE, AND GENEALOGY SUPPLY VENDORS

Abebooks.com   http://www.abebooks.com/
This service searches for used and out-of-print titles of all types.

Amazon.com   http://www.amazon.com
This online mega-store is best for new and recently printed titles, but they can also do searches for out-of-print books. Their prices for out-of-print titles are not based on condition, so buyer beware. However, they always confirm prices before ordering a title they're searching for you.

Avotaynu   http://www.avotaynu.com.   They can also be reached by phone at 1-800-AVOTAYNU or (201) 387-7200. Write: P.O. Box 900, Dept. W, Teaneck, NJ 07666; E-mail: info@avotaynu.com.
Avotaynu carries its own publications, including CD-ROM and microfiche as well as genealogy books by other publishers.

Barnes and Noble   http://www. barnesandnoble.com
Barnes and Noble carries new books on genealogy. The retail stores will order books that are in print for you that they may not ordinarily stock. You can also order books from them online.

Association of Jewish Book Publishers
http://www.avotaynu.com/ajbp.html
This Web site features Jewish book publishers and their wares.
The page is hosted by Avotaynu.

Yizkor book specialists:

- J. Robinson & Co., 31 Nachlat Benjamin St., P.O. Box 4308, Tel Aviv 65162, Israel
- Moshe Schreiber, 16 Mea Sharim St., Jerusalem, Israel
- Chaim E. Dzialowski, P.O. Box 6413, Jerusalem 90163, Israel
- Pinat Ha-Sefer, P.O. Box 46646, Haifa 31464, Israel

Institutions with major Yizkor book collections:

- The New York Public Library, Jewish Division (see page 292 for information on how to contact)
- Jewish Theological Seminary Library
- University of California Library—UCLA, Jewish Studies Collection
- Yad Vashem (see page 292 for information on how to contact)
- Hebrew Union College—Jewish Institute of Religion, Klau Library
- Library of Congress, Hebraic Section
- Brandeis University Library
- Harvard University, Harry Elkins Widener Memorial Library, Hebraic Collection
- Yeshiva University Archives (see page 292 for information on how to contact)
- Jewish National and University Library
- YIVO Institute for Jewish Research (Manhattan) (see page 292 for information on how to contact)
- Holocaust Center of Northern California (San Francisco)
- Price Library of Judaica (University of Florida, Gainesville)
- Jewish Public Library of Montreal

Everton Publishers   http://www.everton.com/ or write: Everton
Publishers, Logan, UT 84323-0368; (800) 443-6325.

Everton carries a full range of genealogy supplies including
research forms, binders, and software.

Frontier Press   http://www.doit.com/frontier/frontier.cgi or write:
Frontier Press, 10 Cadena Drive, Suite 2, Galveston, TX 77554-6329;
tel. (800) 772-7559, fax: (409) 740-0138, E-mail: KGFrontier@aol.com.

This company specializes in providing genealogical and historical
books. Although they are a general genealogy supplier, they have an
extensive number of books and audio tapes related to the subject of
Jewish genealogy. They also publish the *Genealogical Helper*
magazine.

Personalized Family History Book. Write to: Peggy Halverson,
Route 1, Box 210, Deer River, MN 56636; (218) 326-4177. Peggy
Halverson works with individuals and families to create custom-
designed family history books.

Heirloom Histories   http://heirloom.inetz.com/.   Write to: 3058
E. Sundrift Circle, Salt Lake City, UT 84121; (801) 773-5038.
Another resource for creating a lasting family album for your
descendents.

MICROFILM/MICROFICHE AND CD-ROM

In order to use microfilm or microfiche, you must have access to a
machine that reads material in this format. Some libraries have machines
that can be used. Some genealogical societies may also have this equipment. It's also possible to purchase this equipment yourself. Before you
buy information on one of these formats, be sure that you will be able to
make use of it.

The CD-ROM requires a computer with a CD-ROM drive. Besides
making sure that you have access to this equipment, you need to make
sure that the program on the CD-ROM can be run on the kind of computer to which you have access. Most of the time, material that is in
CD-ROM format indicates the type of computer needed to run it.

Below are listed some basic information available in these formats that may be of special interest to Jewish genealogists. Except where otherwise indicated, they are available from Avotaynu.

Avotaynu on CD-ROM (1985–1996). This is a comprehensive reference work on Jewish genealogy featuring more than 2,300 articles that are accessible with a full-word search engine. It requires an IBM or Mac computer with CD-ROM drive. It is also available in a printed edition.

Gazetteer of Central and Eastern Europe (microfiche). This is a tool for locating towns in Central and Eastern Europe; 350,000 towns are shown with latitude and longitude. An important aid to finding a town that is "missing."

Jewish Residents in the 1861–1901 Censuses of Canada (microfiche). This is a list of all Jews found in five Canadian censuses between 1861 and 1901.

PROFESSIONAL GENEALOGISTS

Working with a professional genealogist can help you move your research along. The genealogists listed here were selected because of their areas of interest and specialization. Inclusion in this book does not indicate an endorsement.

If you would like to know more about one or more of these professionals, you can contact him or her directly. If you contact a genealogist by snail mail, write a brief note about your proposed project and enclose a self-addressed, stamped envelope for a reply. Don't forget to include your own address, phone number, fax number if you have one, and an E-mail address if you have one. You should also feel free to ask for references before beginning a project.

Norma Arbit, 4530 Woodley Avenue, Encino, CA 91436-2722, (818) 981-0590

Specialties: Russia—especially Ukraine, U.S. records services; cemetery research in L.A. area.

Jordan Auslander, 321 W. 24th Street, No. 16-G, New York, NY 10011-1556, (212) 691-9428, jausland@pipeline.com
Specialties: Metro NYC; New York City area cemeteries; Slovak and Hungarian records.

Charles B. Bernstein, 5400 S. Hyde Park Boulevard, 10C, Chicago, IL 60615-5828, (312) 324-6362
Specialties: Chicago, California, rabbinic genealogy services: record searching (Chicago, including courthouse), book publisher (for clients), American German-Jewish.

Warren Blatt, 27-1 Georgetown Drive, Framingham, MA 01702, (508) 620-0659, wblatt@jewishgen.org
Specialties: Polish vital records and translations, immigration, naturalization services.

Shalom Bronstein, Rechov Hizkiyahu Hamelech 47/4, Jerusalem 93224 Israel, (02) 561-0047, sygaa@netvision.net.il
Specialties: Resources in Jerusalem: Yad Vashem and Central Zionist Archives Services: Pages of Testimony, Yizkor books, translations from Hebrew to English.

Jeffrey Cymbler, 94-01 64th Road, No. 4G, Rego Park, NY 11374, (718) 896-0028, jcymbler@aol.com
Specialties: Russian, Poland, and Galicia; Holocaust; Yizkor books services; translations (Hebrew and Yiddish).

Nancy J. Deutsch-Sinderbrand, 111-32 76th Avenue, No. 3C, Forest Hills, NY 11375, (718) 544-6721
Specialties: Cleveland, New York; Czech, Slovakian and French resources; cemetery research, oral history, interviews.

Boris Feldblyum, 8510 Wild Olive Drive, Potomac, MD 20854, (301) 424-2654, bfeldbly@capaccess.org
Specialties: Archival research in the former Soviet Union, historic and contemporary photographs of Eastern Europe, translations.

Alex E. Friedlander, 169 Stratford Road, Brooklyn, NY 11218, (718) 693-7169

Specialties: Polish and Lithuanian archival records and other sources on nineteenty-century Polish and Lithuanian Jews; Suwalki Gubernia.

Lucille Gudis, 600 West End Avenue, New York, NY 10024, (212) 799-8660, lgud@aol.com
Specialties: New York City; England family research, record searching.

Ladislau Gyemant, Str. Tarnita 1, BL. B5, Sc. III, ap. 283400, Cluj-Napoca, Romania, (011) 40-64-167256, gyemant@mcarmilly.soroscj.ro
Specialties: Transylvania and Moldavia (Romania); family research and record searching.

Sherrill Stern Laszlo, 34 Craig Avenue, Piedmont, CA 94611, (510) 655-6789, laszlo@uclink4.berkeley.edu
Specialties: San Francisco area; California; Austria and Hungary; Czechoslovakia (Bohemia, Moravia, Slovakia); family research; record searching (U.S. public records, published and archival records); translations (Hungarian).

Herb Mautner, 6507 Longridge Avenue, Van Nuys, CA 91401, (818) 761-1856, hmaut70937@aol.com
Specialties: Germany (Bavaria and Duchy of Anhalt); Bohemia (Czechoslovakia) up to 1933; family research, translations.

Adele Miller, 5445 N. Sheridan Road, No. 1605, Chicago, IL 60640, (312) 275-0941
Specialties: Translations (Polish to English, Yiddish to English, English to Polish/Yiddish).

Gary Mokotoff, 155 N. Washington Avenue, Bergenfield, NJ 07621, (201) 387-7200, garymokotoff@avotaynu.com
Specialties: General Jewish genealogy, Holocaust research.

Barbara Sora Shpack, Box 1527, Salt Lake City, UT 84110, (801) 322-2877
Specialties: Polish, Russian, German, and Hungarian records at Latter Day Saints services; record searching.

Regina Wassercier Spiszman, 5921 Simpson Avenue, North Hollywood, CA 91607, (818) 769-5326

Specialties: Poland, Brazil, Australia, England; U.S.: Illinois, Michigan, and New York services; access to extensive genealogical library.

Betty Provizer Starkman, 1260 Stuyvessant Road, Bloomfield Hills, MI 48301, (810) 646-0332, bettejoy@aol.com
Specialties: Eastern Europe, Holocaust services, family histories, record searching, locate relatives, Jews of China.

Miriam Weiner, 136 Sandpiper Key, Secaucus, NJ 07094, (201) 866-4075
Specialties: Holocaust sources; author, *Routes to Roots,* genealogy tours; customized visits to ancestral towns; and research in Ukraine, Moldova, Belarus, and Polish archives.

Geraldine Frey Winerman, 4660 Varna Avenue, Sherman Oaks, CA 91423, (818) 784-7277
Specialties: U.S., New York, England, Sephardic research.

GENEALOGICAL SOCIETIES

This is a list of genealogical societies that may be of interest to Jewish researchers.

Association of Jewish Genealogical Societies, 7604 Edenwood Court, Bethesda, MD 20817, http://www.jewishgen.org/ajgs/ajgs-jgss.html. There are affiliates throughout the world.

Jewish Genealogical Society of New York, P.O. Box 6398, New York, NY 10128, http://www.aol.members/jgsny/main.html. This is a very active and well-established chapter.

Polish Genealogical Society of America, 984 N. Milwaukee Avenue, Chicago, IL 60622, http://members.aol.com/pgsamerica. This organization has local societies all over the United States.

INSTITUTIONS AND ORGANIZATIONS OF INTEREST TO JEWISH GENEALOGISTS

Family History Library, 35 N.W. Temple Street, Salt Lake City, UT 84150, (800) 346-6044, http://www.lds.org

HIAS (Hebrew Immigrant Aid Society), 333 Seventh Avenue, New York, NY 10001-5004, (212) 967-4100, E-mail: info@hias.org. HIAS is a Jewish aid organization that helps Jews and others with immigration and emigration issues. HIAS assisted more than 70,000 Holocaust families in the 1940s and 1950s. They maintain case files on these persons, and will search for a modest fee.

Jewish Heritage Council, World Monuments Fund, 949 Park Avenue, New York, NY 10028, (212) 517-9367, http://www. worldmonuments.org. This organization researches and preserves important Jewish landmarks worldwide.

Lower East Side Tenement Museum, 66 Allen Street, New York, NY 10002, (212) 431-0233, http://www.wnet.org/tenement. Outstanding museum dedicated to researching the New York immigrant experience.

New York Public Library, Jewish Division, 42nd Street and Fifth Avenue, New York, NY 10018, (212) 930-0601. This is a major Jewish general reference and genealogy library.

Routes to Roots: http://www.routestoroots.com. This is a company that specializes in Jewish research in Eastern European archives. It also arranges customized tours to Eastern Europe.

United States Holocaust Memorial Museum, 100 Raoul Wallenberg Place SW, Washington, DC 20024, (202) 488-0400, http://www.ushmm.org

Yad Vashem, P.O. Box 3477, Jerusalem, 91034, Israel http://www.yad-vashem.org.il

Yeshiva University Archives, 500 W. 185 Street, New York, NY 10033, (212) 960-5451

YIVO Institute for Jewish Research, 555 W. 57th Street, 11th Floor, New York, NY 10019, (212) 246-6080, http://www. baruch.cuny.edu/yivo

RABBINIC ORGANIZATIONS

Central Conference of American Rabbis (CCAR)—Reform, 355 Lexington Avenue, New York, NY 10017, tel. (212) 972-3636; fax: (212) 692-0819, E-mail Infor@ccarnet.org, http://ccarnet.org/index.html.

Rabbinical Assembly (RA)—Conservative, 3080 Broadway, New York, NY 10027, (212) 678-8060.

Academy for Jewish Religion Alumni Association—Pluralistic, 15 West 86th Street, New York, NY 10024, tel.: (212) 875-0540, fax: (212) 875-0541, E-mail names18@aol.com.

Reconstructionist Rabbinical Association (RRA)—Reconstructionist, 1299 Church Road, Wyncote, PA 19095, (215) 576-5210.

Rabbinical Council of America (RCA)—Orthodox, 305 Seventh Avenue, New York, NY 10001 (212) 807-7888.

OVERVIEW OF JEWISH GENEALOGY AND GENERAL GENEALOGY RESOURCES ON THE INTERNET

Cyndi's List of Genealogy Sites on the Internet: http://www.CyndisList.com. An excellent site of general genealogy information in cyberspace.

Everton Publishers: http://www.everton.com. Genealogy supplies.

Federation of East European Family History Societies: http://feefhs.org.

Genealogy Homepage: http://www.genhomepage.com. General genealogy information.

Genealogy Toolbox: http://genealogy.tbox.com. An excellent general genealogy Web site for finding books, software, and research help.

Jewish Appleseed Foundation—Geneology Web page for beginners: http://www.jewishappleseed.org.

JewishGen: http://www.jewishgen.org. The premier Jewish genealogy Web site.

National Archives: http://www.nara.gov. Home site for NARA.

Sephardic Genealogy Web site: http://www.orthohelp.com/geneal/sefardim.html. Outstanding Web site for genealogists interested in Sephardic genealogy.

Yahoo Genealogy Index: http://www.yahoo.com/Arts/Humanities/History/Genealogy. Excellent search tool for genealogy sites on Yahoo.

Glossary

Genealogy, like any specialized science, has a language all its own. In addition, Jewish genealogy has some specialized terms that are used to describe situations that are unique to the Jewish experience. The purpose of this glossary is to provide basic information that will help the novice Jewish genealogist gain a better understanding of genealogy in general and the special nature of Jewish genealogy in particular. This is not an exhaustive list of genealogy terms. Such lists can be found both in more advanced books on the subject of genealogy and on many of the genealogy Web sites on the Internet. Rather, this is offered as a basic vocabulary for the novice Jewish genealogist with the idea that, as the reader becomes more interested and proficient in this work, he or she will search out the knowledge that seems most personally relevant.

JEWISH AND GENEALOGICAL TERMS

AJGS Association of Jewish Genealogical Societies
AJHS American Jewish Historical Society
Anti-Semitism Hatred and/or fear of the Jewish people, of individuals who are Jewish and of Jewish things; discrimination against or persecution of Jews.

Aramaic   Sister language to Hebrew, spoken in the land of Israel during the first century of the Common Era.

Ascendant/Pedigree Chart   Family chart that starts with the individual doing the genealogy and lists all ancestors.

Ashkenazi   Jews of Eastern European descent, especially Jews from Germany, Poland, Lithuania, Hungary, Romania, Ukraine, and Russia.

B.C.E. (Before the Common Era)   This is a term used by Jews and increasingly by academics as a substitute for B.C. The objection to the term "B.C." is that it refers to the birth date of Jesus. Dating time in relation to one individual is seen today as viewing time through a very narrow lens. The term "B.C.E.," while not a perfect solution, makes it possible to widen our focus from a particular religious view of history to a broader understanding of the forces that have shaped our modern world.

Bar Mitzvah/Bat Mitzvah   The designation for a Jewish boy of thirteen (bar) and a Jewish girl of twelve or thirteen (bat) which signifies that he or she has become responsible for the personal fulfillment of God's commandments as transmitted through the Torah and interpreted by the rabbis. Literally, "son" or "daughter" of the commandment. Also used as a term for the synagogue ceremony during which the young man or woman is called to the Torah as a sign that he or she has reached the time of Jewish religious maturity.

Bencher   A small prayer book containing the blessing after meals and other prayers.

Bris   Eastern European pronounciation of the word *brit*. This term refers to the ritual circumcision, covenant, and naming ceremony performed for a Jewish male infant at the age of eight days old.

Brit Banot   Covenant ceremony for a baby girl, usually performed on the eighth day after birth.

Brit (Bris) Milah   Ritual circumcision performed on a male infant by a mohel or a mohelet when the baby is eight days old. The brit milah ceremony welcomes the baby into a covenant with God.

C.E. (Common Era)   Designation for the time period traditionally labeled "A.D." beginning with the year "1" of modern history. (See B.C.E.)

Cohen/Kohen   Male descendent of the line of Aaron, the Kohen Gadol—the High Priest. Aaron belonged to the tribe of Levi, one of the twelve tribes of Israel. The members of the Kohen group had special ritual and administrative duties within the Temple and were restricted in certain areas of their lives in order to allow them to retain the necessary ritual purity required for their tasks. The designation of "Cohen" is passed down through the patrilineal line and is marked by the appellation "Hacohen"—the Cohen—as a suffix to a man's Hebrew name.

Descendent Chart   Family chart that starts with the individual and tracks only the individual's descendents.

Family Group Sheet   A document that keeps track of all individuals in a specific family group.

Guberniya   A Russian term used for Russian and Polish provinces prior to 1917. There were fifteen guberniyas in the Pale of Settlement, plus ten guberniyas in the Polish provinces which was known as the Kingdom of Poland.

HIAS (Hebrew Immigrant Aid Society)   HIAS focuses on helping Jewish and non-Jewish immigrants around the world with issues related to the many legal procedures involved in immigration.

Inquisition   A campaign of religious persecution begun in Spain by the Catholic church in the thirteenth century and lasting for four hundred years. The focus was on discovering and converting or putting to death all nonbelievers and "heretics." Jews and converted Jews were a particular focus of the Inquisition. Eventually the Inquisition spread to other Catholic countries, including South America.

JGS   Jewish genealogical societies.

Kohen/Cohen   See above.

Ketubah   Jewish wedding contract.

Kippah   The Hebrew term for a Jewish religious head covering. See YARMULKE.

Ladino   "Secular" language spoken by Sephardic Jews containing both Hebrew and Spanish words.

Levi/Levite   Traditionally a male who belongs to this tribe. The tribe of Levi was entrusted with responsibilities for maintaining the Temple in Jerusalem (which no longer stands.) The designation of one as a Levi is passed through the patrilineal line and is indicated in one's Hebrew name by the suffix appellation "Halevi"—the Levite.

Liberal Judaism   Jewish practice in which Jewish law is seen as somewhat flexible.

Matrilineal   (1) The genealogical line based on one's mother's family; and (2) a family history based exclusively on the female descendents in the family.

Matronym   A suffix indicating that one is the descendent of one's mother.

Microfilm/Microfiche   A standard and inexpensive way to reproduce and store docoument images. The documents are miniaturized so that a microfilm/microfiche can hold a large amount of data. The microfilm/microfiche is viewed through a special viewer suitable for that format. Microfilm and microfiche viewers are available at most libraries and archives.

Mohel/Mohelet   A Jewish man or woman trained in the surgical procedure of circumcision and in the rituals involved in the brit milah ceremony.

NARA   National Archives and Records Administration

Patrilineal   (1) The genealogical line based on one's father's family; and (2) a family history based exclusively on the male descendents in the family.

Patronym   A suffix indicating that one is the descendent of one's father.

Pedigree/Ascendant Chart   Family chart that starts with the individual doing the genealogy and lists all ancestors.

Pogrom   Violent, unprovoked attack on Jews and Jewish property by non-Jews, often with the assistance of or through the instigation of local non-Jewish authorities.

Pale of Settlement   Territory established under the Czarist Russian regime to confine and control its Jewish population. The Pale included parts of Poland, Lithuania, Bessarabia, and the Ukraine. This area, approximately four percent of the Russian Empire, contained approximately ninety-four percent of the Jewish population. The Pale of Settlement was abolished in 1917.

Progenitor   The earliest documented person in a genealogical line

"Refusenik"   A Jew living in the former Soviet Union whose request to emigrate was refused. The reasons for refusal were generally arbitrary and without merit.

SSDI   Social Security Death Index

Sephardic   Jews descended from ancestors from Spain, Portugal, Latin America, and the Middle East.

Siddur   Hebrew term for a prayer book.

"Step" brother/sister   Child of one's step parent. No blood relationship exists between step siblings.

"Step" father/mother   Spouse of one's parent as a result of a remarriage.

Temple in Jerusalem   The Temple in Jerusalem was the center of Jewish worship from about 900 B.C.E. to 70 C.E., when it was destroyed by the Romans in an effort to subdue Jewish nationalism. Religious Jews believe that the Temple will be rebuilt and ritual sacrifices as described in the Torah will be restored when the messiah comes.

Traditional Judaism   Jewish religious and ritual practice in which Jewish law is interpreted in a strict manner.

Transliterate   The use of the letters of the English alphabet to spell out foreign words and place-names. While a standard "scholarly" system for transliteration exists, this approach is often not universally applied. For example, the word *Shalom* could also be transliterated as "Sha-lome" or "Sha-lohm."

Wimple   A Jewish family heirloom created from a baby's blanket that is usually embroidered or decorated with family names and symbols. The wimple can be used to bind a Torah scroll. There is a tradition of using a wimple to tie the Torah during a young man's bar mitzvah ceremony and when he is called to the Torah prior to his marriage. This custom was prevalent in Eastern Europe, especially in Germany, and is being revived in the United States today.

Yarmulke (pronounced "yar-mul-kah" or more commonly "yam-a-

kah")   A small head covering, traditionally used by men, but today also used by women. Very traditional Jews wear this head covering all of the time. Some Jews wear a yarmulke during study, prayer, or ritual celebrations. *Yarmulke* is a Yiddish word. The Hebrew word for this item of head covering is *kippah*.

Yahrzeit   The anniversary of a person's death. A yahrzeit is observed by the lighting of a special candle in the home on the evening before the "day" of death. Most synagogues also have yahrzeit lamps that are lit in memory of members of the congregation, or friends and family of members of the congregation, who have died. Either the secular date or the Hebrew date of death can be observed.

Yiddish   "Secular" language common to many Ashkenazic Jews based on a mixture of German, Polish, Russian, and other Eastern European languages.

Index